Advanced Marketing Techniques for Architecture and Engineering Firms

Advanced Marketing Techniques for Architecture and Engineering Firms

Margaret Spaulding

William D'Elia

Previously published as *The A/E Marketing Handbook*
by the *A/E Marketing Journal*

Original drawings by Peter M. Hasselman, FAIA

McGraw-Hill Publishing Company
New York St. Louis San Francisco Auckland Bogotá
Caracas Hamburg Lisbon London Madrid Mexico
Milan Montreal New Delhi Oklahoma City
Paris San Juan São Paulo Singapore
Sydney Tokyo Toronto

Library of Congress Cataloging in Publication Data

Spaulding, Margaret.
  Advanced marketing techniques for architecture and engineering
firms/Margaret Spaulding and William D'Elia.
    p. cm.
  Bibliography: p.
  Includes index.
  ISBN 0-07-016248-4
  1. Architectural services marketing--United States. 2. Engineering services mar-
keting--United States. I. D'Elia, William. II. Title.
NA1996.S63 1989
720'.68'8—dc20   89-34422
                                                    CIP

1234567890 HAL/HAL 895432109

ISBN 0-07-016248-4

*The editors for this book were Harold B. Crawford, Wendy L. Grau, and Nancy
Young, the designer was Naomi Auerbach, and the production supervisor was Richard A. Ausburn. This book was set in ITC Garamond Light. It was composed by the
McGraw-Hill Publishing Company Professional & Reference Division composition
unit.*

Printed and bound by Halliday Lithograph.

*For more information about other McGraw-Hill materials,
call 1-800-2-MCGRAW in the United States. In other
countries, call your nearest McGraw-Hill office.*

DEDICATION

In this book the authors have rethought and rewritten an earlier book on A/E services marketing. That handbook, published in 1983, was a joint effort of the two present authors and their beloved colleague Jim Ricereto, who passed away in 1985. Jim was an inspiration to the first book, and to this one as well. Most important, Jim was a source of knowledge, insight, and humor to a family of marketers who helped pioneer this often misunderstood "profession." He let us know when we missed the point, and taught us perhaps the most important lesson of all, that doing good work and having fun are not mutually exclusive. We trust this book is true to his spirit as well as his intellect.

Contents

Chapter 6. What You Need—Clients 109

Chapter 7. Your Roadmap—The Marketing Plan 130

Preface to This Edition

A lot has changed since we wrote the first version of this book, *The A/E Marketing Handbook,* published in 1983 by Michael Hough and *The A/E Marketing Journal.* He is no longer a publisher. Jim Ricereto's tragic death in 1985 left only two authors. Before then we all worked for mid-to-large-sized firms—architecture, A/E, and engineering, respectively. We now have our own firm as consultants to this field. Other changes include: the rapid growth of the total number of design firms and the number of marketers in them. Automation—both CAD and in marketing systems—became a standard tool. More people select marketing as a career, and marketing A/E services draws people from product sales and other business backgrounds. More firms began to explore, if not embrace, the concepts of a true client-centered practice and what it takes to achieve it.

Some things have not changed: the marketer is still under pressure to help the firm "get work," while trying to organize the information, paper, and people upon which the firm's marketing efforts rest. Many designers, engineers, and managers fail to acknowledge the importance of marketing, giving only lip service to the efforts of the marketer. The marketer still experiences the intensity of the effort in pursuing a job: the disappointment of losing and joys of winning.

We also made major changes in this book: Each chapter, rethought and rewritten, incorporates new insights and reflects changes in the practice. We have added to our original perspectives through our consulting to a wide range of architecture, engineering, planning, and interior design firms.

Some things about the book have not changed: it remains a "doer's manual," taking the approach that the marketer in the trenches needs a quick reference of suggestions and advice for handling specific questions. Although this book takes a broad perspective and provides useful information to anyone responsible for marketing—coordinator and principal alike—this is not an academic work but a pragmatic one drawn from experience, both our own and that of others.

Margaret Spaulding
William D'Elia

Preface to the First Edition

The idea to write a manual on marketing came to us through our experience in the trenches and the realization (sometimes brutal) that we didn't always have the resources we needed to do our jobs well.

Each of us learned how to market architectural and engineering services in several offices, by doing, listening, taking chances, making mistakes, and experiencing the rush of success. We learned in situations where we, and often our bosses, did not know what to expect or how to reach our goals. We learned through the phone calls that went unanswered and the proposals that didn't open the doors.

Although there are several excellent books on the subject, we felt a lack of "hands on" reference material. So we set out to close that gap with a manual that catches the spirit of the job.

Because we are all active in our local chapter, our initial discussions often took place after Society for Marketing Professional Services (SMPS) steering committee meetings. We began to review the need for a "doers" approach to the subject of marketing. The ideas started coming together one summer evening over day-old pizza, some beer, and a long sheet of butcher paper. During this session and others like it, we recorded our thoughts on marketing, our experiences, lessons learned, profiles of clients and bosses, critiques of our jobs, and the books that had helped define those jobs. All the, "Remember that client who ..." and, "You know what drives me crazy about ..." were placed on the butcher paper until we had covered many of the marketing experiences and growing pains of our careers. From this effort, the manual took shape in style and content.

This manual represents the collected advice of three people—an architect, an engineer, and a former journalist—who have spent the last several years marketing. We know that marketing design services is not an academic subject, and we have not had time to read everything on the subject. As a result, this is not an academic book. Encyclopedic, maybe, but it is based strongly in our experience, observation, and insight into a growing profession. It concentrates on "how to," not "why." But we must tell you there is advice we ourselves do not always follow. As you probably know, marketing cannot always be done by the books, and we are the first to admit that.

We teamed up to write this book. Each author wrote three chapters. We did not always agree on what the others said (still don't) and we critiqued, edited, and argued over each other's chapters. However, we pushed forward, added important information, and took out unnecessary advice. We wanted to capture the spirit of marketing, which, though frustrating and exhausting, is also exciting and fun.

This book is an accumulation of experiences and insights, something we have come to love and believe may be of help to you.

William D'Elia
James Ricereto
Margaret Spaulding

AUGUST 1983

Acknowledgments

This book draws on our first-hand experience as marketers for architecture and engineering firms and from our experience as consultants to these professions. It is impossible to thank everyone who contributed—during the decade-plus of our work—to each author's insight and the information contained in this handbook. We owe thanks to our first bosses who, when we were baby marketers, extolled us to "think like our clients" as we squirmed in our chairs. We owe thanks to those "good ole' boy" marketers who helped guide our first steps in creating a career out of professional services marketing. And to SMPS, whose San Francisco chapter we helped to found, for providing a national network of contacts who gave freely of their knowledge to help us learn as much as we could about the complex business of A/E marketing.

In writing this book, we relied on many marketers from a great range of firms to provide comments and insight to our draft chapters. These people, both technical and nontechnical, senior marketers with key positions in their firms as well as junior marketers with new approaches to their responsibilities, helped to bring clarity and reality to our points of view. Marketers who contributed to this book include: Diane Creel, Sharon Gray, Kristin Kline, Dianne Ludman, Rose Reichman, Nina Saint, George Wittenberg, and Howard Wolff.

Our careers have been guided, inspired, and driven by some very special people—colleagues, bosses, and clients. We owe special thanks to people like the following for kicking and cajoling us to think harder and learn faster: the late George Agron and Howard Friedman, Weld Coxe, Bill Hankinson, Michael Hough, Gerre Jones, Roz Koo, Carol McConochie, Herb McLaughlin, Bill Mittleman, Dell Palmer, Darlene Weidert, and Art Zigas. Special gratitude to Tim Allen and Peter Loeb for their insight and analysis.

On a personal level, we want to thank our spouses and families for putting up with the insanity writing a book like this imposes on one's personal life, not to mention the impact it has on the cash flow of a small practice like ours. And we should thank Charlie at the gym for trying to keep us sound in mind and body through it all. We especially want to thank Liz Eckstein in our office for putting up with us, contributing logic, humor, and production skills to the effort and keeping our heads screwed on straight during the process.

But perhaps most important of all, we want to acknowledge the clients we have worked with in recent years, who have struggled to learn the hard lessons of marketing and shared their successes with us. Their good work makes it all worthwhile.

*It must be remembered that there is
nothing more difficult to plan, more
doubtful of success, nor more dangerous
to manage than the creation of a new
system. For the initiator has the enmity of
all who would profit by the preservation of
the old institution and merely lukewarm
defenders in those who would gain by the
new ones.*
NICCOLO MACHIAVELLI
The Prince, 1514

Chapter One

Your Overview— Marketing Evolution and Structure

INTRODUCTION

Marketing, in a professional service firm, is primarily a tool for creating and managing change. It involves introducing new systems, and it very often involves defending the validity of marketing in a hostile environment. Professionals—architects, engineers, planners—are highly educated, dedicated to their fields, and inclined to feel (if not to admit) that "marketing" is something they wouldn't have to do if they were as good at their discipline as they want to think they are. So, as a participant in this "dangerous" enterprise of marketing, you may find yourself subject to Machiavelli's warning. And, you may be pleased to know you have allies, among them the authors of this book.

About this book: It's for people who don't have time to read books—those who do the actual day-to-day marketing for architecture and engineering firms. In fact, it is mainly for the person who coordinates the marketing, whatever his or her title—from principal to assistant. That person not only has a frequently thankless job, but it is one in which there is never enough time. Here's how this book can help. This first chapter, for example, does three things:

- It provides an overview of how planning and design professionals have faced the challenge of marketing.

- It discusses the classic structures that architects and engineers have used to do their marketing.

- It offers insight into what seems to work well in marketing today.

If you are not interested in this kind of background now, go on to any one of the other chapters, each of which stands on its own and does not need to be read in sequence. They are:

- Getting marketing systems organized (Chap. 2)

- Developing a direct marketing program (Chap. 3)

- Marketing techniques—PR and sales tools (Chaps. 4, 5)

- Making it work—understanding clients (Chap. 6)

- Creating your marketing plan (Chap. 7)

- Determining what marketing should cost (Chap. 8)

- Overcoming Machiavelli's prediction—or, how to succeed through internal politics (Chap. 9).

This book does not spend much time on person-to-person sales techniques to use with clients; see the resources section for more comprehensive books on that subject.

WHAT YOU NEED TO KNOW ABOUT MARKETING

What Is Marketing?

Some people say marketing is finding a need and filling it. Other definitions we have heard include: "Marketing is what we do to guarantee a revenue stream for the firm." ("Revenue stream" is a 1980s word for income.) Marketing, according to the American Marketing Association, is the process of planning and executing the conception, pricing, promotion, and distribution of ideas, goods, and services to create exchanges that satisfy individual and organizational goals.

Philip Kotler, in his textbook *Principles of Marketing,* describes marketing as "a set of principles for choosing target markets, identifying customer needs, developing want-satisfying... services and delivering value to customers and profit to the company." John Simonds, a management consultant, refers to marketing as staff functions of planning, market assessment, analysis of opportunities, strategy development, marketing information systems, staff training, and coordination and direction of business development. He refers to business development as the line function of direct client contact for the purpose of acquiring new or expanded contracts.

We define marketing as planning, executing, and evaluating your efforts to get new work. (We like it because it's quick to read, easy to remember, and will outlive the '80s.) The important points here are:

- Marketing is not just selling.

- Marketing is not just public relations.

- Marketing is not just responding to requests for proposals (RFPs).

Marketing is an umbrella that covers all the things that need to be done to close the sale, including:

- Planning
- Research and analysis
- Developing strategies
- Selling (direct client contact)
- Designing and producing sales tools
- Public relations
- Evaluating results

In product marketing and even in nonprofessional services marketing, pricing plays a large part in the marketing strategy. We omit it from this list because in professional services we usually try to focus on value rather than price. In this respect we try to be like doctors and lawyers who tend to accept a range of "prices" or fees that have been long established for services we know people need.

More importantly, pricing—whether percentages of construction costs or hourly rates to a maximum—has traditionally been negotiated *after* selection, not before, which tends to remove it from under the marketing umbrella. Of course, if negotiations fail, you don't have a sale. Furthermore, this sequence has changed in many markets, with fees becoming a major or primary selection criterion, even though attitudes throughout the professions toward pricing have not changed. See Chaps. 6, "Clients," and 7, "The Marketing Plan," for more on this subject.

According to Diane Creel, a veteran design firm marketer who has become president of a large engineering firm, "Every business decision is... a marketing decision. You can only do as much business as the market will bear. . . ." Marketing is an interactive series of processes that depend on each other to be effective. Staffing and productivity, financial management decisions, office size and location, specialization or diversity—all these elements affect marketing and vice versa.

And, you can't always predict what you'll have to do or what will work at a given time. We've all experienced emergency crunches—jobs we "won" get put on hold or canceled by the client; we suddenly get 4 or 40 requests for proposals all due at the same time—that could not have been predicted. We've also experienced the "perfect" strategy that didn't win the job. Welcome to marketing.

Finally, we should mention what we call, for lack of a better term, the "Zen" of marketing. We have often found that in the eager pursuit of a market, a client, a project, or an entire program, we fail spectacularly to obtain that specific objective in that pursuit, but, by some miracle, we have entered an unexpected new market, obtained an unanticipated new client or project, or emerged in the midst of a surprisingly successful new program. We can't explain it except to say that the unpredicted results were well worth the energy expended.

A Brief History of Marketing

Marketing first dealt with the selling of products such as packaged goods, commodities, or equipment. In the 1960s marketing concepts were first applied to consumer services such as banks and hotels. In the 1970s the concept of marketing began to interest a few professionals—attorneys, physicians, and accountants as well as a small number of architects and engineers. According to Kotler in *Principles of Marketing,* service firms have traditionally given the following reasons for neglecting marketing:

- They thought it would be unprofessional.
- They thought it would be too expensive.
- They had so much business that they thought it wasn't necessary.

Sound familiar? Today, much marketing goes on around us from which we can learn. For example, we can learn from our prospective clients who use effective marketing techniques to sell their products or services. We have found it effective to take good ideas from the world around us (such as that beautiful new Mercedes Benz brochure and all those inventive consumer ads) and integrate them into the specific needs of our firms.

THE EVOLUTION OF ARCHITECTURE/ENGINEERING (A/E) MARKETING

The Emergence of A/E Marketing

Back in the old days, you didn't start your firm unless you had a couple of friends who would give you some work. Prior to the 1960s some government officials had private consulting practices on the side. They would get their work from colleagues in sister agencies. Today we consider this kind of practice a conflict of interest.

Actually the "ole-boys" who operated that way were marketing their businesses. They would do some research on client needs, target a few clients, sell their services, and close the deal. The ole-boys would do their business at social gatherings and meetings of clubs, associations, and civic groups to which they belonged. Friendship, based often on social class, created a network from which projects developed and were passed around. It was simple from the client's point of view: you hired the person you liked to work with. In those less litigious days, confidence and trust were more important than a design philosophy or even technical qualifications.

In some ways, not much has changed. The best way to obtain a job is still to develop a personal relationship with a client, and most clients still select a design professional on trust. Sophisticated firms today continue to use the ole-boy network as part of their marketing program. Marketing directors are well advised to encourage the social butterflies of the firm to frequent events at which they can meet and cultivate potential clients. (More on this technique in Chap. 6, "Clients.")

During the 1970s, a number of A/E firms incorporated and began to look into the future. Founding principals began to think about retirement and ownership transition. Their practices were changing, becoming more business-like. Some sought the advice of management consultants who advocated planning a marketing program. They began to target their markets and plan for the long term. A number of factors accelerated this interest in marketing:

- The recession of the mid-1970s

- Double-digit inflation

- Increased competition for hard-to-come-by projects

As a result, firms had to work smarter as well as harder to break new ground. Larger firms saw the benefit of having marketing departments. Nontechnical marketers (those without architecture or engineering backgrounds) emerged in A/E firms and became responsible for research, communications, and selling. They assisted in the marketing effort and participated in business decisions.

To meet the growing needs of the professional services marketer, the Society for Marketing Professional Services (SMPS) was begun in 1973 and now has a membership of several thousand. For more information on the history of A/E marketing, refer to Weld Coxe's book, *Marketing Architectural and Engineering Services*. In the first edition, published in 1971, he documents the evolution of the ethical questions posed by design professionals regarding marketing. The second edition, which was published in 1983, notes that by the end of the 1970s, professional societies (such as the American Institute of Architects and the American Consulting Engineers Council) finally accepted that they could no longer legally regulate the marketing of members' services.

What Succeeds Today: The Third Generation

What works today in marketing professional services is what we might call "third-generation" marketing. In the first generation, firms generally based their practices on friends and relationships deriving from friendships, often characterized not only by the ole-boy network but by a tendency to market by sitting in the office, waiting for the phone to ring. When the market for design services began changing in the late '60s and early '70s, firms began embracing the rituals of product marketing, including activities such as "cold calling" to get "prospects" and "leads," attending conventions, and hiring staff to represent them with potential clients. In many firms, however, these second-generation tactics have not been very successful, largely because they have not been integrated into the fabric of the firm. They are activities taking place at the perimeter of the firm, often without the full blessing of most members of the firm or of the profession as a whole, and are looked upon by many professionals as an unsavory business.

Today, third-generation marketing attempts to capture the best of both preceding stages, observing the following:

- Basing a practice on obtaining clients with whom the professional has rapport and shares common values

- Creating a balance of direct (specific client) and indirect marketing activities

- Planning carefully and monitoring the plan to find and follow marketing strategies that work best

Within this third-generation framework, we have found that the following four activities, if undertaken regularly, sort of like eating from each of the basic food groups, will lead to a workable marketing program:

- **Planning** Setting goals, not just for marketing but for the overall business; selecting key markets to target, then evaluating the firm's ability to meet those goals in two key ways—determining the strengths of the firm as compared to those of the competition, both technical and marketing, and determining the strengths of the targeted markets; and monitoring the firm's progress.

- **Direct client contact (sales)** Developing and maintaining effective communication with your client base; rewarding technical staff, from the top down, for having good client relations; and placing emphasis throughout the firm on clients, not just projects.

- **Effective marketing and sales tools** Creating systems that tell you about your clients, and your clients about you in cost-effective, beneficial ways; other systems can tell you how well you are doing (hit rates) and what else you need to do to meet your goals.

- **Public relations** Establishing a program to create an image of your firm as experts in selected fields, which lowers the cost of direct client contact (they call you instead of vice versa) and "educates" clients about the value of your services before you sit down to negotiate fees.

Marketing has continued to grow as an accepted part of the A/E practice; we estimate that 20 percent of all new firms seek marketing assistance from consultants or "friends" as part of their start-up activities. Of the approximately 15,000 architecture and 12,000 consulting engineering firms in the United States, we estimate as many as 40 percent have someone in-house who has marketing as a major and acknowledged part of his or her tasks. Among smaller firms, even under 15 persons, as many as 20 percent now have a full- or part-time person dedicated to marketing.

Remember, even in these firms, where marketing is recognized as essential to the practice, organized marketing still represents change, with all its attendant potential for problems.

THE A/E WAY

The Evolution of Firms

In order to understand marketing you must first understand your firm and where it stands in its evolution. We have observed that the sophistication of a marketing organization closely parallels the evolutionary pattern of a typical A/E firm. As the firm evolves, a marketing organization within it tends to emerge. No one can expect to hit the ground running with a full-blown marketing program. The idea usually has to be sold to others in the firm, funding must be authorized, the program must be developed and modified into what will work for each firm. The following are the five evolutionary stages of a typical architecture or engineering firm.

- **Stage I: Creation** A new firm is started by an entrepreneur with some creative thoughts as to what he or she wants to do and, perhaps, what the market needs. If you are contemplating starting your own firm, don't do it unless you have a few clients already under your wing. This is your ole-boy stage, and your first goal is to get the firm going. During the ole-boy stage, the owners market by the seats of their pants, and, if their intuition is right, they succeed.

- **Stage II: Growth** The entrepreneurs are pretty good, so the firm grows. The problem is that the firm grows beyond the capability of the existing management structure. New people are brought in or are promoted to assist in managing the firm. They, however, are only an extension of the original principals and do not have either decision-making authority, or, usually, the entrepreneur's innate marketing savvy. This is the time that most firms recognize the need for someone to coordinate the marketing effort. Typically, this person will start without a very clear idea as to the requirements, responsibilities, and challenges of the job.

- **Stage III: Maturation** The firm continues in spite of itself. It goes through a number of up-and-down cycles. The principals develop a sense of security in their business capability and begin to delegate authority. At this time marketing really starts to work in the A/E firm. Delegation of authority permeates the organization, and teamwork is what makes marketing and the firm successful.

- **Stage IV: Power struggle** It is time for the original principals to retire and to be paid for their ownership in the firm. This is an emotional time, and the rational behavior exhibited in the maturation stage does not necessarily prevail. The big question emerges: Who is the heir apparent? Sometimes a struggle develops between a senior technical professional and the marketing director who has been responsible for obtaining recent business. Lines may be drawn, games played, with teamwork and marketing success diminishing. Frustration develops in the marketing department, reflected by a high turnover in positions.

- **Stage V: Re-creation** If the firm ever makes it out of the power struggle stage, it is re-created, and new creative marketing concepts emerge. Actually, what has happened is that you have reentered Stage II.

Note that, if you are in a branch office, your evolutionary stage may be different from that of your parent company. In fact, branch offices tend to be more volatile, and their evolution (or demise) can occur much more rapidly than it does in the firm as a whole. Branch offices can also proceed through these stages without logical sequence as a result of senior people being moved in and out of the office.

The Marketing Organization

When we discuss marketing organizations, we may seem to describe large, sophisticated marketing departments which only large firms can afford. Larger firms, usually national in scale, were the first to implement marketing, but marketing techniques can succeed in small firms as well. In smaller firms, instead of assigning each job to a different person, consider each one a task, many of which can be done by one individual. In these firms, the marketing department is often one person—the same person who does the design, the calculations, and the contract documents also pays the bills.

Figures 1.1, 1.2, and 1.3 illustrate three types of A/E marketing organizations based on size and evolutionary development.

In the small firm (Fig. 1.1), the principal in charge of developing business is usually in charge of all sales and marketing. This principal will generally borrow from the operations staff for support in marketing. In the very small

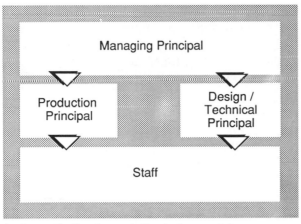

Figure 1.1 Typical organization for marketing in the small firm.

firm, the operations, business development, and managing principals may be the same person. That individual is fortunate in some respects in that he or she seldom has a problem developing loyalties and assigning priorities.

Figure 1.2 shows a larger organization, probably on the order of 50 people, which is more sophisticated in its organizational structure. One principal is generally assigned all responsibility for sales and will build the marketing organization around a secretary and a coordinator (who may be the same person). Support for this effort will often come from the technical staff.

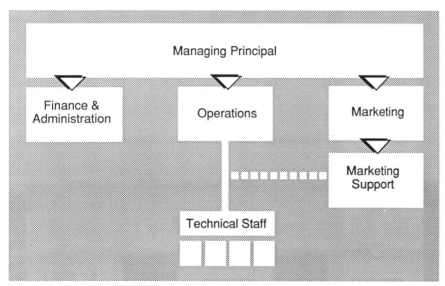

Figure 1.2 Typical organization for marketing in the mid-sized firm.

In the marketing organization shown in Fig. 1.2, the person responsible for marketing will often use key project managers and other operating principals to assist in calling on clients and making sales presentations. Be careful if this is your organization because, although the firm often talks about marketing and long range plans, it is often only concerned with sales. This kind of organization is often employed by the A/E firm in its stage II evolution, growth. Confusion and anarchy may be rampant, but have faith; as the marketer, it's your job to help the organization evolve into stage III, maturation.

Figure 1.3 represents the most sophisticated marketing organization. Here, a real *marketing* director is responsible for both sales and marketing. Sales goals are generally assigned to individuals committed to selling, even though it may not be a full-time assignment. In this type of organization, the salesperson must motivate project managers and operations principals to assist in the marketing effort. The salespeople may be principals themselves, and it wouldn't be unusual for them to be in charge of operating divisions or branch offices.

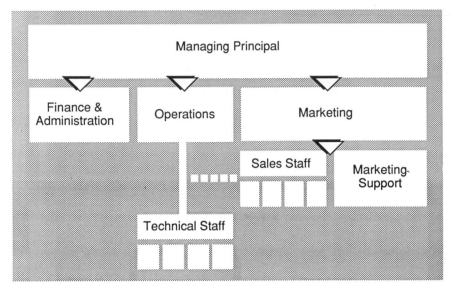

Figure 1.3 Typical sophisticated marketing organization for a larger firm.

Kotler, in *Principles of Marketing,* makes an observation which we find applicable to many A/E businesses:

> A company can have a modern marketing department and yet not operate as a modern marketing company. The latter depends upon how the other company officers view the marketing function. If they view marketing as primarily a selling function, they are missing the point. . . . Only when they see that. . . marketing is the name not of a department but of a company philosophy will they become a modern marketing company.

The Marketing Operation

We have discussed three types of marketing organizations. The type of organization in which you find yourself depends on the size of the firm and its stage in the evolutionary process. Unless you are the owner, there is generally very little you can do to change the type of organization.

On the other hand, you can operate your marketing organization based on one of two models described by author and consultant Weld Coxe. How you operate your marketing organization depends on who you are or who your lead marketing person is. Essentially, marketing organizations are either directed or facilitated. Coxe referred to these models as the "M1" or "M2" organizations. They relate, also, to second- and third-generation marketing, as we show here.

In the directed (M1) organization, the principal in charge of business development believes in marketing (as opposed to just sales) and directs both. This model is most effective in a firm that understands third-generation concepts. Realistic sales targets are established. Strategic and action plans help the firm meet sales targets in a priority sequence. Figure 1.4 illustrates the directed marketing organization.

In the facilitated (M2) organization, marketing is a support activity, gener-

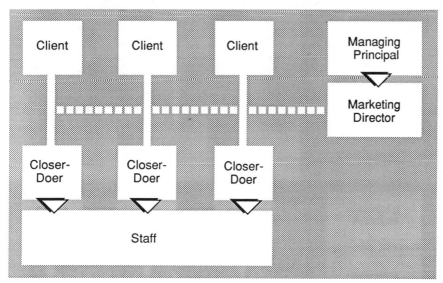

Figure 1.4   The directed marketing operation.

ally managed by someone other than a principal. This firm may still be struggling to apply second-generation concepts. The marketing manager usually prepares plans for approval by the principals and provides support to those principals responsible for sales. In the facilitated or managed system, it is often not clear which principal or what market area has priority. There may be no principal in charge of sales and marketing, but if there is, he or she must mediate disputes between marketing and other interests of the principals while encouraging the marketing manager. Figure 1.5 illustrates the managed marketing organization.

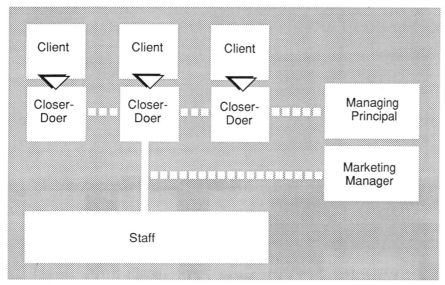

Figure 1.5   The managed marketing operation.

When Coxe introduced his concepts of the M1 and M2 marketing structures at the SMPS national convention in 1980, many people in the audience commented that their marketing organization was not exactly either one but fell into a hybrid category which was dubbed "M3." Three things were happening:

- Marketing personnel were not admitting to themselves that they were not in charge of the marketing effort.

- Confusion arose among marketers as to who was in charge of their programs.

- In fact, most firms are somewhere in transition, between generations, with part of the firm still in first-generation mode, and part of it learning to apply third-generation principles: The majority of firms are somewhere in between.

We know from experience that these conditions continue to exist in A/E organizations today. In Chap. 9, "Internal Politics," we tell you how to determine who is really in charge.

Regardless of your marketing structure, remember what is most important: You need an organized set of priorities that the management of the firm endorses and the marketers understand. These priorities should be set forth in a marketing plan; more is said on that subject in Chap. 7, "The Marketing Plan."

The Jobs to Be Done

The jobs to be done in marketing can be divided many ways. A common and effective method is between *sales* and all other *marketing* tasks.

First, let's look at sales, because it should be a significant part of the marketing effort. We use the word "sales" here even though architects and engineers go through all sorts of gyrations to avoid using it. It is usually called "business development," "marketing," "job development," or some other more professional-sounding term.

While we profoundly respect the need for professionalism in architecture and engineering, design firm marketers can learn a lot from the techniques of successful salespersons in other fields, though we should adapt these lessons to our own field. Good salespeople understand the importance of thinking like their clients and we recommend the practice of putting oneself in the client's place to understand his or her concerns and then addressing those concerns through benefits statements, packaged in an eye-catching, appealing manner. In a professionally managed marketing program we employ sales techniques such as the following to help us understand our clients and ensure the success of the sales effort:

- Conducting client research
- Developing leads
- Handing off (information and clients to the appropriate person)
- Presenting
- Closing
- Maintaining good client relations

Who, in a professional service firm, should lead the sales effort and perform these functions? There is no simple answer, and the best person, of course, depends on factors such as the size and diversity of markets you serve, the goals, "culture," and size of your firm, and the technical sophistication of your clients. Regardless of who it is (or who they are), your firm must have one or more persons responsible for and qualified to represent the firm; and, their efforts in this area must be considered as important as the technical work the firm produces. Ah, what did Machiavelli say?

Your firm's representatives—whether principals, project managers, dedicated sales representatives, or a combination—need to accomplish the following tasks:

- *Gather research* about clients to uncover opportunities and information about them and the markets they are part of.

- *Develop leads* to new work, often through developing a client's trust and by demonstrating that your firm has experience at solving the client's problems.

- *Hand off* an individual client from the representative to the technical person who will actually work on the project, a step that is necessary even if the representative is also a technically trained person but not the one to head up a specific project.

- *Present your firm's qualifications*—either in general, to introduce your firm to a client, or in terms of specific and distinguishing qualifications for a particular project—in both informal interviews and formal presentations.

- *Close "the deal,"* that is, convince the client that your firm or project team is the one the client wants above all others for a specific project and that the client is ready to make a commitment to that effect.

- *Maintain good relations* with existing clients to assure that the things that sold the client on hiring your firm are being delivered to his or her satisfaction, preserving a good reference for other clients and creating the possibility of future work with this one. This last step is the most cost-effective form of sales and often the most overlooked.

The tasks described above are discussed in more detail in Chap. 3, "Direct Marketing."

Every sales representative, the person who most often initiates meetings with prospective clients—whether trained as an architect or engineer or not—needs marketing support. In a small firm, the salesperson may get support from a part-time coordinator, a part-time secretary, or freelance marketing person. In a large firm, all these people may be assigned full time to marketing but work only part of their time for each representative or salesperson.

The People Who Do the Jobs

The people who do the marketing tasks are often nontechnical. Their backgrounds can be anything but are likely to be one of the following:

- Librarian

- English major, journalist, or communications expert

- Well-educated secretary who may have been underpaid or bored with a previous position

- Recent architecture, design, or engineering school graduate who leans toward the business side of the practice

A series of job titles has evolved in the A/E marketing business. The responsibilities assigned to each title are sometimes confusing and often overlap. In defining roles, we know from experience that one individual, regardless of his or her title, may play a number of roles in a firm. The role often, but not necessarily, corresponds to the tasks previously mentioned and may not be reflected in the title on the marketer's business card. The key roles are:

- Marketing principal

- Marketing director

- Marketing manager
- Marketing (or sales) representative
- Marketing coordinator

The *marketing principal* is the officer or principal in charge of the sales and marketing effort. The buck stops here. This person may be the chief executive officer, the chairman of the board, or a vice president of marketing.

The *marketing director* makes decisions regarding planning, implementing, and evaluating the marketing effort. He or she typically makes the day-to-day "go/no-go" decisions and defers only major policy decisions to the marketing principal. In the small firm, this person often is the marketing principal.

The *marketing manager* in a large firm reports to a marketing director and generally manages the marketing support staff. In the small firm this person reports to the marketing principal. This individual defers most policy decisions to the marketing director or principal. Nevertheless, this person often acts as a facilitator, manages a staff or a group of subcontractors, and ensures that the day-to-day marketing activities are organized to meet objectives.

The *marketing representative* is the firm's outside salesperson. Besides sales, this person may be responsible for internal marketing functions under the authority of the marketing director, or principal in charge, such as development of special brochures and other promotional activities. This person is often assigned to a specific geographic area or to sell a specific service or to serve a specific type of client.

The *marketing coordinator* reports to the marketing principal, director, or manager, depending on the size and complexity of the firm. The marketing coordinator monitors the marketing effort and maintains marketing information. He or she schedules and coordinates proposals, presentations, and brochures and often serves as an intermediary between the marketing director and the technical staff.

Marketing support roles in the A/E firm may be shared with other divisions of the firm or filled by subcontractors. They include:

- Word processing
- Data management
- Filing
- Graphics
- Writing/editing
- Public relations

All firms must somehow get these jobs done. They are often handled by the marketing coordinator or the marketing manager. Word processing, filing, writing, and editing may be done by a marketing assistant, who might also act as the marketing secretary in the small firm. Depending on the size of the firm, the marketing assistant will report to the marketing coordinator, manager, or principal.

Graphics and public relations are sometimes provided by subcontractors. Firms that have graphics specialists on their staff for billable work often attempt to share graphics time with the marketing department. Very few firms are big enough to afford full-time public relations specialists on staff. Very large firms have specialists on staff and also use subcontractors for special assignments. We say more on public relations and graphics in Chap. 4, "Indirect Marketing," and Chap. 5, "Sales Tools."

Remember, your own job title is what you use to present yourself to the

Thank heavens our marketing coordinator is here; now I don't have to do it.

outside world, and it may be very different from your job description, which defines your responsibility inside your firm.

How Many Marketing People Do You Need?

Statistics from nationwide polls of architecture and engineering firms vary widely on this question. And, the answer should vary, depending on the nature of the practice and the people involved. However, on average, you can expect that for every 20 people in a planning or design firm you will need the equivalent of one full-time marketing person. (By full-time equivalent we mean that if you take all the marketing time spent by various people in your firm it would add up to one full-time person, i.e., 40 hours per week.)

In *small firms* you may have 1 full-time equivalent marketing person for every 10 people. For example, in the 10-person firm, marketing time probably consists of one-third of a principal's time, one-half of his or her administrative assistant's time, and some miscellaneous time for technical people who occasionally work on a proposal or make a presentation.

In *large firms,* the ratio is likely to be 1 marketing person for every 25 staff members. It may be an even higher ratio if the firm has a large administrative staff. You can plan on needing 1 marketing principal (who can close a deal) for every 10 people in your firm. The person who closes will probably not be full time in marketing. In fact, expect this individual to spend less than 50 percent of his or her time in marketing; the rest of the time will be spent on projects and/or in administration.

The next question that must be answered is "which positions are appropriate to fill for our size office?" We've answered this question by preparing a matrix (Fig. 1.6) of marketing positions typically required for various sizes of firms. We have also answered it by filling all the various roles in some capacity.

NO. OF TOTAL STAFF	PRINCIPAL–CLOSER		MARKETING DIRECTOR	MARKETING MANAGER	MARKETING COORDINATOR	MARKETING STAFF
	NO.	F.T.E.				
1–15	1–2	0.5			1	
15–30	2–3	1			1	
30–50	2–6	1–2		1		1
50–100	4–12	2–3	1		1	1
100–200	8–24	3–6	1		1	2
200+	16+	6+	1		1	2+

Figure 1.6 Marketing positions by firm size.

Actually, the number of marketing people you use in your firm depends on how much money you are willing to invest in marketing and how you plan to attack your marketing program, as well as the structure of your firm, the type of clients you decide to pursue, and the degree of change your firm is undergoing. Much more is said on the cost of marketing in Chap. 8, "The Marketing Budget."

What Will Work for Your Firm

We've discussed the various types of marketing organizations, organizational models, the tasks to be done, and roles people must play to get the tasks done. Your own marketing program should be molded around the people who lead the firm and the influences that surround you. You should not attempt to mold the firm's leaders to fit your preconceived notions of what an A/E marketing program should be. It won't work. On the other hand, you may have to train or replace middle- to lower-level staff to get effective implementation of a marketing program.

Now let's get organized and go to work.

INTRODUCTION

A few years back we received something in the mail from a marketer whom we had recently helped find a job with an architecture firm. She had returned some material to us and instead of a cover letter in her usual cordial, thoughtful manner, she had stuck a "Post-it" and scrawled "I know I have fully arrived at BVS and as a marketer—I DON'T HAVE TIME FOR ANYTHING!!!"

First, we should note that, for most marketers, this is not a 9 to 5 job; it is more often a 7:30 (breakfast with consultant's marketing person) to 6 job, ending with an SMPS program. It is all too often a 7:30 a.m. to 9:30 p.m. or midnight job as the deadline for a proposal submittal comes down to the wire. Don't feel you are the only marketing person who can't get on top of your schedule. But, keep trying.

Most marketers for professional design firms envision a perfectly organized marketing operation, primed to anticipate needs, prepared for expanded responsibilities, and responsive to crises in a cool, efficient manner. But, they envision it in someone else's firm. The reality of our own situations has always been very different from this stellar ideal.

"If only we had time to get organized," goes the familiar refrain. Having worked in the trenches for many years, we can say that few marketers ever work in a state of complete efficiency and calm.

Marketers' lives are destined to be hectic, and the struggle to get ahead of the RFPs and slide filing is akin to Sisyphus ever pushing his recalcitrant stone up the mountain. Of all the talents and skills needed to be a marketer, none is more critical—over time—than the ability to organize and stay organized. Figure 2.1 illustrates the organization learning curve.

ORGANIZING YOUR JOB

This chapter takes you through the basics of organizing your work as a marketer. We discuss from our own experience what and how things can be organized and describe a few specific systems that have worked for us or for others we know.

It may help to think of getting organized in four distinct areas:

- Your personal job tasks, schedules, and responsibilities
- Information about your firm's markets, potential clients, leads, and prospects
- Information about your firm—its strengths, capabilities, track record, people, and projects
- Success rates—your own, in terms of your job-related objectives, and the firm's (hit rates for proposals, presentations, etc.)

This chapter provides techniques for getting organized in each of these areas.

One of the first tasks you may need to tackle if you are new to the job or new to the firm is to gather all the marketing material into one place, even if it's only a file drawer next to your desk. You need to create a distinct marketing department, separate from other parts of the firm, where things can be put and found. Others may have access to this space, so it may need to be kept impersonal. But, you need your own space in order to start getting organized. No matter how organized it is, how big or how compact, there is one thing you will never find in it—enough time.

Chapter Two

Getting Organized— Order from Chaos

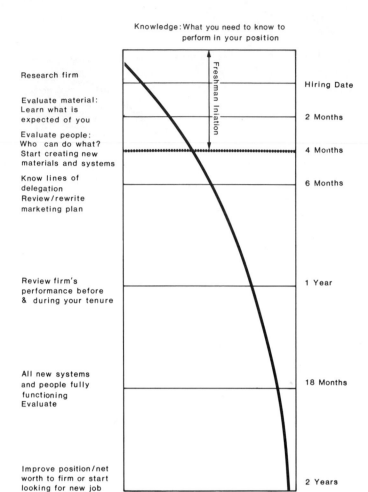

Knowledge: What you need to know to perform in your position

Freshman Iniation

Research firm — Hiring Date

Evaluate material:
Learn what is
expected of you — 2 Months

Evaluate people:
Who can do what?
Start creating new
materials and systems — 4 Months

Know lines of
delegation
Review/rewrite
marketing plan — 6 Months

Review firm's
performance before
& during your tenure — 1 Year

All new systems
and people fully
functioning
Evaluate — 18 Months

Improve position/net
worth to firm or start
looking for new job — 2 Years

Figure 2.1 Organization learning curve.

ORGANIZING YOUR PERSONAL JOB TASKS

Managing Your Time

Much of getting organized is time management, organizing priorities. Books that may help you in this are *The Time Trap* by R. Alex Mackenzie, *How to Get Control of Your Time and Your Life* by Alan Lakein, and *The One Minute Manager* by Ken Blanchard.

All marketers have tricks that work for them to help keep ahead of the clock. For example, one marketer we know says, "Keep a file folder filled with 5-minute projects—e.g., file one or two slides away, read an article that's routed to you, etc. Little tasks like these tend to get waylaid by major tasks and never get done. If you discipline yourself to do a few small tasks every day, they'll never become overwhelming."

Organizing Your Thoughts

The toughest part of getting organized is sorting out all the information you need access to at a given moment. You need a systematic way of thinking about marketing in general and about your job in particular.

Regarding your job, the organization process probably began before you assumed the marketing position. If you are new to the firm, do some research to learn what your options and priorities are (as in "If we do not study history, we are condemned to repeat it"):

But you should see me when I'm not organized.

- Read everything available to you about your firm: articles, pamphlets, existing brochures, any and all publications concerning the work of your firm and its people.

- Search out and read memos regarding projects, budget analyses of the firm in general, and about specific projects, correspondence with consultants and with friends of the firm.

- If possible and appropriate, interview the person you are replacing to determine what worked and what didn't. You may not agree with his or her analysis, but there may be some useful insights.

As a result of this survey, evaluate what in marketing has worked in the past and what has failed in order to see what may continue to work, what must be changed, and what new approaches may be worth trying.

Understanding Your Role

A prime factor in getting organized is understanding the expectations of others in the firm regarding your position. You must understand key people's priorities for your position and analyze them against your own perceived priorities. Therefore, we strongly suggest that before you tear apart the slide collection and restructure it in order to end loss or thievery, do a little research. Contact key people in the firm to cull their views on marketing needs and on the firm in general.

These interviews will show you how and whether other people are involved in marketing and, if you are new, will help you get to know others in the firm while showing them how you work. Keep the interview professional, serious, and short, using a prepared set of questions. Remember, important people in the firm will have little time to chat and may have been interviewed by a marketing person before, with few visible results. Gaining the trust of your colleagues means they will share responsibility and information with you (*the* primary complaint of all A/E firm marketers who deal with these issues).

The following questions can serve as a guide:

1. What types of projects do you think the firm should pursue? Do these projects differ from what is being done now? Should we look for work with different types of clients? Do you think the firm should offer services, for example, other than those now offered? Should we pursue work in other geographic areas?

2. What are the special talents of the firm? What are its drawbacks?

3. Are there any special talents among the staff that are not currently being promoted by the firm?

4. How were existing projects brought into the office?

5. What, if any, have been recent breakthroughs in the marketing effort? Who initiated them?

6. What, specifically, can be done to improve the marketing effort?

7. How should the firm handle public relations and indirect marketing, publishing, awards programs, seminars, group participation, press relationships?

8. What growth or change should take place in the direction or nature of the firm?

9. What intelligence on relevant markets already exists within the firm, and who is responsible for this information?

10. What talents for marketing are available in-house and for which must consultants be used?

11. What type of support will the marketing effort be given and to what extent will marketing ideas be funded?

12. Is there a marketing budget?

13. In your opinion, what is the single most important marketing activity and who is responsible for it?

Use the answers to these questions to draft a brief marketing history of the firm. You may also want to draw an organization chart illustrating the marketing functions in your firm and how the people committed to marketing relate to one another (more on your firm's organization in Chap. 9, "Internal Politics").

Getting Agreement on Your Role

The last question above leads us to the next thing you need to do. When you have started to understand your firm, its goals, its position in desired marketplaces, and how it is seen by the outside world, it is time to look inward. You need to know what is expected of you and to define your priorities.

Even if you don't have time or the opportunity to interview everyone, talk to as many of the owners of the firm or its decision makers as you can. Most important, know to whom you report and what his or her objectives are and what do you need to do to satisfy this person first. Develop what we call a short-term action plan in outline form (tasks, assignments, deadlines, budget) as shown in the two examples below:

- Boilerplate development—20 new project descriptions by August 1; TK and SJC to do; est. 50 hours and $450 for repro.

- Leads—develop/obtain two new qualified prospects per week starting in two weeks; TK and FJL to do; est. 10 hours per week.

At some point this short-term action plan needs to fit into the overall marketing plan, but you may not get to that for months (or years). In Chap. 7 we offer a detailed approach to writing a marketing plan. In his book, *How to Market Professional Design Services,* Gerre Jones devoted the entire chapter, "Getting Organized," to writing a marketing plan. While the marketing plan is the organizational frame of your marketing program, first you need to establish systems for dealing with the day-to-day pressures and responsibilities you confront.

In addition to writing your short-term action plan, write your job description. *It may not be the same one you were given when you were hired.* You should write it or revise it as soon as you have conducted the interviews. Pass this description around, with your action plan, or present them at a marketing meeting and get agreement on them from those in charge or with whom you will be working. This agreement should address your responsibilities, both long term and day to day.

Distinguish your short-term, high-priority tasks from those you will be tackling later on (say, in 6 months). When you complete this step, compare your short-term action plan to your earlier historic analysis. Would Machiavelli think you are in trouble?

To Do Lists

A marketer's most crucial piece of equipment is probably a list. Marketing is a topsy-turvy experience, and keeping up with the sheer complexity of the role sometimes defeats your efforts to get organized. (If you take "to do" and combine the words you get the Spanish word, *todo,* for "all"—that's what our to do lists seem like.)

But, there are two distinct schools of thought on these lists: one says it should be a "todo" list, with all your tasks entered daily. Others say this omnibus document becomes overwhelming, oppressive, and inefficient—you can't set clear priorities on a three-page agenda.

The other school says keep only high-priority items on the list, just enough for 1 day. Keep other tasks on a calendar (which can also be used for a to do list) or in some other system. However you organize your to do list, always tie it back to a calendar, because whatever your tasks are, their priorities will reflect due dates, deliverables, and other time concerns. So, take your choice. If you need everything in one place and can deal with sorting through the mess, make one list at the first or end of the week and add to and delete from it daily. Use the following guidelines for making up your list:

- Date and evaluate each entry; note priorities, either by numbering tasks or starring some—we sometimes use colored highlighters to mark those that have a shorter deadline.

- Date the to do list.

- Place a deadline by each task (you can then cross-file by deadline to your "tickler" file).

- Keep the list where you can get at it easily; some people keep them in a notebook and carry them everywhere; others keep them on their desks where they see them constantly.

- Keep the entries simple—they are for you alone; if you need to explain a complex task or break it down, do it in some other place, not on this list.

Keep your old lists in a file to review periodically. You'll be amazed at how much you accomplished; it will help you plan your time in the future and help you explain to others what you do all day.

Tickler Files

A tickler file is a chronological file that tells you when you need to do things such as make calls, send letters, and have photos taken or sent to a printer. It also tells you what others should be doing so that you can light fires under them, remind them, or just plain nag. One effective method is that of "monthly/daily":

- Set up a file for each month of the year.

- At the same time, make up a series of folders labeled 1 through 31, a folder for each day.

This simple filing system lets you log in and out your specific marketing duties. Anything that requires action has a ready-made slot in the tickler file: travel and meeting data, things to read, letters to answer. Empty each day's folder as part of the day's work. Act on the items or relocate them. Use the tickler file to coordinate the work of others, as in awaiting response to questions asked of a consultant.

The tickler file does have some drawbacks as it will not force you to look ahead. (For this, a large poster-type calendar with note space for each day may be helpful.) Avoid the situation of opening the file for January as if it were Pandora's box and finding in there a due date that is impossible to meet because you didn't look ahead.

Many marketers now use the computer for their tickler file, checking first thing when they log on each day. You may need special software to create a system that works for you. (See Chap. 3, "Direct Marketing," for more information on software for marketers.)

ORGANIZING INFORMATION: YOUR FIRM'S MARKETS

One of your highest priorities may be lead finding and qualifying prospects. You need systems to help you keep this fast-changing information current and distributed to the right places—where it can be acted on. The following section describes methods for organizing information about markets, specific projects, and clients, as well as methods for developing networks and other resources for exchanging information. You will find more information on developing information on clients in Chap. 3, "Direct Marketing."

You can start organizing information on your markets by developing a tickler file similar to the one described above. Only this time you can use a card file, organized by date, to keep track of all active leads and contacts. These leads can be organized alphabetically by project or client. The information consists of your last contact, what you must do to follow up, and when your next contact will be made, how, and by whom (Fig. 2.2). Remember, the card is not your meeting notes but a guide to keep you up to date.

Another example is a running tickler file which we have used to keep up to date with on-going sales activities (Fig. 2.3). Systems like tickler files often serve you, the maker of the file, better than anyone else. There is a certain discipline in writing down this information that can really help you stay cur-

```
              Ernestine Entrepreneur
              Dogood Development
              123 Main Street, Midtown
              123/456-7890

          November 10, 1988:  lunch w/Ernestine re:  intro to our
          firm; discussed plans to renovate Dogood Bldg.; promised
          to send info on our renov. projects; call back early 1989.
          (FILE JAN 89)

          January 11, 1989:  called Ernie, arranged walk-thru of
          bldg. on 2/5.

          February 5, 1989:  walked thru Dogood Bldg.; renovation
          job - warehouse to offices; lunch and promised to send info
          on office interiors projects and have her meet RB, principal/
          office dev. projects (FILE 2/8)

          February 12, 1989:  called and arranged for Ernie to come
          to our office on 2/18 to meet RB (FILE 2/16)
```

Figure 2.2   Information card on client.

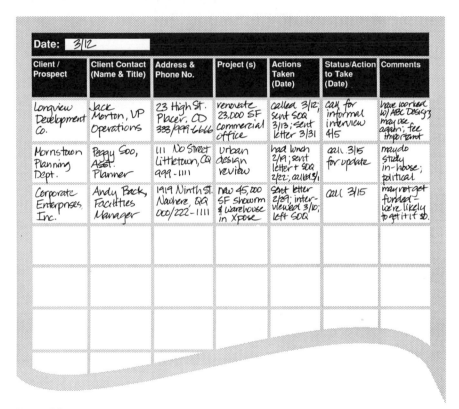

Date: 3/12						
Client / Prospect	Client Contact (Name & Title)	Address & Phone No.	Project (s)	Actions Taken (Date)	Status/Action to Take (Date)	Comments
Longview Development Co.	Jack Morton, VP Operations	23 High St. Placer, CO 333/999-6666	renovate 23,000 SF commercial office	called 3/12; sent SOQ 3/13; sent letter 3/31	call for informal interview 4/5	have worked w/ ABC Design; may use again; fee important
Mornstown Planning Dept.	Peggy Soo, Asst. Planner	111 No Street Littletown, CO 999-1111	urban design review	had lunch 2/19; sent letter + SOQ 2/22; called 3/1	call 3/15 for update	may do study in-house; political
Corporate Enterprises, Inc.	Andy Back, Facilities Manager	1919 Ninth St. Nowhere, QQ 000/222-1111	new 45,000 SF showrm & warehouse in Xpose	sent letter 2/29; interviewed 3/10; left SOQ	call 3/15	may not get funded— we're likely to get it if $$.

Figure 2.3   Running tickler file.

rent, whether you review it frequently or not. By updating this tickler every time you make or receive a contact—not hard to do on a computer—you can quickly check what to do next on every important opportunity. By printing it out weekly or biweekly, you can report your progress to others in the firm.

A note of caution on tickler files: others in the firm have to keep you posted on their marketing activities. If your tickler file includes assignments for others, the file will help you keep aware of and help organize their marketing activities. A simple memo or note on the back of a cocktail napkin will suffice, but somehow the lines of communication must be open in both directions.

Network Files

Some marketers say that the most important element in their lead-finding efforts is an effective network. This network can provide information about your markets, your competition, prices and services, and who is looking for work or just found a job. The best information usually comes directly from people in your network. You will learn in time whose mouth (both within and outside the firm) provides the best information.

The network is a system of "live wires," connected to the key marketing people in your firm, into which you must tap. There are many ways to organize a network. Ideally you have an active card file or printout from a word processor or computer on which are printed the names of people who are in the network. These names, updated constantly, should be cross-referenced and described as much as possible and may even be subdivided by type or rated as to relative value to the firm. The network is not a dead file or a telephone directory; it is a living "hot line" and a spontaneous reference system. Figure 2.4 shows an example of an organized network entry. (Some marketers keep much of this information on the person's business card, including, of course, when and where you met, and sometimes a brief description of his or her looks.) Increasingly, this information is kept in a computer database, often on software specifically designed for the purpose.

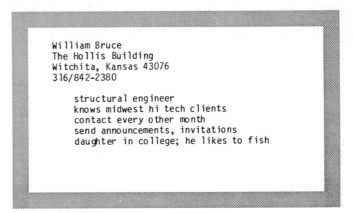

```
William Bruce
The Hollis Building
Witchita, Kansas 43076
316/842-2380

    structural engineer
    knows midwest hi tech clients
    contact every other month
    send announcements, invitations
    daughter in college; he likes to fish
```

Figure 2.4 Organized network entry.

If you use a card file, either one that rotates or the old recipe box type, you may want to organize by names only, rather than by company, remembering that, if the network is active, the people who use it will know the people in it. However, you may also want to cross-reference by firm, so that, when you need to know who are your contacts at Murphy Land Development, you can quickly find out if someone there knows you.

Another method is simply to break down the network into its basic types and organize these separately, though still by name within the given type. This method may yield groupings such as:

- Consultant
- Prospective client
- Existing and/or past client
- Agents, writers, public figures
- Special friends (of the firm or its principals)
- Project type (health care, retail centers)

However, remember that the more filing cubbyholes you create the more nooks and crannies there are in which information you need can hide and the more places you need to check when updating information. Therefore, whatever approach you use, keep it simple.

Warning: the names on a list such as this are usually personal contacts developed by people in your firm over many years. Note whose contact within your firm this person is. Colleagues within your firm may feel proprietary about sharing these quasi-intimate contacts with you. People whose contacts form the network must stay in touch with them until they hand them over to you (along with a personal introduction). The point is, really, that these contacts must be nurtured and used. They cannot simply be stuffed into a "dead" file.

Your job is to see that the network is used and that it grows, not to sit on it until it hatches leads of its own accord. People will use the network more efficiently if you get in and organize it, help evaluate it, and see to it that people really do use it.

Your CIA

Some marketers keep comprehensive files on clients and potential clients, sometimes by market, either on the computer or in hard copy. File folders let you include newspaper clippings and annual reports, for example, or copies of pending legislation or other data near and dear to a marketer's heart, as well as brief notes from interviews with individuals in the client organization. As with many other systems, the best way to organize these data is from general to specific, most likely by project type. As an example, a file on waste water facilities might begin with information on national, state, and local legislation, move on to specific areas experiencing growth or other needs, and from there move to specific water districts funding projects and/or those with whom you have met.

Some perfectionists even keep notes in these files on the personal taste and interests of executives or decision makers in the client organization (e.g., wears yellow argyles and knit vests; has two kids, one in college at State State).

ORGANIZING INFORMATION: YOUR FIRM'S CAPABILITIES AND EXPERIENCE

The undertakings described so far will help you organize your basic approach to marketing and keep track of information about clients and projects. Now we will look at systems to help you keep track of information *about your firm* that you want to give to clients. (See also Chap. 5, "Sales Tools, and Chap. 3, "Direct Marketing.")

The following is a quick overview of methods we have used for organizing this material. It includes what goes into the computer and what should be kept in hard copy.

Boilerplate

The stock statements about the firm—its people, history, design philosophy, and significant projects constitute what we commonly refer to as "boilerplate." It is generally off-the-shelf information used in proposals or statements of qualifications, sent along with introductory letters or stuffed in with a brochure sent to a prospective client. This material should be written by you, or to your specifications, in such a way that it can be:

- Assembled to apply to general audiences

- Manipulated to contain variations applicable to more specific audiences

Creating, maintaining, and updating boilerplate is an important marketing activity. The information should all be on a word processing system, one that you have mastered and have easy access to. You may want to suggest new or different systems if the one your firm uses doesn't meet your marketing needs. In addition to word processing for boilerplate, many firms now use a database management system as well to help them call up what boilerplate exists under specific headings or "fields." Several software programs combine data and word processing and at least one system is designed to perform these functions specifically for A/E firm marketing. They enable you to call up whatever already exists in the system under a given category and then make whatever changes you want to it using word processing. A typical boilerplate database might include the following:

- U.S. government Standard Forms 254, 255
- Standard form letters of interest or intent (by market)
- Standard outline proposals (by market)
- Project descriptions (short and long forms)
- Résumés for all senior technical personnel (by specific version for different markets)
- Project lists by market

In terms of hard copy for boilerplate, we recommend you keep a supply of completed sheets convenient to your work station for quick assembly of packages but also keep an original set of all pages in a more secure place. You never know when the printer will be jammed up and you need to put something together quickly. You can at least make photocopies from the clean original (unless that machine is broken, too).

To keep track of both originals and copies, you may want to develop a filing system that is indexed as follows:

I. Introductions
    A. General introduction to the firm
    B. Introduction to the firm—industrial market
    C. Introduction to the firm—health care market
    D. Introduction to the firm—(other specific markets or situations)
II. Résumés
    A. By personnel (general and alphabetical)
    B. By specific market (alphabetical; version tailored to industrial or health care, for example)
III. Project descriptions
    A. Comprehensive—master file of all available data
    B. Industrial market (alphabetical)
    C. Healthcare market (alphabetical)
IV. Project lists (by market)
V. Cost or budget control statements
    A. Approach
    B. Track record, statistics
VI. Other key issues
    A. Schedule control
    B. Awards
    C. Other

Proposal Files

Set up a filing system to store hard copies of proposals and statements of qualifications, by client or project type, alphabetically and possibly by year. If you keep them on a book shelf, you may need to store the smaller ones in special containers—pamphlet cases, for example—so they don't get lost among the big binders. These files help you find the great descriptions of your approach to solving some esoteric problems that you (or someone) wrote about 18 months ago and is somewhere in the computer but you aren't sure where. Having access to all your proposals by type of project will help trigger your memory and save hours of rewriting, or worse, reinventing the approach statement. When you have all your proposal material in your database, cross-referenced for easy access, you may still want the actual proposals for those in your firm who want to "see" how the material was used previously.

Along with the proposals, be sure to keep the RFP and all notes on client and project research conducted at the time of the submittal. (You may want to put copies of these notes in your CIA file as well, if the client is one you will want to talk to again.) You will also want to file any debriefing notes here, regarding why you did or did not get awarded the project. Among other things, these files will help you create or double check on your "hit rate" record.

Keeping Track of Photos

A simple rule for photos: all originals and first-quality negatives should be kept out of the hands of anyone other than yourself or your designated appointee. This prohibition includes principals in your firm. Organize and file *your* originals by project and by type (e.g., Project: Newark Office Park. Type: color negatives or original print or transparencies). These leave the office only when you need prints to be made from them or when *Architectural Record* calls, in which case you make duplicates for yourself and send the originals by special handling. (You will send originals, albeit nervously, to magazine editors because you want, in print, the best quality graphics possible.)

Our experience indicates it is better to have many prints of a few agreed-upon favorites than to have a few prints of everything. First, find out the favorites, then build your supply. Spend all the time you need editing and reducing photo files to include only those that are really first rate.

Prints are expensive, and giving them away should be a serious undertaking. A good brochure will reduce your need to mail prints to prospective clients. However, brochures can fall out of date quicker than Italian furniture, and prints of recent projects (usually not in the brochure) will tell an audience where your firm is *now*.

File photos and other graphics by project or description (e.g., construction management, medical office buildings) to reflect the organization of your written material. Cross-reference projects that fit into two or more categories.

Where Are the Slides?

It is a simple fact of life that slides disappear. They "walk," are left on airplanes, or find their way into portfolios when people leave the firm.

Slide organization is much like the organization of photos outlined above, only more so. Some firms use slides frequently, exposing slides to destruction and loss. Periodically review all new slides; cull them to a reasonable number, retaining those that are commonly liked and make several duplicates of each. Then lock up the originals and throw away the key.

Whatever you do, keep the slide filing system simple by avoiding complex numbering, indexing, and cross-referencing. Follow these simple rules when filing slides:

- Weed out bad or useless slides before they even get into the system.

- Organize slides according to how they are used, such as "presentation" slides and "historical" or "record" slides. Within these basic divisions, organize slides by project type or in some way that reflects your firm's markets.

- Assign one person to maintain order in the slide system (with a little luck, it won't be you).

- As stated before, keep the master slides safe from everyday use.

In a firm we know, the slides are filed alphabetically by project within categories of project type. The system also contains two separate groups of slides: "first" slides (the best, most used) and "second" slides (ones of less quality, unique or special topics and ones which are less frequently used). The first slides contain three or four copies of less than 20 slides per project. The second set contains fewer copies of a larger variety of shots. In addition, each principal or project architect who makes presentations has his or her own slide show arranged in a carousel tray ready to be used on a moment's notice or adapted for a special presentation. Every slide itself is labeled as to where it should be filed and marked to show how it should be placed in the carousel (Fig. 2.5).

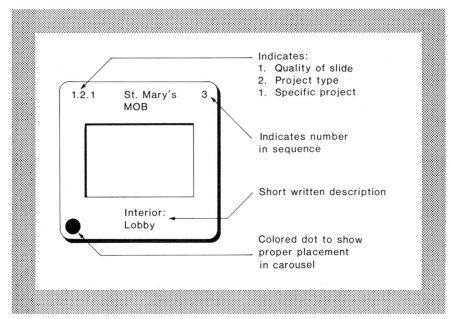

Figure 2.5 Sample slide (labeled).

Let's quickly review this particular system, bearing in mind that it is only an example of how you might organize slides without purchasing a manufactured system. In a drawer or drawers of a filing cabinet (they use large lateral files) were sections labeled "First Quality":

- 1.1 City Planning
- 1.2 Health Care
- 1.3 Housing
- 1.4 Renovation
- 1.5 Hotels/Restaurants

These drawers held heavy-duty plastic sheets of slides, each sheet labeled, in labeled file folders or three-ring binders.

In another drawer labeled "Second Quality: Special Slides" they kept the next generation or less frequently used slides filed under the same sub-headings:

- 2.1 City Planning
- 2.2 Health Care
- 2.3 Housing
- 2.4 Renovation
- 2.5 Hotels/Restaurants

A light table and portable slide viewer were nearby for easy viewing and to discourage people from taking the slides. A sign-out sheet was taped to the top of the file cabinet for recording who had what. In a separate, literally fireproof room (you may consider a safe deposit box), they filed the original 35-mm slides, transparencies, and negatives (for prints) with the same numeric system. No one but marketing staff had access.

This is just one example of how slides may be filed in-house. There are a number of manufactured slide-filing systems on the market. If you decide to purchase a system rather than creating your own, ask questions such as the following:

- What is the capacity?
- Can we add on to the system for a reasonable cost?
- Does it protect the slides from the elements and (very important) from handling?
- Can it be secured?
- Can we view the slides without touching them?
- Can the system be organized with enough individuality to work with our other filing systems?
- Does it require a lot of space or special ventilation?
- For the cost, is it worth more than some other item we could use (like another computer)?

Brochures and Other Printed Matter

Other means of telling clients about your firm are brochures and newsletters—from general, image pieces to more focused, market-specific ones. We describe these items in Chap. 5, "Marketing Tools." However, you do need efficient filing systems for keeping them organized by subject and especially for monitoring inventory: how many got sent out and to whom they were sent. One marketer we know, for example, placed a numbered sticky-back label on each brochure. When people in the firm took a brochure to hand out, they peeled off the labels and put them in a log book by their name.

Another important printed item may be reprints of articles. Magazine articles or other published descriptions of your work, not written by your firm, are always good marketing tools and should be kept in reasonable quantities. Unlike boilerplate, this printed material is usually not altered. For this reason, you can have many copies printed in the best quality you can afford. File this type of written information, organized to reflect its subject matter and placed close enough to your boilerplate so they can be pieced together quickly for a general or specific audience. Again, our experience has led us to organize all material by project type or market.

ORGANIZING FOR SUCCESS: MONITORING

Another set of systems we recommend will enable you to review periodically how well you and your firm are doing. In a broad sense, monitoring occurs on two levels—reviewing what you said you would do (in your action plan and in your job description) to see *if you did it* and reviewing what you did to see *if it worked.* We talk more about both of these systems in Chap. 7, "The Marketing Plan," but they are also part of getting organized. Let's look first at how you review to see *if you did it.*

Monitoring Your Own Success

Depending on your job, the specific tasks you need to monitor and the volume of things to track, you may want to keep tabs on any or all of the following on a weekly or monthly basis:

DIRECT MARKETING

RFPs received: (#)		
Proposals:	In progress (#)	Submitted (#)
SF 255		
SOQs		
Fee submittals		
Other:_____		

_____

Presentations:	In progress (#)	Completed (#)
Leads acquired (#)		
Prospects uncovered (#)		
Comments:_____		

_____

Contacts made (#)
Contacts scheduled or attempted, not completed (#)
Comments:_____

_____

Contracts awarded: (# and fees) (You may want to compare what you actually won against a target figure and show the percent variation).
Prior backlog (from end of prior reporting period)/Current backlog

SALES TOOLS

Project descriptions (#)	Revised	New Entered
Résumés (#)	Revised	New Entered
Other boilerplate	Revised	New Entered
Photography (#)		
Graphics (#)		
Brochure development: Progress_____		

PUBLIC RELATIONS

Press releases	In progress (#)	Submitted (#)
Announcements	In progress (#)	Sent (#)
Articles queried or submitted (#)		
Articles:		
Progress:_____		
Awards submittals:	In progress (#)	Submitted (#)
Lectures:_____		
Seminars, etc.:_____		

REPORTS/PLANNING

Market Research:_____
Image Survey:_____
Other:_____

You can see from the above that your own progress report needs to respond to the job you do and what you and others in your firm think are the priorities. The point is to be able to track progress and review the volume of work against the results, which is the other thing to track.

Monitoring the Firm's Success

These analyses assist in determining how well your marketing and sales efforts are working. Are you pursuing the right markets? Is there enough volume to sustain the firm? Are you getting all the leads you need? Are you making the short lists and winning the presentations? These are major questions that need to be discussed with the firm leaders, ideally out of the office, perhaps in a retreat organized to help develop a marketing plan. You need systems to develop the information that will become the basis of a plan (see Chap. 7, "The Marketing Plan").

If you are responsible for marketing policy, you will also want to know if projects are profitable and, if not, why—should you avoid this client in the future, should you get out of the entire market, or do you just need to be more careful with the scope description, your internal cost estimating, and project management? The following gives some ways to get a handle on this information, but the list is by no means exhaustive.

Market Share This measurement is widely used in product marketing but difficult to track in the professional services field. However, you can keep a record of all the projects of a certain type that you hear of, for which your firm could or does compete. Even if you don't actually pursue them, these jobs indicate the volume of work in a given market and give you an indication of what percentage you are capturing. Compare this volume to the number of jobs your firm is awarded. Look at both the number of jobs and the total fee volume (or construction value).

These figures will also help you assess if there is adequate volume in the market to justify further marketing expense and other investments to improve your position. It will also indicate if you are loosing share to the competition and if you aren't getting information about prospects and leads early enough. You will want to see an increase in market share from year to year.

Hit Rates—Proposals This category records the number of short lists your firm makes based on proposals submitted. If you make short lists based on other criteria (referrals, phone conversations, etc.), keep a separate list of those. Keep track of how many proposals you submit per month or year and how many are winners. If you mainly submit your qualifications to be a subconsultant to another firm, track which of the prime consultants you submit to have the best success and which have the lowest. See if you can work with the primes that have poor track records to help them improve.

Hit Rates—Presentations Record how many presentations you go to and how many of them you win; again, as a subconsultant it's important to track which prime consultants have the highest success rates and see what you can do to help the others improve.

Hit Rates—Fee Proposals If your firm has to submit fees as the primary or a major criterion for obtaining work, keep careful track of your win-loss rate by scope, fee, client, and project.

Volume of Repeat or Add-on Work from Existing Clients Keep track of how much additional fee volume you obtain from clients for whom you are currently working; you will need the accounting office's cooperation for this one.

Volume of New Work from New Clients and New Markets   This assessment will let you evaluate whether you met your marketing goals, especially if you identified specific targets by market and client in an annual plan.

Analyzing the Costs and Results   These are only some of the reports you may want to generate on a regular basis. The advent of relatively easy-to-use database management software has made reporting more sophisticated and less time consuming than it once was. One warning: we have seen firms in which the marketing coordinator's or manager's time was so consumed with report generation that the person had almost no time for marketing or sales support. In a very large firm (several hundred people or more) this dedicated effort will make sense; in a firm of less than 200 people it should not take up more than a few days per month.

The point of all these analyses is to provide material on which to base future marketing decisions and from which to create or revise your marketing plan (see Chap. 7, "The Marketing Plan"). They will also help others in your firm understand the value of marketing (although we don't guarantee these data will convince the diehard disbelievers).

In large firms, or in any firm with a numbers-oriented managing principal, the ability of a marketing person to justify expenses and show a cost-benefit relationship will pay dividends. We know of at least one marketing person who was promoted to chief administrative officer based largely on his ability to make sense of the numbers.

INTRODUCTION

Most of us have said or heard others in our firm say things like, "Why didn't we know about that lead?" or "How do we get the next job?" or "We have to find a way to get in the door with this client."

Direct marketing involves the effort to procure work and culminates in the sale of your services to a client who needs and will pay for them. Architects and engineers tend to think in terms of getting the next job; marketers need to think in terms of developing clients. If you have a client, projects will follow. We describe some specific types of clients and strategies or tactics appropriate to each in Chap. 6, "Clients." In this chapter we describe both how to develop a client relationship and how to turn that relationship into a job.

We assume you have a marketing plan in effect (Chap. 7), you have most of the systems and tools you need (Chaps. 2 and 5), you understand the types of clients you will be pursuing (Chap. 6), and you now need to launch a campaign to court a client or type of client.

DIRECT MARKETING: STEP BY STEP

In our experience, obtaining a client usually follows a sequence that includes at least some of the following actions (see also Fig. 3.1):

Market research and lead finding A combination of literature search (reading about markets and potential clients) and phone calls or personal interviews with potential clients and those who know about them to determine who is likely to be planning projects, what the projects are, how much money will be spent, and what are the client's selection criteria.

Courting clients A series of steps, often involving letters of interest, brochures and other qualifications statements, invitations to informal (sometimes social) meetings, a visit to and/or from the client introducing key people in your firm, and reviewing your experience and qualifications.

Writing proposals Stating in clear, specific terms how well you understand the client's requirements for services relative to a specific project and the unique (if possible) ability of your team to meet those requirements.

Making presentations Having your project team leaders address the client's selection team in regard to the key criteria and concerns they have about the project and persuading them that your team is the best qualified to do the job.

Closing Signing a contract with the client to perform the services.

Evaluating the process Obtaining a debriefing from the client and reviewing the strategy and techniques with in-house colleagues in order to learn what worked or did not work.

Now, let's take a closer look at each element in the direct marketing sequence.

MARKET RESEARCH: A PRO-ACTIVE APPROACH

In this case "pro-active" means "professionally active," with emphasis on professionally. Research is a very professional activity and can put your firm ahead of the competition in a respectable way. It epitomizes third-generation marketing techniques.

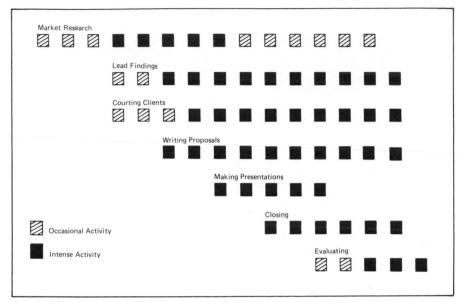

Figure 3.1 Direct marketing time line.

In this book we talk about market research in two time frames: In Chap. 7, "The Marketing Plan," we describe research that you do as part of developing a plan; it has a starting and ending point and the findings direct your firm's decisions as to clients and projects to pursue at a particular time. Another kind of market research is on-going; it takes place every time you pick up the morning paper or read a trade magazine or have lunch with a business friend. It is this latter research we want to talk about in this chapter, what you do with the information you are taking in all the time.

This kind of research can also be called "lead research" and can be used to identify potential clients within already targeted markets (those you uncovered for your marketing plan). We want to emphasize that you benefit from knowing a lot about your markets before you start to sell to them. We continually test the goals of our firms against the findings of our research.

For each market, identify initial sources whom you can contact to obtain the information needed. Sources to consider include:

- Past clients
- Potential clients
- Directors of trade associations (in specific market)
- Editors of trade publications
- Market analysts (stocks and bonds)
- Decision makers in federal, state, and local agencies
- Experts in the field (consultants, investors)
- Other engineers, architects, planners, etc.

Listen, Listen, Listen

Generally, the most current information available on a given market comes from talking *and listening* to people. The perceptions of people active in your area of interest, their gut reactions to the market's potential, and their views concerning your firm's place in that market will help you focus your sales efforts.

Even before you interview some of the people listed above, start with your own firm. Interview your principals, key staff persons, other colleagues, and even competitors. To get this information, try some of the following techniques:

- Hold a roundtable luncheon in your office with some well-informed people to discuss trends in each market you have identified.

- Talk to your current clients concerning their views of this market.

- Talk to bankers, venture capital investors, brokers, and other financial specialists concerning their perception of this market.

- Talk to lawyers, accountants, and other legal and financial experts who know the market.

- Attend seminars and workshops given by others in this market segment; talk to other attendees, not just the speakers.

We recommend expanding your network from in-house resources to colleagues, then to interested observers, and finally to potential clients so that when you do start talking to clients you will be conversant in their areas of interest.

If there is one thing to remember from this chapter, it is: *Do not wait until a specific project is identified before you approach a client.* Talk to possible clients as part of your oral research. We have found this approach is non-threatening because you are recognizing them as experts as opposed to looking for work from them. They are sources of information, not necessarily sources of projects in the short term. If you hit on a project along the way, consider it a bonus. Your real goal is to collect information so that you can make informed decisions when you do uncover leads.

Follow these steps in interviewing people to get market information:

- Prepare a general list of questions you want answered.

- Prepare more specialized questions aimed directly at each contact.

- Remember to gear your questions to the special knowledge of each contact.

- Begin with a person who is best able to educate you on the trends, concepts, issues, jargon, and scope of the market.

- Do not be afraid to admit ignorance. *You are learning, not selling.*

- Build from what you have learned to become more conversant in the subject area.

- Ask open-ended questions wherever possible (who, what, when, where, why), not yes or no questions.

- Encourage your source to express opinions; evaluate them as such.

- On every call, be sure to ask for names of others who might be worth talking to.

- Stop when the data start repeating themselves or when you run out of time.

- Follow up on a call with a note of thanks or an agreement to meet.

Read, Read, Read

While you should talk to as many resource people as possible, you should also read about trends and issues in the selected markets. Your reading will include the following types of periodicals:

- General circulation (daily newspapers and weekly news magazines)

- Financial interest (e.g., *Wall Street Journal, Barrons*)
- Trade press for your firm's disciplines (e.g., *ENR, Building Design and Construction, Interiors*)
- Trade press geared toward your client's market (we know you can't wait to dig into the next issue of *Shopping Center World*)

As you develop knowledge about a market, maintain intelligence files on that market. These may include an up-to-date record of major projects and other activity in the market area. This information, such as newspaper or magazine articles, annual reports, or technical papers, will also help you to discuss issues of concern to your intended clients. Include information about past and present clients of your firm as well as intelligence on potential clients. We recommend that this research be filed by project types (e.g., shopping centers, libraries, convention centers) or client types (e.g., municipalities, bio-technical, NAVFAC, etc.).

Analyze the Findings in Terms of Your Firm

Determine if your firm can compete successfully in a given area by continually analyzing your experience and talents against what is required by clients. If you need to improve your firm's competitive edge and establish credibility in a market, we suggest several ways to begin:

- Promote key people on your staff who have relevant prior experience, can lead projects, and can deal directly with clients.
- Hire a person known in the field to lead a marketing effort in the targeted area and act as a "closer-doer" (see Chap. 6, "Clients," for more on closer-doers).
- "Marry" the required skills by forming an association with a firm well known in this market, first on a trial basis for one project, potentially for a longer term (but remember, there must be a logical reason for your own firm's presence on the team).
- Work with consultants and/or specialty contractors who have successfully completed projects of a similar nature and know clients in the field and will recommend your firm. Once you have sold your skills and are actively working in the area of interest, you may then lay claim to experience in the market.
- Review the reasons your firm is hired by clients in other areas and evaluate these reasons to see if they apply to the market under consideration (Fig. 3.2). Evaluate these reasons and, where possible, apply the strong points to your marketing efforts in the new area of interest.

In summary, the primary activities of your research include:

- An analysis of the current and future trends of the market
- The development of intelligence files on the market in general and on key clients in particular
- Lists of clients in that market and potential clients your firm may approach
- An evaluation of your own firm's strengths and weaknesses in the market
- An evaluation of the strengths and weaknesses of your competition and potential affiliates

Project:		
Your evaluation	Strong	Weak
Fee		
Design		
Approach to problem solving		
Staff involvement in project		
Personality of firm		
Cost Control		
Location		
J.V. partner		
Other		

Figure 3.2   Reasons your firm gets hired.

DEVELOPING LEADS: THE SOONER, THE BETTER

Developing leads is probably the single most important concern of most marketers. For this discussion we'll call a lead any useful information about a potential project in a market targeted in your firm's marketing plan. Genuine leads meet certain criteria, including:

- The project is real and likely to go ahead.
- It is or can be funded.
- Your firm is qualified to provide the services required.
- No other firm has been selected; it is not "wired."

Marketing people are trained to identify and evaluate these factors and can usually do so more effectively than their technical A/E colleagues. But, once a lead has been established, the marketer should look to the technical staff for help and begin planning the handoff.

How many calls does it take to get a nibble? It depends, of course, on how active the market is, which is one reason for doing market research first. But in a "mature" market (one with lots of competition for relatively little work), you can expect to complete up to 50 calls before you uncover a really hot prospect. In the process you should have learned a lot and filled up your tickler file. You will also have made lots of incomplete calls to the wrong person, who refers you to the next wrong person, who leaves you on hold..., etc.

Talk to People; Don't Be Shy

As with market research, lead finding begins with talking to the right people. Use your existing contacts to expand your knowledge of a given market and begin to look for leads that are directly linked to projects. Talk to:

- Consultants and suppliers
- Real estate agents
- Former, current, and potential clients
- Contractors
- Friends of the firm who are in the field and often know first hand who is developing—or thinking about—a project of interest to you

Nurture the relationships you have with people who are reliable sources of information. You cannot sit by the phone waiting for others to give you leads; you must also pass leads along to them.

Phone Techniques: What to Say After You Say. . .

Much of the talking we do to develop leads takes place over the phone. Salespeople often refer to these contacts as "cold calls" because they involve calling someone you may not know (and their reaction may be decidedly cool). Before making the call, outline questions you will ask, information you expect to receive, and how you want to "close" the conversation. (Make this outline brief and informal, but do it.) Include reminders such as, you want to come away knowing you will have a meeting, send résumés, propose for the job, gain other leads, or plan a fishing trip. Here are some guidelines to follow:

- Try to talk to the specific person you ask for, but find out who else you can talk to.

- If you can't reach your target, ask when you should call back rather than expecting them to call you.

- If you can't get through, try to develop a professional friendship with an assistant or administrator and get whatever information you can from this person.

- The best relationships are those between equals, and that is the way a lead-finding call should feel.

- Think about ways you can assist the person you called, usually by providing him or her with information.

Remember, you are making the call and are initiating the communication, so don't hesitate to direct the conversation. And don't worry about what time to call. But always start by asking if you've called at an inopportune time and offer to schedule a later call at a specific agreed-upon time. If you can't reach a key person during regular business hours, try in the early morning or late evening; you can sometimes by-pass a receptionist or secretary.

Figure 3.3 shows a list of questions that should be asked of a contact when first developing a lead. This method works best under two conditions: when you have done some research on this client and when it is a client with many projects and on-going work. This list can be used by either a marketing or a technical person making an initial call to a potential client. The list is designed to be used with the actual client, but you can modify it if your source is a third-party informant. We incorporate information from a form like the one above into our tickler system or into an abbreviated tickler form like the one shown in Fig. 3.4, a lead or prospect update list.

Back to the Books

In addition to your information network, you can use some of these publications, which are devoted solely or in part to providing leads:

- *Commerce Business Daily* (*CBD*), a federal publication that lists all government-funded contracts over a certain size

- *Dodge Reports*, private subscription publication outlining upcoming projects in several key industries

- *Engineering News-Record*, a weekly magazine

```
QUESTIONS TO ASK PROSPECTIVE CLIENTS

1.  Please tell me something about your firm's/institution's/
    agency's (etc.) past projects [It's good to know something
    about them before you call!], e.g.:  Which projects would you
    call successful, and why? _____

    _____

2.  In what ways would you change the way you develop projects --
    why? _____

    _____

3.  What growth or major changes do you anticipate in your market
    in the next year or two? _____

    _____

(if applicable)

4.  What planning/architectural/engineering/interior design
    (etc.) firms have you worked with, or are you currently
    using? _____

    _____

5.  What do you think of their service? _____

6.  What would you like to get -- in terms of services, experi-
    ence, knowledge or skills -- from consultants you work with?

    _____

7.  What upcoming projects can you tell us about? _____

    _____

8.  What is your selection procedure? _____

    _____

9.  What would you suggest we do to introduce our firm to you?

    _____

10. Who else in your organization (or other organizations) do you
    recommend we contact? _____

    _____
```

Figure 3.3 Questions for prospective clients.

- Local news and business publications
- Lead-finding services

Don't overlook the business section of the local newspapers as well as national publications concentrating on business news. Articles about upcoming developments or land sales are often good sources for generating leads.

You can also use lead-finding services. You pay for the service, and leads are channeled to you. A conscientious service will limit its subscribers and try to avoid any conflicts of interest. Experience has taught us to be wary of lead-finding services. Before you subscribe to a service, find out how they work; be sure they do limit their clients and that they can deliver. Contact noncompeting firms who have retained the service to get their reactions. Some services use old or erroneous information, resulting in a waste of time and money, not to mention embarrassment, if you pursue a dead lead. We have all made the mistake of contacting a potential client in order to be considered as designers for a project that just started construction. Lead-finding services are most helpful when you have no established network of your own, such as when your firm enters a new market or when you open an

Project	Contact (Your Firm)	Contact (Client or lead consultant)	Action (Taken or to be taken)	Date of Last Activity	Estimated Fee or Project Cost	Probability
Southwest General Hospital	D.M.	J. Thomas	Submitted fee proposal; DM to follow	8/13	$185 K (fee)	Good - they know us
Metro Center	J.B.	Metro Bldrs & 3-Z Arch. W. Jones	Discussion of scope/ role on team	9/12	$125 M (project)	Lao- uses TBG; does not like JVs
Tucson Transit Mall	M.B.S.	A. Franks City Plan.	Interview held	7/10	$425 K (fee)	Lost - fee too high

Figure 3.4 Lead or prospect update list.

office in a new area. And they are of more benefit to contractors and interior architects than to planners and others involved in early project development.

Gerre Jones' book, *How to Market Professional Design Services,* has some excellent insights on the subject of lead finding.

Make Your Own Leads

Many potential clients, especially in the private sector, have vague ideas of projects they would like to develop but 'have not brought their ideas to a point where they can review consultants' credentials.

We have submitted successful proposals to clients who have not requested them. To do this, describe the potential project and a definite direction that it may follow. A firm we know often works with repeat clients, in part by helping them determine the value of land or investments they have. Some firms propose to do a limited amount of work to assist clients in evaluating a project's potential. You may be helpful in finding an investor for a client who has property but no financing.

Through your contacts in real estate, leasing, and public agencies, you may be able to structure a team that can develop a project where no potential existed before. To initiate action requires intellect and patience. You are part of a creative process and must be prepared to invest money and time before this effort turns into a real project.

What to Do with Leads Once You Get Them

Leads are best nurtured by professionals who speak the language of their clients. To follow up on a lead, use *one* individual in your firm who is familiar with the project type, feels comfortable representing the firm, and, preferably, who stays in touch with the marketing arm of your firm. At best this person should be a "closer-doer," able to manage a project for this client once you are awarded the contract which he or she helps "close."

The handoff between the initial contact (often a principal or marketing person) and the person who will nurture the client relationship should be made very early in your dealings. Once you feel a contact has true potential to produce a project, develop rapport between the client representative and the person in your firm who will work with the client over a period of time.

After completing the handoff, you, as the marketing person, may no longer deal directly with the client representative. But, the client has not yet given you a job, so your work has not yet ended. How do you stay abreast of progress (or lack of it) in pursuing this prospect?

To help us stay informed we ask our technical colleagues to use forms like those shown in Fig. 3.5. Even when they don't use the actual form, they know—from our having gone over it with them—what they are supposed to find out about the client. They sometimes give us this information in memos, either the formal type or scribbled notes on cocktail napkins and the like. We also use these forms ourselves to get information. Ask your technical colleagues and other marketers in your firm to give you completed forms on client contacts. To get them started, ask them to comment on the forms you've prepared for their use and modify them as needed.

COURTING

Courting is one of the best ways to develop leads, and it consists of developing a close, long-lasting relationship between two parties. It may take place prior to your developing an actual lead but only if you know the client will have one or more leads in a reasonable time frame. "Reasonable" may be 3 to 6 months or 1 to 2 years, depending on the size and resources of your firm, the type and size of the project, and the type of clients (slow-moving bureaucracies versus fast-acting developers).

Courting a client involves making the party aware of your presence and abilities. During this phase you spend your time keeping the client current on your firm's activities. You want to raise the comfort level of this client about working with your firm. During the courting phase the client's representatives will get to know the technical people and managers with whom they may be working.

In Chap. 6, "Clients," we profile typical client groups, including those in both the public and private sectors. Activities described in this chapter are generally geared toward the private sector, though many are applicable to all clients. If the public sector makes up a significant portion of your target market, apply the following techniques to your lead development and courting. ("Public sector" refers to federal, state, and local governments; all branches of the military; publicly owned utility companies; many schools and hospitals; and numerous institutions.)

- Pay a personal call on the director (or targeted person) of the local or regional office of each agency you believe will have work suitable for your firm. Maintain the contact through repeat visits.

- Determine which agencies of the federal government contract for the type of services your firm provides by reviewing the *Commerce Business Daily*.

- Develop relationships with local agency representatives far in advance of any project notification.

- Be certain to complete all prequalification forms that you are given and update them regularly.

- Approach major institutions as you would private clients, but remember that any decision will be made by a committee. It may take time to determine who the real decision makers are.

- In general, don't even try to wine and dine federal government representatives as part of your courting efforts; but, varying degrees of courtship are appropriate at the state and local level.

CLIENT CONTACT REPORT

Your name _____ Date _____

Please answer the following questions as fully as possible. If you need
more space, use the back of this sheet. Send original to marketing
coordinator, keep a copy.

Contact name & title _____

Business or institution _____

Date of initial contact _____ How contact was made _____
(telephone, letter, personal, etc.)

By whom contact was made _____

Address _____ Phone _____

Type of business _____
(manufacturing, municipal, etc.)

Project type _____
(office, hospital, etc.)

Project cost _____ Size _____
(number of beds, sq. ft., etc.)

Project profile: replacement, renovation, addition, new construction? _____

Other _____

If replacement, renovation or addition, when was original built? _____

Size _____

Plans available _____ Master plan available _____

Special services required _____

Who is funding/administering project _____

Scope _____

Other consultants being considered (don't call them "competition" in

interview) _____

Have other consultants been pre-selected? _____

Selection procedures/criteria? Proposals, letter of interest, SOQs,

interviews? _____

Dates: Proposal return _____

Interview _____ A/E selection _____

Contract award _____ Construction start _____ Occupancy _____

Has client worked with other (_____) firms before? How successfully? _____

Does client have a particular kind of firm in mind (local, national, large,
small, etc.) _____

How do they perceive the consultant's role for this project? (extension of
staff, little direct interchange with staff, etc.) _____

Are they familiar with any of the subconsultants we would consider? Do they
have any problems with them; would they recommend others? _____

How detailed a proposal is expected? _____

Preferred fee structure? (lump sum, cost plus, time & materials, etc.) _____

Do they want cost estimate in the proposal? If so, how should we present it? _____

What are the key issues of this project? Who supports it, who is against
it, and why? _____

If we get the contract, to whom will we be accountable? With whom will we
work? _____

What is the contact's role now? What will it be? (try to qualify the
interviewee) _____

Information source for this prospect _____

Next contact _____ Type _____

Other data and comments _____

Figure 3.5 Client contact report.

Eating and Drinking Your Way to a Job

Breakfasts, lunches, and dinners are important social events at which you can get to know your potential client (or the person who connects you to a client). We know marketing people who rarely have a lunch to themselves because they use this time to nurture leads or work their network. The luncheon provides the opportunity to meet in a friendly environment on equal terms. It's important in courting to develop a feeling of equality between the client and consultant since clients want to work with people sharing common interests and, above all, similar values—from agreement on ethical practices to the relative merits of private versus public universities. Things as simple as how you treat the waitpersons in a restaurant may influence a client relationship and the business that can come from that relationship.

You can use a luncheon to introduce your contact to that expert in your firm (e.g., principal or project manager) who will continue to develop the relationship and land a project. The handoff between the marketing person who has established the lead and the technical or expert person should be handled carefully. As with passing a rod from one who has hooked a fish to one who will reel it in, at any moment the fish may slip away.

The Handoff: A Delicate Operation

The personalities and scenarios involved in a handoff may be as follows:

- The lead may be discovered by a marketing researcher or technical person (e.g., architect or engineer) who describes it to a marketing coordinator or director (someone who makes contact calls).

- The marketer establishes communication with the potential client or contact and makes an assessment of whether or not this effort will lead to a job.

- If the assessment is positive, the marketing person will want to hand off the contact to someone in the office who has experience and is conversant in the type of projects to be developed. In our experience, this handoff should take place as soon as possible, but not before you have analyzed the potential and found the prospect worth further pursuit.

If this relationship leads to your firm's being considered for a project, there may be an "embrace," not a handoff, by the technical professional who has nurtured the contact to welcome the closer or principal of the firm who gets the client to sign on the dotted line. The entire process can be handled by one person, and traditionally the principal of a firm did complete all lead-finding-to-closing activities. However, in most offices today, the handoff often comes into play.

We recommend that you have some overlap—time in which the present and next contact within your firm deal with the prospective client concurrently. Try to perform the handoff in person, not over the phone, and in the context of a working or information-gathering session so you have an honest reason to bring a new player into the game.

A scenario for a handoff may go somewhat like this:

MARKETER:: "Well, Ms. Alcott, we certainly have learned a great deal about your company. We knew you were developing industrial facilities in Venezuela but had no idea how fast moving the South American operations will be in the next few years."

CLIENT:: "When we entered that market we were also surprised at the growth potential. It was only very recently that we decided to commit our resources to this type of development. So you can see, we are not necessarily old hands at this and will demand quite specific, related experience from our consultants in order to give us the information we need to protect our investments."

Marketer:: "I can see where this could be a very important field for your company and that your projects must be particularly noteworthy. For this reason I really think you should meet Joe Beets, one of our chief engineers, who recently joined our firm and has experience on the types of projects of interest to you as well as very recent work experience in Venezuela. [Notice that we did not say that Joe had actually worked on the same kind of project in Venezuela.] Perhaps we could have lunch next week and I could introduce you to Joe. I'm sure he can give you insight into the state of industrial facilities development in South America, including his own first-hand experience with your primary competition."

Client:: "I think a meeting such as this could be most beneficial. I'll bring one of my partners along, and we'll discuss some of our plans and how you may help us realize them."

Lead Follow-Through

As you nurture a potential client and start developing a file about a company, ask the following questions:

- What additional leads can be generated from this contact?
- What talents or experience will this potential client require of consultants?
- Will your firm need to expand its capabilities through consultant firms (or by hiring the right talent) in order to be fully responsive to the clients needs?
- In what geographic area is this client most likely to develop a project?
- Can your firm work profitably in this location?
- How will your firm help the development of a project for this client, and can you be assured of a role in the project?

From the answers to these questions and others like them you can decide if the prospect will really lead to good opportunities for your firm. You can assign priorities to these prospects.

In Chap. 2, "Getting Organized," we discussed the use of a tickler file or a calendar to help keep you organized and establish priorities for marketing activities. As we mentioned above, lead contacts should be assigned to a person in your firm with the most appropriate technical background. (Make sure principals in your firm approve and support the marketing efforts of key technical people.) However, in most instances the marketer must remind that person of his or her responsibility. List your leads according to priorities based on a number of factors, primarily:

- Probability of selection (how qualified and well positioned you are with the client)
- The strength of your competition
- How close the project is to going ahead
- Whether the probable budget makes it worthwhile

A Question of Doubt

We move now from nurturing a lead to actually selling our services for a definite project. Therefore, the issue is not so much whether your firm is "good" or staffed with "nice folks" but whether your staff can perform on a project with specific requirements. To eliminate doubt regarding the services you perform, look first at the areas where doubt may arise and answer questions before they are asked or become points of concern. We continually deal with issues raised by clients such as the following:

- Your firm does not have much, if any, experience in the project type.
- Your firm is not organized to handle this type of project.
- You have not worked with the consultants needed for this project.
- The time schedule is too tight for a firm like yours.
- Your personnel are not technical enough (or are too technical) to understand the project.
- Your client is a tenant and you have only worked with owners (or vice versa).
- Your firm is perceived as too:
  - Expensive
  - High end
  - Low end
  - Distant
  - Unresponsive
  - Slow and methodical
  - Quick and dirty

If you have courted a lead well, many questions of this type will never be asked. But when they are, be prepared. For example, build an effective project team organization. The earlier you can assemble a project team that meets all the client's concerns, the more credibility you have and the better your chances of winning the job. While principals usually close the deal, more and more clients want to evaluate first hand the project leaders with whom they will be working.

Choose key personnel who can win the job. This selection presents a problem: what do you do about the skilled technical project director who does not present him- or herself well to the client? Almost every marketer has to face this situation. How do you deal with it?

- Structure client meetings so that this technician can respond to questions about specific technical issues.
- Brief the technical expert on the client's critical concerns.
- Send the technician to communications training seminars and presentation workshops.
- Rehearse *all* meetings with potential clients.
- If there is any doubt about the technician's ability to deal professionally with a client, try not to leave them alone together.

To Go or Not to Go—Not a Prom Queen's Decision

At some point you have to decide whether or not a client is worth pursuing further. If the client is worth your efforts, your firm must also decide if a particular project under consideration is worth further pursuit.

The go/no-go decision should be made before much of your firm's principals' time is invested, time and money for travel are spent, and expensive brochures or handouts are made. Often, decisions of this nature are made behind closed doors without the participation of the marketing staff. We have all been in the position of knowing that a job was impossible to obtain but being told to spend a lot of time and effort in its pursuit, sacrificing more viable prospects in the process.

As the marketer, you can add a perspective to the go/no-go decision through your knowledge of the client's major concerns and your own marketing program, what other opportunities exist, their relative priorities, the time and effort this particular attempt will take, and how prepared the firm is to make those investments.

When and how you make the go/no-go decision depends on the individual situation, but we list below some points to consider in making it:

- Is this project consistent with your marketing plan?

- What are your firm's chances of procuring this contract?

- Are the skills of your project team and consultants well matched to the client's needs?

- If your firm cannot complete the project alone, will the client respond favorably to an association?

- If your firm probably will not get this job, should you pursue it nevertheless in order to be "in line" for future work from this client?

- Might this client recommend your firm for work with other clients if your effort is strong but you do not get this job?

- Can the project be accomplished profitably? (Consider the marketing costs and potential liability.)

- Will a successful job be useful to the firm as publicity?

Mr. Abercrombie Fitzmaurice, meet your project architect, Joe Beets.

- Will the project help your firm achieve a balance in project and client types?
- Is the project funded? Does the client pay?

In our experience, few firms review these questions rigorously and, as a result, pursue too many projects without strong conviction. Once the firm decides to go for a client or project, do everything you reasonably can to get it, including passing up other, less promising opportunities if necessary.

STATING YOUR CASE

Stating your case to a client may require written documents, graphic illustrations, and/or personal interviews. Regardless of the medium, stating your case effectively requires building a case around the client's concerns and expressing your credentials in a way that helps the client see the benefit and value of what you bring to the job.

Written Submittals to Potential Clients

Written qualifications are usually expressed in one or more of the following methods:

- *The letter* usually responds to an informal request for information about your firm's qualifications in general or for a specific project. For small projects, the letter may include a fee proposal and double as a contract.
- A *statement of qualifications* uses boilerplate material primarily and is often submitted as part of a preselection process; it is sometimes used as a brochure though it shouldn't be.
- A *proposal* in response to a request for proposal or questionnaire includes much original information and modified boilerplate to respond to a client's stated concerns or direct questions.
- A *scope statement with fee proposal* identifies the services in detail (often including a schedule) and provides a fee related to the scope of work. These can be part of a proposal or follow as a final submittal to obtain a project.

Preparing Qualifications Statements

A qualifications statement may be sent in response to a request for qualifications or sent unsolicited to a prospective client. A statement of qualifications is not a proposal (we discuss proposals further on) and is usually sent before a proposal. Most of the organizational techniques described here can be used for all types of submittals, including proposals.

In dealing with most branches of the federal government, your firm's qualifications will be described in Standard Forms 254 and 255. We devote a section of this chapter to those submittals.

If there is a deadline for submitting information (there always is, and it is always too soon), work back from the due date, identifying all tasks and personnel needed. Use the following as a guide.

- Assign someone to manage the production effort (yourself or the technical professional who has been dealing with the client).
- Establish a budget (including personnel time) to develop the submittal.
- Determine a schedule for writing and production.
- Make an outline for all contents and be certain someone is responsible for each of them.

- Arrange for production of graphics (covers and charts).

- Assign appropriate staff to write responses to specific concerns.

- Have someone available to tailor the boilerplate to fit this submittal. (That someone will most likely be you, so budget your time accordingly.)

- Make sure someone with mothering instincts is available at the proper time to produce, print, bind, and deliver the material.

- Have someone assume responsibility for overall quality control (again, probably you).

When you know about a project for a client but you have not received a request for proposal (RFP), you can submit a qualifications statement to ensure that your firm will be included in the client's prequalification list. The contents of a qualifications statement vary depending on the client and the situation surrounding the submittal. Many elements of a qualifications statement will also be included in a proposal. These contents may include:

- *Cover letter* expressing interest (and summarizing key qualifications; can also be included in an executive summary)

- *Relevant experience* including lists of projects and descriptions of specific projects

- *Résumés of specialists* in this project type or other firm leaders

- *Reprints* of relevant articles by or about your firm

- *Photos* and plans of projects

- *References*

The Proposal: Suddenly It's Real

A well-written qualifications statement will assure the client that your firm has the ability to perform the required services for a specific type of project. A proposal is the sales tool that can edge your firm past the competition. Even if you are not competing for the job, a successful proposal will assure the client that the project can be developed successfully. A winning proposal depends on your having done your research well and will

- Make evident your awareness of the client's specific concerns

- Respond to questions the client wants answered (whether asked or not)

- Be as short as possible, direct, and to the point

- Reflect the style of the client as well as that of the submitting firm

Proposals are prepared in response to several client-generated situations, such as:

- Public sector RFP (from *Commerce Business Daily* or other source)

- Private sector selection group or long list

- Private sector fee proposal (short list)

- Unsolicited (when you know a client has a project in mind and you submit a proposal as a prompt)

How to deal with the perpetual time crunch? Principals and project managers often receive RFPs and sit on them until the last possible minute. One way to minimize this situation is to talk frequently with the project managers and principals involved in marketing and send them frequent marketing updates reminding them to pass information along to you. Develop boilerplate ahead of time: résumés, project lists and descriptions, and general statements about the firm (refer to Chap. 2, "Getting Organized," and Chap. 5, "Sales Tools"). Have selected photos, reprints of articles, charts, graphs, and other graphics ready to use. More things to do include:

- Retain all charts and graphs used in past proposals to help you develop new ones for specific proposals; file by service, project, or client-type.

- File and reference all hard copy material used in proposals so you can retrieve it quickly, i.e., keep résumés, project descriptions, and approach statements in binders or folders by category—service, client, or project type.

- Keep all information—boilerplate and examples of applications from prior proposals—in your computer.

Like project schedules, proposal schedules contain elements of a critical path, such as decision points and coordination; therefore:

- Assign tasks to people and hold them accountable.

- Note areas in which you will need technical or outside consultants. Start these areas soon since they will require coordination.

- Allow time for printing graphics and covers. Check with printers to be certain they can produce work in the time allotted. If not, adjust your schedule *while you have time*.

- Try to keep the proposal coordination (project management) separate from the writing and editing (design).

Figure 3.6 shows an example of a simple proposal production schedule.

Select your project team. Actually, you need three teams: one to produce the proposal (see our overview below), your firm's project team, and the subconsultant group you will propose. Because it takes time and "jawboning" to get all the information you need from subconsultants, review consultant files and select those you will use as early as possible. Review in-house skills (see Chap. 5, "Sales Tools") for the most qualified project team. Rewrite résumés if necessary, and keep new résumés on file for future use.

Assess the need for a joint venture (JV) or association. Review the pros and cons of a JV relationship; make sure the proposal stresses strong points and mitigates weaknesses. (Actually, the decision to form a JV should be made well in advance of receiving an RFP. If you have been tracking the client, you'll know ahead of time what type of team will work.) Answer questions the client may ask, (after all, you should know the client pretty well by now); especially answer, "How will this joint venture benefit the client?" Develop all new graphics the association will need: new logo, letterhead, address, officers-in-charge. Analyze costs and time commitment for producing a joint venture proposal. Arrange in advance regarding who pays for what; don't wait to find out if you got the job.

Consider graphics and printing. The appearance of the proposal makes a statement about the firm's quality of design or professionalism and interest in the project. Be certain your graphics are well integrated, charts all have similar title blocks, letterhead and covers work together, and that labels, all in the same typeface, appear in the same location on each graphic. If possible, reenter all consultant information and print it out to conform with your own material. As more firms turn to desk-top publishing, submittals look more professional and more attractive. (See Chap. 5, "Sales Tools," for more information on desktop publishing.)

```
PROPOSAL PRODUCTION SCHEDULE                    Proposal/job # _____

Date due to client _____    Time due (e.g. 5 p.m.) _____

Proposal title _____

Client (attention of) _____

Proposal production leader _____

Type of proposal:  letter style ____ full-blown ____ estimated length ____

                   qualifications ____ fee ____ other _____

Summary of RFP requirements (attach CBD or other) _____

_____

_____

Our role:  Prime _____  JV _____  Consultant _____

           Other prime _____

           Other joint venturer(s) _____

Initial estimate of proposal cost:  time _____ expense _____

      If shared, with whom _____ Agreed to by _____ Date _____

Proposal Production and Submittal

      One-sided ____ Two-sided ____ Stapled ____ Bound (how) _____

      Number of copies to client _____

      Number of copies to subs _____ Who _____ Mail _____

                              _____  _____    _____

How it will be delivered _____

To what address _____ _____

Special instructions _____

_____

_____
```

Figure 3.6 Proposal production schedule.

The following are also important:

- Plan for timely delivery: don't trust the mails. (But if the client is the U.S. Postal Service, don't use a competing carrier.) Spare no expense. Put someone (or just the submittal) on a plane if that's the only way to make the deadline.
- Call to be certain your proposal arrived and to see how well it was received. Ask if you can provide anything else.
- Plan for an interview and handouts.
- Review your proposal to see what you can use in the future.

Although you may exceed your budgets of time, money, and energy, if your firm really wants the job, you will do whatever is necessary to get it, and this overexertion is often justified. Figure 3.7 shows a form you can use to help you manage the proposal schedule.

Proposal Content: Not an Afterthought

If you have to respond to a client's questionnaire, complete it exactly as you are directed. Use an executive summary or cover letter to highlight or intro-

I. Proposal Production Team

Our Firm	JV		Date Assigned
Principal			_____
Coordinator			_____
Editor			_____
Writer(s)			_____
			_____

Graphics			_____
Covers	Dividers	Charts	_____
Graphs	Stationery		_____
Other			_____
Photography			_____
Printing			_____

II. Project Team (as listed in proposal)   Resumes Required (long, short, other)

(P-I-C) _____

(Project Engineer/Architect) _____

(PM) _____

(Job Captain) _____

(Other) _____

III. Consultant Team

Indicate: Have/Need/Need Revision

Consultant	SF255	SF254	Resumes	Project Descriptions	Back-ground	Specific RFP	Other Response
(Firm A)							
(Firm B)							

IV. Project Descriptions (attach list)

V. Project Lists (needed/revised)

_____

_____

VI. Other Boilerplate

Cost Control	Reference List
Schedule Control	Other: comments _____
E/O Record	_____
Letters of Recommendation	

Figure 3.7 Proposal schedule management form.

duce the points you think are critical. But, if there are no stipulations as to what you must submit or the order in which you submit it, make sure your proposal contains the following in roughly this order:

- A cover letter, which can also serve as an executive summary (brief overview of the proposal's key points).
- Table of contents with page numbers (if more than about 15 pages).
- Problem statement, background, situation analysis or other euphemism for the client's key concerns, e.g., what could cause this project to fail?
- Your approach: How you propose to solve these problems and meet the client's concerns.
- Scope of services: What will you do to address these concerns?
- Your project team: Describe each person's role on the project and his or her specific, relevant experience to fill that role; include a clear organization chart for the project team and consultants.
- Schedule for delivering the project: Show you can do it.
- Relevant project experience: Lists and descriptions of prior projects that involved solving similar problems that the client will understand and that relate to them.
- Fee: If required, and based on a clear scope definition.

Other sections you may include but are not essential are

- History of the firm
- Philosophy of design
- Long form résumés
- Printed project descriptions
- Other charts and graphics not related to this project
- Awards (unless requested in the RFP)
- References (unless requested)

The following supporting material should go into an appendix if space allows and the information is relevant:

- Brochures
- Article reprints
- Project photos

The following rules, if followed, will help improve the content and effectiveness of your proposals:

- **Put yourself in your client's place**   Address his or her concerns first. For example, in a cover letter, executive summary, or any introductory piece, start by identifying the key issues you think the client is facing ("hot buttons"). Then, explain why and how your firm can resolve those issues, emphasizing your relevant project experience. If you think of issues you can't resolve, omit those issues, change your strategy so you can respond, e.g., add a consultant, or realize you may not be suited for this project.
- **Experience alone is not enough**   It's a given; you must almost always have experience in a project type or with the same type of client to be

considered for a short list. To distinguish your submittal from others, you must *also*:

- **Use statistics** Avoid the "we have experience" and "unusually well qualified..." type of comments unless you can immediately verify the statement with facts and figures—how many square feet; how many dollars of construction put in place; how many actual projects; how many years?

- **Use examples** When you say you have experience, indicate how you actually did something—use a project case study (abbreviated) or just briefly describe a real problem and your solution. At a minimum, refer the reader to relevant project descriptions ("On pages *xx-xx*") for more details.

- **Use benefit statements** When you state something about your firm, e.g., "We understand the importance of efficient planning," continue the idea by telling the client *why* your understanding will improve the project or make the client's life easier. Every firm says things like "We have experience in controlling costs" or "We use the team approach." Instead, describe how your experience will result in the best possible cost containment for this project—"We will use the XYZ computer tracking system to assure accurate biweekly reports" or "We will seek innovative solutions as we did on the QP2 project" or "We won't reinvent the wheel or experiment on your budget" or "The 'team approach' means *you* have a say in every decision throughout the project, which results in a more workable solution, a minimum of surprises during construction, and a finished project you will be proud of."

Proposals, like advertisements, serve to persuade, perhaps even to modify someone's behavior. To do so, they have to:

- Grab attention and retain it.
- Convey useful, relevant information.
- Capture the imagination of the reader.
- Do it in somewhere between 30 seconds and 5 minutes.

None of this means being unprofessional or misrepresenting the truth (especially not that). In fact, if you don't have a strong cost control system, you're better off avoiding the subject than using a wishy-washy platitude that raises doubt in the client's mind or clutters up the message about the real value you bring to a project. But remember, if cost control is critical to the client, you shouldn't submit for this project without a good track record in this area.

- **Focus on your key strengths** Decide what can really set you apart on this project. Limit the points to about six; then state them clearly, using the devices described above and repeat them often. Theme and variation, just like a symphony.

- **Make your writing style active and interesting** Practice rewriting to use the active voice—"We will summarize the finding," "The design team will prepare a diagram," "The entire project team will review the plans" *instead of* "A summary will be provided," "A diagram will be prepared," "The plans will be reviewed." Final editing note: *When in doubt* (about an idea or the structure of a sentence) *leave it out*.

- **Format, also, contributes to success** Proposal reviewers may have to look at 50 to 100 submittals to make the first cut. Therefore:
  - Make lines of text short and the margins wide (the human eye can't

track long lines and tends to skim to the start of the next paragraph). Text should look like a newspaper—easy to read.

- Use "bullets" and indentation.
- Use lists whenever possible, instead of lengthy paragraphs to describe your attributes or experience. (When you can't figure out how to make a statement shorter or tighter, try to convert the ideas to a list and take out all "the's" and "will be's" and other passive statements.)
- Use subheadings, type, and underscore. _____
- Use page numbers.
- Use graphics with headings to explain why the graphic is important or describes a benefit to the reader.

Once you decide to go for the project, back away from the delivery date by one day; set an artificial deadline for yourselves; allow that extra day to *proofread* the proposal and *revise* it to make it shorter. No one can write briefly in the first draft or even the second. You won't end up with a whole day, of course, but even a few hours to review will result in tighter prose and fewer glitches. Use a spell checker on your computer (one marketer was told by a client that they threw out all proposals with typos). Make this time a high priority. If possible, have someone other than the author do this review.

George Orwell said in a famous essay, "Politics and the English Language," that the last rule is to *break all of the foregoing rules rather than be boring.* In professional proposals, of course, you can't violate all the conventions. You can, however, employ some of the creativity that makes you and your firm excellent at what you do. Your writing and your presentations, after all, do reflect the quality of your thinking as problem solvers and designers. So, when it comes to trying out a new format, including new graphics, or even experimenting with humor, be willing to take risks rather than disappear in the pack.

Making a Proposal: Who Does What?

When preparing a proposal, remember that you may not be able to do it alone. When possible, we involve the people listed below in writing selected portions of proposals:

Principal in your firm (or in a very large firm, a project manager):

- Establishes overall approach to project
- Reviews editorial and graphic content
- Writes cover letter, problem statement
- Selects project team
- Selects consultants
- Attends "bidders" conference or other client meeting
- Conducts site visit and prepares photos or sketches if appropriate

Project manager:

- Contacts client to clarify technical issues regarding the project
- Writes project approach
- Provides analysis of technical issues
- Develops project schedule
- Describes project team organization

Marketing coordinator:

- Calls client to clarify format, deadline, and other nontechnical issues

- Monitors overall production of proposal

- Writes or modifies boilerplate qualifications statements, résumés, and project descriptions (may often work with project manager)

- Organizes, orders, and tailors graphic material to fit into submittal

- Maintains the schedule for review and rewrite of all materials

- In some firms we know, the coordinator may also have to coerce the word processor or desk-top production person into staying late to get it done and may organize the group lunch or beer and pretzel party when it's over.

STANDARD FORMS 254 AND 255

Although practically everything we have said regarding proposal preparation can be applied to private and public sector clients alike, various agencies of the federal government—and many state and community agencies—use Standard Forms 254 and 255 in the selection of consultants. For most federal projects the 255 actually does serve as a proposal, although the *CBD* announcement may say, "This is not a request for proposal." They mean you should not include a fee—it's not a bid.

Here are some guidelines for responding to *CBD* announcements and preparing SF 254s and 255s.

CBD: Your Tax Dollars at Work

The *CBD*, hard to read, full of typos, and often incomplete information, is published every weekday by the U.S. Department of Commerce in Chicago and identifies most A/E projects initiated by federal agencies and their subcontractors. (It is available by priority mail and electronically by modem.) The publication is divided into alphabetical and numerical sections covering various types of procurements. The alphabetical sections (A through Z) primarily describe needed services; the numbered sections are for the procurement of goods and supplies. *CBD* announcements do not include projects under a certain construction value or emergency projects (such as structures damaged in a storm). These can be authorized by local agents, another reason to maintain good communication with area managers and officers.

Most *CBD* notices contain one or more numbered notes. Explanations of these notes are published only on Mondays. A numbered note referenced in the *CBD* announcement *should be read as part of that announcement.* (Note 62 refers to requirements of the Department of Defense—Army, Navy, Air Force, Marine Corps. Note 63 refers to all other federal agencies.)

The last page of each *CBD* contains a legend explaining the meaning of the small numbers inside black circles which often appear at the beginning of the announcement. The black circled "1" indicates 100 percent small business set-aside. Projects designated by this number can be obtained only by firms with gross annual fees below a specified level, stated on the back page. A black circled "3" indicates the procurement is set aside for labor surplus areas as designated by the U.S. Department of Labor. When the U.S. unemployment rate exceeds 10 percent, a city or county must exceed that rate to qualify as a labor surplus area. Figure 3.8 illustrates a *CBD* announcement.

SF 254

The Standard Form 254 gives an overview of your firm and should be updated and submitted every year to each agency for which you want to work.

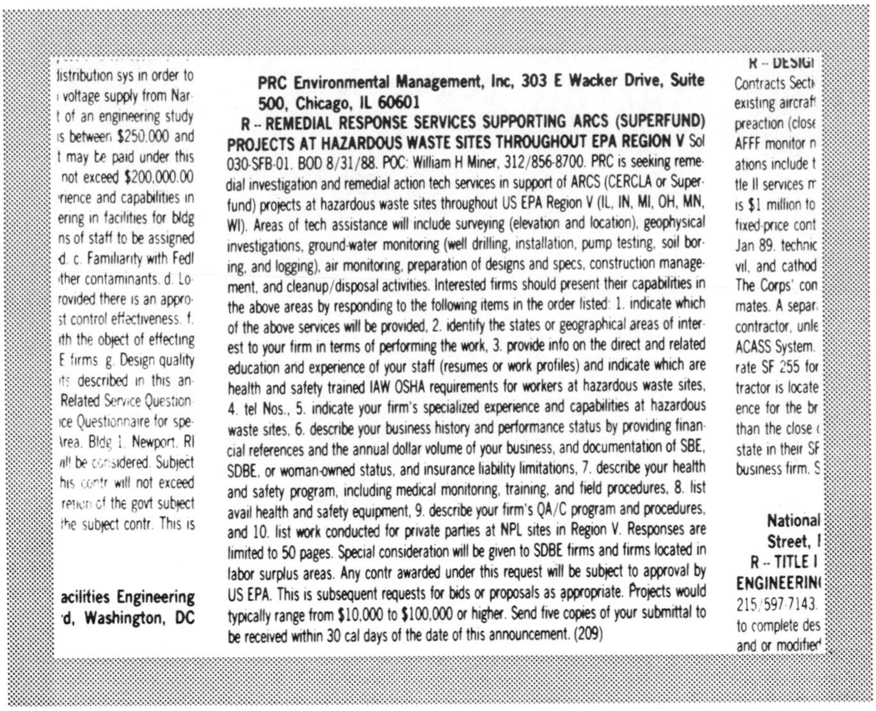

PRC Environmental Management, Inc, 303 E Wacker Drive, Suite 500, Chicago, IL 60601

R -- REMEDIAL RESPONSE SERVICES SUPPORTING ARCS (SUPERFUND) PROJECTS AT HAZARDOUS WASTE SITES THROUGHOUT EPA REGION V Sol 030-SFB-01. BOD 8/31/88. POC: William H Miner, 312/856-8700. PRC is seeking remedial investigation and remedial action tech services in support of ARCS (CERCLA or Superfund) projects at hazardous waste sites throughout US EPA Region V (IL, IN, MI, OH, MN, WI). Areas of tech assistance will include surveying (elevation and location), geophysical investigations, ground-water monitoring (well drilling, installation, pump testing, soil boring, and logging), air monitoring, preparation of designs and specs, construction management, and cleanup/disposal activities. Interested firms should present their capabilities in the above areas by responding to the following items in the order listed: 1. indicate which of the above services will be provided, 2. identify the states or geographical areas of interest to your firm in terms of performing the work, 3. provide info on the direct and related education and experience of your staff (resumes or work profiles) and indicate which are health and safety trained IAW OSHA requirements for workers at hazardous waste sites, 4. tel Nos., 5. indicate your firm's specialized experience and capabilities at hazardous waste sites, 6. describe your business history and performance status by providing financial references and the annual dollar volume of your business, and documentation of SBE, SDBE, or woman-owned status, and insurance liability limitations, 7. describe your health and safety program, including medical monitoring, training, and field procedures, 8. list avail health and safety equipment, 9. describe your firm's QA/C program and procedures, and 10. list work conducted for private parties at NPL sites in Region V. Responses are limited to 50 pages. Special consideration will be given to SDBE firms and firms located in labor surplus areas. Any contr awarded under this request will be subject to approval by US EPA. This is subsequent requests for bids or proposals as appropriate. Projects would typically range from $10,000 to $100,000 or higher. Send five copies of your submittal to be received within 30 cal days of the date of this announcement. (209)

Figure 3.8 **CBD** listing.

Even though *CBD* announcements usually say you need not submit an SF 254 if one is already on file, we recommend submitting one every time you submit a qualifications statement. Some agencies take your most recent 254 and use it to replace any previous form on file. So, if you change your SF 254, the agency may have only that version.

In completing an SF 254, be as accurate as possible about your firm's background and financial earnings. The form gives space to list 30 projects on which your firm has served as prime contractor, consultant, or as part of a joint venture. Although new firms and very small firms may not have 30 projects to list, large firms should develop an SF 254 for each project type they wish to pursue, using the spaces to describe projects relevant to that type with a few general projects to show broad experience.

Remember, a relatively new firm can list projects completed by directors while they were employed elsewhere. Use the special category for this designation (IE).

SF 255

The SF 255 should be considered a proposal. It is always tailored to a specific project. For federal government submittals, you usually have 3 weeks to respond. In preparing an SF 255, read the *CBD* announcement carefully, determine that your team's qualifications suit the job requirements, and note all numbered or specified requirements in order of priority.

Because *CBDs* are hard to read, with very small print, some firms enlarge them. Read each description several times to be sure you get all the critical information. Do not prepare a submittal unless your firm has completed several similar projects; *CBD* announcements typically attract as many as 40 to 60 submittals or more. Unless your firm is exceptionally qualified—by experience—don't waste your time.

Once you have your project team in place, consultants contacted, and relevant projects identified, you are ready to complete the form. Let's run through the preparation of an SF 255, bearing in mind the following key points:

- Be relevant—list information that relates to this project *only*.

- Be brief but not so short that you can be misunderstood.

- Do not exceed allotted typing space, except on the last page (Section 10), unless you have checked in advance and know the agency doesn't care if you modify the form.

- List projects in order of relevance and explain how they relate.

- Do not leave any blank spaces.

Below are descriptions of each section of the form:

SECTION 1: Project Name/Location for Which Firm Is Filing.
Enter the name of the project exactly as it is stated in the *CBD* announcement.

SECTION 2A: Commerce Business Daily Announcement Date....
List the date the procurement was announced in the *CBD*.

SECTION 2B: Agency Identification Number, if Any.
The Navy's NAVFAC divisions are almost the only ones using identification numbers. The number is listed right after the name of the project. If the *CBD* announcement does not contain an identification number or there is no *CBD* announcement, enter "none" in this section.

SECTION 3: Firm (or Joint Venture) Name and Address.
Enter the name of the office that will be the prime consultant.

SECTION 3A: Name, Title and Telephone Number of Principal to Contact.
Use the name of a principal or other senior person in your firm who is authorized to negotiate this contract.

SECTION 3B: Address of Office to Perform Work.
If different from Item 3. Enter address of branch office or consultant's office where majority of work will be performed. If the office is the same as 3 (generally the case), enter "Same as 3."

SECTION 4: Personnel by Discipline.
Enter in the appropriate discipline lines the number of people in your office plus people in any joint venture offices. Do not include proposed consultants in this count.

SECTION 5: If Submittal is by a Joint Venture....
If there is not a joint venture, enter "None."

If you have formed a joint venture (as opposed to a prime-consultant relationship), be certain the responsibilities of each firm are clearly described, as briefly as possible.

SECTION 6: Outside Key Consultants/Associates....
List only those you feel are necessary to complete the project as described.

Try to use consultants familiar with the project type and the agency involved *and* with whom you have worked before.

Include consultant firms' SF 254 forms with your submittal as well as SF 255, Section 7, Brief Résumés of Key Persons, for all project team members from consultant firms.

Section 7: Brief Résumés of Key Persons....

List only personnel who have a definable role on the project (principal in charge, project manager, job captain, project engineer, etc.).

Keep the information brief and relevant to both project experience and role on the project team as defined for the job you are pursuing.

Follow instructions as directly as possible, giving the role the individual will play in the project, years of experience, education, and registration.

If your background information is not up to date or your consultants do not fill out this form completely, you can get caught in a time bind. So, have *your* firm's personnel data ready ahead of time and contact the consultants as soon as possible.

In describing the individual's experience, name specific projects and be sure that both the project and the person's role are relevant. See Chap. 5, "Marketing Tools," for an example of an SF 255 biography.

Section 8: Work...Which Best Illustrates Current Qualifications Relevant to This Project.

Remember that it says "Relevant to This Project." It is better to list six applicable projects than ten that are only remotely similar to the project under consideration.

Enter all the information requested.

Describe *briefly* what your firm did. Use enough space so that you will not be misunderstood, but do not use an entire column.

If you feel a project your firm did is so great or so relevant that it needs additional comment, use Section 10 of the form to expand on your description of the project.

Do not forget to include the address of the owner for projects listed.

Show the completion date (past or anticipated) by year.

The cost of the entire project can be estimated but be as accurate as possible (in thousands).

Work for which your firm was responsible can be listed as a dollar amount (in thousands) or as a percentage of the total fee.

Section 9: All Work...Currently Being Performed Directly for Federal Agencies.

If your firm is very large, has many branch offices, or does a lot of federal work, you should keep a list of ongoing projects which includes (at least) the information requested in this form.

The more work you show, the less likely you are to get the job.

Section 10: Use this Space....

And they do mean "use this space."

This is the only place you have to describe your firm's unique qualities and why your firm is perfectly suited to this project.

Cover all the stated and perceived issues from the *CBD* announcement and from your own research of the project. Emphasize how your team can respond to them.

Include both technical and management capabilities in your office.

Expand on relevant projects listed in Section 8.

If you have special knowledge about the project type or the location, stress that here.

If your firm has won awards or published papers on projects of this type, mention that here.

You can type or print Section 10 on a larger sheet and then reduce it but be careful that the material can still be read.

Use two columns for better readability.

Attachments to the SF 255

Attach a clear project team organization chart to your SF 255. Also include general information about your firm with your submittal, but check to see if you should attach it directly to the SF 255. Some agencies throw out everything but the 255.

Transmittal Letter

Your cover letter will accompany the SF 255 (bound in with it) and should include reference to the *CBD* announcement. If you mention your consultants, explain why you selected them and indicate that their SF 254s are included with the submittal. Your transmittal letter can summarize the key points made in Section 10; keep it brief but not so brief that you are misunderstood. In completing any form, check with the specific agency's procurement office to see what their preferences or restrictions are, including such matters as use of photos, covers, and appendices.

There are several software programs that will help you generate forms 254 and 255. If your firm produces more than three or four of these forms each month you may want to obtain one of these programs (see "Resources" at the end of the book).

THE PRESENTATION

Presentations have been described as the point at which every firm goes in a winner, but only one firm comes out a winner. They depend, increasingly, more on personalities and planning than on the technical skill of the presenters. As with a proposal, you need to manage, staff, and budget the preparation for a presentation. One of the most difficult tasks a professional marketer faces is preparing for an interview. Most principals and project managers loathe rehearsing for an interview, but the results will improve if they do it and you need to help them.

To begin with, collect and review research information you have on this client and this job. Be aware of all the client's major concerns and subtle considerations. Spend time "putting yourself in this client's shoes" to determine your strongest message.

Convince a firm principal or the project director for the proposed project that a rehearsal is absolutely necessary. (Keep a record of your hits and misses; we can almost guarantee that the rehearsed interviews are more successful.) Tell everyone from the outset that there will be a rehearsal so that they will come to accept this as part of the process. By rehearsal we don't mean the presenters need to memorize their speeches. There are, of course, gifted, extemporaneous speakers whose charm and intelligence will prove irresistible to the client. Unfortunately, you probably have only one or two of these, at best, in your firm.

Many firms are now rehearsing their teams on video, often doing more harm than good, despite the best of intentions. The following guidelines from professional video trainers Tim Allen and Peter Loeb may help you make the best use of this tool and prevent your presenters from getting more anxious and stiff or refusing to participate in rehearsals:

- Seeing yourself do something is more valuable than listening to other people tell you what to do.

- There is no right way to do anything; the best way is the one that works for you.

- An ounce of criticism neutralizes a pound of support; be *very* supportive of good points; offer concrete suggestions, not just criticism regarding weak points. The natural response to criticism is defensiveness; the natural response to encouragement is growth.

- It's hard for people to take in new information until they've had a chance to say what they think; give presenters a chance to say what they think and feel after seeing themselves, before you offer your comments.

- You're much more likely to change something if it's your idea to change.

- Big changes that last are a result of small changes that work; don't ask a presenter to do anything differently the first time. Build change slowly.

- Practice may not make you perfect, but without it, you won't even get better.

- Videotape only *small* portions—3 minutes maximum—of each person's presentations. No one can absorb more than that at one time. Work on improving just that part; the lessons can be applied to the remainder of the presentation.

- Always, always have a person do the same 3 minutes again, making the changes he or she wants to make. Repeat as soon as possible after the person sees the first taping and has discussed how it looks.

A winning presentation hits home at the client's critical concerns, avoids self-aggrandizement, yet assures the client of your capabilities. A winning presentation establishes a mood and comfort level that say to the client, "These people will be good to work with." In a presentation, personality is very important. We think it is a good bet that no client has ever wanted to hire a consultant he or she cannot stand, no matter how technically competent the consultant was.

Heed some of the unwritten rules of chemistry:

- Humor—but don't force it if it isn't natural.
- Dress—as conservative as you can *comfortably* be.
- Manners—you can never be too courteous, but don't be phony.
- Self-assurance—comes from knowing what you're talking about.
- *The ability to listen.* Most important of all.

The client will value these as much as the ability of your team to work together and get the job done.

Manage the Presentation

Use this checklist to prepare and rehearse your presentation. (Use another sheet or put information on a flip chart. Distribute this information to your total presentation team, including consultants if appropriate.)

- Are we truly committed to obtaining this project?
- What do we *know* about the project, the client, and the client's concerns?
- What *questions* do we have about the project, the client, and the client's concerns? What *answers* did we get? From whom?

- *Who's* on the selection committee? Who are the decision makers? Name, position, and key concerns.
- *When* will we rehearse? Dates and times:
  1st time:
  2nd time:
- What's the presentation agenda?
  Client concerns to be addressed:
  Order of presenters and topics:
- Specific examples to support major points—facts, figures, dollar amounts, time, names, anecdotes, successful solutions to problems.
- What materials do we need—flip chart, handouts, graphics?
- Why would the client select us for this project?

Make sure you know and respond to:

- The client's criteria for selection.
- Who is the competition.

Make sure also that:

- Your project team has a leader who is knowledgeable about both the client and this project.
- All the attendees have a clear purpose for being at the presentation.
- The comfort level and ability to communicate with the client are already strong.
- Your associated firms or consultants are well represented.
- All presenters have met and are comfortable with one another.
- All your material—boards, flip charts, handouts—fit together graphically: color, typeface, logo.
- You know where the presentation is, how to get there, when, who takes what props and other material.
- You know the location and accessibility of electric outlets, lights, shape and size of room, curtains (for slides), etc.

You will not have enough time, so be sure you know early on what materials you need to produce for the presentation. If time allows, you may want to develop a handout or leave-behind that will recount for the client the key points made at the interview. Leave-behinds, however, are *not* as important as the actual presentation; forego this step if it means you can spend more time rehearsing instead.

Will there be a slide show or AV presentation? If so, does the person leading the interview know how to run a slide projector, adjust a microphone, and operate the AV projector? Must special material be produced? Do you know the cost and timing required to produce this material?

Rehearse the presentation to be certain each speaker has enough time. Leave enough time for questions and answers; this period is often the most important part of a presentation because new, critical issues may surface.

CLOSING: DID THE FAT LADY SING?

Marketers are often great openers but cannot close. Just what is closing and who should do it? In the simplest terms, closing is getting the client to sign on the dotted line.

In most cases, the act of closing follows all the proposals and formal presentations and involves negotiating your compensation. A good closer can negotiate a fair compensation for services without sacrificing the goodwill it has taken so much effort to develop. The closer is usually a principal in the firm and always a senior staff person, experienced in the project type, who can commit the firm to a course of action for a specified fee.

The closer should always be a doer; someone who can lead the project (but doesn't have to) and has worked on nurturing the project. Never bring a project to selection and then introduce a stranger to close the deal. Hammering out a contract is a delicate game, and it should not be thrown out of balance by having new people start pounding on it at the eleventh hour.

EVALUATING THE PROCESS: ARE WE MARKETING YET?

We refer more than once to marketing as being, in large part, a research activity. Your research always builds upon itself and does not end when the client does or does not sign on the dotted line. Get debriefed as to why you either won or lost.

Once you are in an interview, it is generally acknowledged that your firm can meet the demands of the project. You can lose the project at this point because of very minor factors. Another firm may have introduced new criteria, turning the momentum away from you, or you simply may not have hit strongly enough on the client's key concerns. Do not settle for being told simply, "Gee it was a tough decision; you came in second. You are well qualified, but. . . ." Try to get specific information.

As you learn from your own mistakes, try to learn from the success of others:

- Who was the winning team?

- How did they present themselves?

- What issues did they discuss?

- Who were their consultants?

- How long had they known about the project and how well did they know the client?

- Did you misguess as to who made the ultimate decision and therefore geared your presentation to the wrong person?

The best marketing tool is a satisfied client; if you have won a new project, maintain contacts to ensure the job goes well. One of the best ways to find new work is through your present clients. Develop mechanisms for expanding the work or obtaining new work with the same client.

Assuming that all is going well with the client, discuss both additional work and other contacts of this client who may lead you to new projects. An active network of people who can share information with you should include present clients who open up more doors.

As a final note, try to maintain some contact with a client you have lost. They may think highly of your firm but felt you were not the best team for this particular project. They may consider you again in the future. If possible, be there in the event that those who received the commission make a critical mistake.

And, start courting for the next project.

Chapter Four

What You Do— Indirect Marketing

INTRODUCTION

In Chap. 3, "Direct Marketing," we talked about how to identify potential clients and go about obtaining the jobs you want from them. In this chapter, we talk about what you do to create a reputation for your firm that attracts clients to you—sometimes even before you have identified them as clients. We call this approach indirect marketing, public relations, or simply PR. Public relations is used to help establish a position for your firm in the eyes of your intended clients. The image you seek to project relies as much on who you are and the way your image is transmitted as on the receiver of the message.

WHO NEEDS PR?

We have learned over the years that there are essentially two kinds of successful design and planning firms: those that use direct marketing most effectively and those that use indirect marketing most effectively. If your firm does its direct marketing functions well, especially the early steps of client identification and courtship, indirect marketing can be a relatively small aspect of your overall marketing program.

However, and this is important, if your firm is one of the many that doesn't spend enough time in lead finding and client development, if your marketing is essentially reactive (not getting into gear until after the RFP arrives), PR must be a high priority if you are to achieve marketing success. In many cases it is easier—and more effective—to get principals to write articles, give talks to professional organizations, and join social clubs—than to get them to call on potential clients directly. So, depending on the type of firm you have, indirect marketing can take up anywhere from 15 to 25 percent of your budget and effort.

Generally, smaller, more specialized firms can use PR most cost effectively, while larger, broad-based firms need to rely more on sales staffs and direct marketing. Smaller firms often need to develop a strong reputation in limited areas—with a few types of clients or types of projects—to get the most out of their marketing dollar. The reputation of one principal, spread through PR as well as client referrals, can often carry a small firm for years. Smaller firms also seldom have aggressive sales staffs and therefore must rely more on indirect methods.

Larger, multidisciplined firms, with a wide range of clients and project types, on the other hand, can develop a somewhat vague image for doing quality work, but only one division or one principal will usually have the reputation as an expert in a particular field. (Other principals may also be considered expert, but often in other fields.) The whole firm does not benefit as much from this reputation as does the division or specific regional office. Because of the volume of work needed to sustain them and their broader scope of services, larger firms must rely on a steady stream of projects resulting from a concerted, on-going direct sales effort. However, many large firms have communications directors on staff whose job it is to make sure that clients and public (through the press and other sources) are kept aware of the firm's activities.

WHAT IS PR?

However much time you spend on it, PR should enhance your firm's credibility as experts at whatever service you want to market. Indirect marketing enables you to develop a "position" for your firm in the eyes of clients you have yet to meet. Indirect marketing may also support your direct marketing efforts by helping to convince those you have met that they should select your firm.

The issue of position is key to indirect marketing. You need to define a position in order for this approach to work. What is a position? In this chapter we use it in the sense of an image, especially an image as experts or specialists in an aspect of the built environment. This position or recognition will make anyone hearing about you *feel* a sense of confidence that you can solve problems, save them money, and eliminate hassles that would otherwise plague them on a project.

Well, the photo's backward and the figures are wrong, but they spelled our name right.

When clients already know your firm before you call on them or when they call you first, your PR has worked well. PR can support the overall marketing effort in these ways:

- PR can contribute to a firm's favorable image, by which the client already knows your firm is expert in projects of a given type, e.g., design of criminal justice facilities or space planning for electronics firms, before a real project comes along.

- This image can make direct marketing faster and easier and improve your ability to negotiate a satisfactory fee.

- A public relations program can make your direct marketing program more cost effective by reducing the time you spend explaining how wonderful you are; your time can be spent talking about the client's specific problem because the client already knows about you.

Here's what PR cannot do:

- PR alone is not likely to obtain a specific job.

- A public relations program cannot be measured quickly in terms of return on investment; only over time—usually 2 to 5 years—can a realistic evaluation be made.

WHO DOES INDIRECT MARKETING?

In many firms we have found the principals want to get published, and they want a new brochure. But they haven't clearly identified their target markets and no one is making client calls. So the question is not only who should do the indirect marketing but how much time should be spent on it. First, let's look at who does it.

Large firms, because they often need to produce a large volume of work, may retain a communications manager or director on staff, who may in turn have writers, photographers, graphic designers, and others working for him or her. These, obviously, are full-time jobs. At Parsons, Brinckerhoff, in fact, the PR director has ended up running an entire profit center for the firm, conducting PR campaigns for the clients of the firm's other, more traditional engineering and planning services.

In a smaller firm PR usually becomes a part of the role of the marketing coordinator, manager, or director. In others it is the responsibility of a principal who enjoys writing or public speaking and the relationships developed in this manner.

In all sizes of firms, PR, or some aspect of it, is often hired from a consultant or freelancer. If you decide to take this route, you will find a wide range of consultants to choose from, from powerful corporate advertising and PR firms demanding hefty monthly retainers (and who may or may not know anything about architecture and engineering) to independent writers who may or may not have established relations with the right publications for you. As former marketing coordinators, managers, and directors decide to leave A/E firms and become consultants themselves, the number of freelance PR people who know something about this business has increased and will continue to do so, to the benefit of all concerned.

Before you decide to hire a consultant for this effort you need to know if you can afford it and how can you measure what it should cost against what you will get. Here are some guidelines:

- Estimate how much of your time you have previously spent on these activities and consider the results you achieved.

- Estimate how much more you should spend to get the results you want (you need some sense of what you want to achieve).

- Estimate how much less you will be able to do in other areas, e.g., lead finding, proposal development, presentation coaching, coordinating, and monitoring, or in project management, etc., if you conduct the PR activities yourself.

- Can anyone else in the firm do either the direct or indirect marketing or should you hire someone else to help in these areas in order to free up your time?

- What would it cost to have someone else do the direct marketing?

Take a look, also, at your projected gross revenue from targeted types of clients for the coming year. As discussed in Chap. 8, "The Marketing Budget," you might want to budget anywhere from 5 to 15 percent of your projected gross budget to total marketing costs for the year. Depending on how reactive your marketing tends to be, you may want to budget from 15 to 25 percent of your marketing budget for indirect marketing. (The balance, of course, will be for direct marketing.)

In terms of your own time, if you're responsible for both direct and indirect marketing, you need to evaluate your firm's needs and allocate your time accordingly. It is difficult to say just *how* much of your time should be devoted to PR. Much of this will be determined by the emphasis your firm places on indirect marketing, how involved you are in PR, and your own talents and interests.

With these ballpark figures in mind, if you decide to bring in an outside person for PR, here are some questions to ask:

- Are the consultants familiar with firms like yours? With your clients?

- What have they accomplished previously that would benefit your firm?

- How well do they know the editors and others who can benefit your program?

- How do they work? How frequently will they report to you?

- Do you feel comfortable with them?

- What is their fee structure and how do they bill (i.e., by monthly retainer, by project, on an open-ended hourly basis, etc.)? Don't expect them to work on contingency, that is, you pay them only if they produce results, nice as that would be for you.

If you decide to go ahead with a consultant, here are some next steps to take:

- Develop a PR plan (described below) and determine with one or more PR consultant candidates which items they can implement.

- Develop a schedule for producing the outlined projects and agree in writing with the selected consultant what he or she will do, when, and what material you will provide, by when, for them to maintain the schedule.

- If the consultant is on a monthly retainer, require meetings at least once a month to review projects in progress and to outline new projects within their stated scope of work. (Most A/E firms that have been disappointed with PR consultants have worked with them on retainer. In defense of the consultant, many firms did not give the PR person or firm enough material or direction and, as a result, their program lost its priority with the consultant. A conscientious consultant in this situation will warn you that he or she is underutilized, but another one may simply collect the retainer, work on some vague projects in a perfunctory manner, and be available when a real need arises.)

- Keep a steady stream of projects, articles, and ideas both going to and coming from the consultant.

PUBLIC RELATIONS: FIRST YOU PLAN

Regardless of who does your indirect marketing, you need to start with some goals, objectives, and direction. You will probably have several options to consider, both in the message you want to deliver and in the choice of media with which to deliver it. Look first at your firm's target markets—particularly the types of clients you want most to reach and the types of services and projects in which you want to be considered expert. (If you don't have any targeted markets, meet with the firm's principals and decide on your priorities. See Chap. 7, "The Marketing Plan," to help you with this step.)

From your research (see also Chap. 3, "Direct Marketing") you will know what issues are most significant to your target client types. How can your firm make an impression on these people—other than calling them up one at a time—and convince them, "We understand your problems and can solve them. Hire us."? Review the following list to see which elements of a PR program will suit your firm best. (Each of these elements, along with some "dos and don'ts" will be covered in more detail later on.)

Oh yes, very impressive figures, but I didn't know this was your firm.

- Articles in trade and mass-circulation publications
- Advertising in these same publications
- Direct mail campaigns (brochures, announcements, postcards, etc.)
- Awards program participation
- Design competitions
- Trade shows and conventions
- Memberships in client organizations
- Public speaking engagements
- Participation in seminars
- Entertaining clients

Of the options shown above, we have found that getting published and developing a direct-mail program have been most effective for our firms and others we know of. They are also among the more traditional PR activities for professional service firms. For those reasons we concentrate more on these than on the other PR activities listed above. For an excellent book on this subject, see Gerre Jones' *Public Relations for the Design Professional* (see "Resources" at the end of this book).

Obviously, with limited time and dollars, choosing the right PR medium (advertising or direct mail, for example) and the right message (what is our area of expertise and who is our audience) will be your most important step. List, in priority sequence, what the firm should do, for example:

- Redo image brochure and mail to potential clients.
- Get published in two client magazines this year.
- Enter two design award programs.
- Speak (on a panel?) at one client conference next year.

Involve principals and others in a roundtable brainstorming session to develop this list. But have your own recommendations and justifications solidly in mind first; few things get crazy faster than a PR wish list. In Fig. 4.1 we show a sample matrix that lists PR projects on one axis and a calendar on the other. You can use this kind of tool to show others in your firm what you are working on to promote the firm and to help a consultant see the whole picture you have in mind.

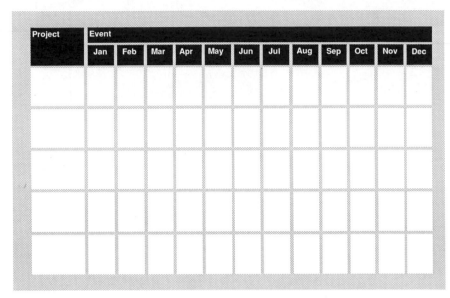

Project	Event											
	Jan	Feb	Mar	Apr	May	Jun	Jul	Aug	Sep	Oct	Nov	Dec

Figure 4.1 PR opportunities calendar.

The following are some methods for handling the major PR elements appropriate to architecture and engineering firms.

PUBLICATIONS

There are several kinds of publication(s) that may serve your needs. They can be categorized as follows:

Trade Publications

Ours (design, engineering, planning publications read by professionals in our own fields). Getting published in these serves five main functions, they are:

- Morale building for those in your firm who are named or who worked on the project
- Recruitment of new talent
- As a source of reprints to send to potential clients
- To obtain referrals to clients from other professionals who see the article
- To influence clients, especially those who have in-house architects or engineers

Theirs (technical or trade publications in your client's field; e.g., criminal justice or facilities management). Getting published in one of these puts your information directly in front of the people you want to read it. Of course, they may miss it or your name may be buried in a list of other consultants, all of them competitors. You can still use the piece as a reprint or direct mail item, however. Try to pick those trade publications that your clients respect since your credibility is linked to that of the publication. Ask your former and current clients what they read.

Local News

Daily papers. These can be useful if much of your firm's business is local. Otherwise, this kind of news just massages the egos of those whose names appear. Articles can be used as boilerplate, especially if the subject is somewhat technical and not too political. (Even though it's better to have your name in the paper than not have it in, don't clip and circulate articles about the garage your firm designed that fell down.) Local articles can link your firm to popular local causes, charities, etc., and with things new and innovative.

National News

Newspapers. The *Wall Street Journal* and *New York Times* are the country's most respected and widely read "national" papers. It is difficult to get articles published in them, but the number of readers and the readers' comparative affluence is high enough to make an effort worth considering. Usually design firms get mentioned favorably only in conjunction with something newsworthy about a particular client, e.g., the decision to build a new corporate headquarters, and unfavorably in connection with a disaster.

News magazines. The same general considerations hold true for magazines such as *Fortune, Newsweek,* and *Business Week* as for newspapers, but, since they tend to put more emphasis on feature stories than on "spot news," their editors may be more concerned with issues (e.g., trends, generic solutions) than with events (e.g., a ground breaking or new corporate leadership).

Getting Published for Fun and Profit

Here are some suggestions and rules for getting published in periodicals:

- The first thing to remember is that those who control the editorial content of the publications in which you are interested are the equivalent of clients, to be researched and courted.

- Make a list of the publications appropriate to your firm. Use a comprehensive guide to publications such as *Bacon's Publicity Checker* and identify publications by their relation to your target clients. Contact each listed publication to get a sample copy and ask your current clients what they read and respect.

- Make a large chart (Fig. 4.2) which will actually be a cleverly disguised matrix consisting of calendar months along one axis and your firm's projects along the other. List only those projects that have some kind of news value for the publications on your list. (Stay tuned for a definition of "news value.")

- This schedule will help you focus on what has to be done and will feed data into your budget (e.g., how much money will you need for project photography? When will you need it?).

- We have found that you derive a dividend from having this chart up in your office to show your colleagues what the opportunities are and what you and they can do to promote the firm.

- Keep in mind it takes a long time to get published in some magazines. Trade periodicals print spot news immediately, but very little informa-

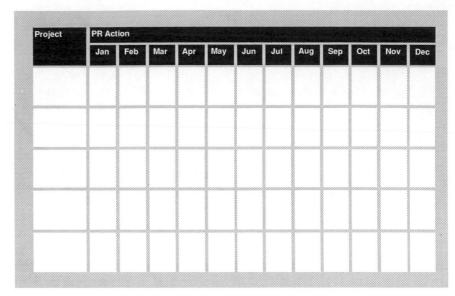

Figure 4.2 PR action calendar.

tion constitutes news. Most information appears as feature articles and gets scheduled for an issue 3 to 6 months in the future.

- Most trade publications have annual editorial calendars you can request that list major topics for future issues.

- To understand the PR and publications racket, we have had to do a lot of reading. What an editor will want to get from you can usually be determined from what he or she has published in the past. Reading will give you the tone, style, format, and basic kinds of information the publication will use. (But, don't start out writing anything until you talk to or exchange correspondence with an editor to see if they are interested.)

- One marketer we know uses another chart to keep track of potential publications and articles or stories of possible interest to them. She lists along one axis the projects of interest to an editor and along the other axis the publications identified as possibly useful to the firm. She puts a number in the box opposite each project indicating which publication has highest priority for that project (Fig. 4.3). The chart really helps her get a handle on projects her firm is doing that can be published and how to get started. It also helps clarify which articles might be used exclusively by which publications.

Getting Published: The "Nitty-Gritty"

Get to know the editors and/or writers on the periodicals in which you want your information to appear. Just like clients, remember? When you read something they have written which you like or to which you can add, write to them. Most writers, incidentally, would rather hear from you in the mail than over the phone. Most are working against tight deadlines and have little time to chat. But they appreciate the written word and enjoy a well thought out letter.

What if you can't write? This is a problem when you want to get published. But do the following:

- Call or write to get information you need from an editor (e.g., what are they looking for, what special issues have they planned for the near future, what kind of graphics do they want to see, what are their deadlines?).

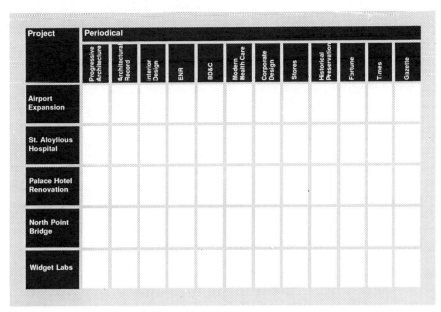

Project	Periodical											
	Progressive Architecture	Architectural Record	Interior Design	ENR	BD&C	Modern Health Care	Corporate Design	Stores	Historical Preservation	Fortune	Times	Gazette
Airport Expansion												
St. Aloylious Hospital												
Palace Hotel Renovation												
North Point Bridge												
Widget Labs												

Figure 4.3 Publications priority matrix.

Have all your questions prepared before you call so that you take up a minimum of the editor's time.

- Tell the editor that you will cooperate in sending information but that you do not intend to write the article yourself. If the editor or writer wants a finished piece rather than a fact sheet or detailed outline, find someone else in your firm or hire someone (see Chap. 5, "Sales Tools," for more on how to get out of writing if you can't do it).

- When you send something in writing, keep it short. Agonize over the cover letter until it says everything you want in as few words as possible. Then use lists, short phrases, illustrations, and diagrams to tell the story; let the writers and editors at the publication shape it.

- Who should contact the press? If someone in your firm already knows and has a good relationship with someone on an editorial staff, use that person as primary contact. If your person hasn't the time to serve the publication, have him or her hand the press contact over to someone who can be effective. If no one knows anyone, use the most senior person in your firm *who has time to do the job well.* In other words, the CEO may be the best person to represent your firm with both your trade press and your clients; but if that person can't respond promptly to phone calls and doesn't delegate well enough to be sure information gets sent out in time to meet deadlines, use a senior designer or experienced marketing person for this important function.

- Try not to entrust your press relations to someone without technical (e.g., design or engineering) background or editorial/PR skills. The best correspondent will be proficient in both technical language and the process of getting published.

- Also be aware of the too-slick advertising and PR outsider who "placed" hundreds of articles for the local shoe merchants and handled the Lower Podunk Prune Pit Queen Festival for 25 years. The editors of design and construction publications may want to be approached by someone who knows the profession more intimately.

- Become a resource for the working press; let people in your community know, for example, that when it comes to real estate developers, your architectural firm has the information the local press may want. Always try to be helpful, but, if you don't know the answer or know it to be confidential, tell the truth.

- In fact, always, always, always tell the truth, even if it means saying, "I can't tell you that; I'm sorry."

- If a garage your firm designed collapses on cars and causes scillions of dollars of damage, don't say you didn't design the garage. On the other hand, don't say it was your firm's fault. Keep in mind that in 6 months corporate and civic executives who hire garage architects may have forgotten your firm was implicated in the collapse, but chances are they will remember your firm's name, "...seems to me I read something about them somewhere...." Remember also that denying something factual will only make any culpability for errors seem more atrocious.

Press Releases and Other "Good Stuff"

How do you get what you do want in print when you want it? How do you get "caught" as PR expert Joan Capelin says, "doing something right?" Let's look at the kinds of material (known in the trade as "good stuff") you can send to various print media types which may interest them in your firm's projects and people.

Press releases are brief statements describing an event of some interest (you hope) to the readership of the periodical (Fig. 4.4). Press releases are effective for various announcements, including:

- Newly appointed senior staff at level of associate, VP, and above

- Senior staff promotions

- New office, new address, new services

- Seminars, lectures, other educational events to which the public is invited, or, after the fact, about which the public may be interested

- Award of a publicly significant new project

- Approval of a controversial project by, for example, a planning commission

- Announcement of a ground breaking to which press is invited

- Announcement of other major milestones on projects of public interest, e.g., topping-off ceremonies, ribbon cutting, and the like

Write your press release in the "pyramid" style: who, what, when, where, why (and possibly how) must appear in the first few sentences, which are called the lead. Assume that anything not appearing in the lead may not appear in print. You may need to practice writing press releases to get the hang of it or hire someone to do them for you.

Always include the date at the top, with your name as the contact and your phone number. You need not write a headline, but it may help to give the person receiving it some idea as to the topic, e.g., "Design Firm Names New Vice President." *Keep it short*. Period.

If not sent in advance, press releases must be prepared and sent soon (within a week) after the event takes place. If one or more photos accompany the release, label them by gluing or taping the typewritten information at the bottom or on the back; don't write directly on the photo. Papers want 4- by 5- or 8- by 10-inch black and white glossy prints; magazines want the same; and, usually, design periodicals require 4- by 5-inch original color transparencies for reproduction.

Always submit press releases on your firm's letterhead, double or triple

PRESS RELEASE

July 28, 1988

Contact Person: Donna Sidel Straus, (415) 236-7435
                   John van Duyl, (415) 398-7088

COIT TOWER RESTORATION RECEIVES TOP HONORS

FOR IMMEDIATE USE

San Francisco — Efforts to preserve one of San Francisco's famous landmarks,
Coit Tower, were honored by the California preservation community at the
Thirteenth Annual State Preservation Conference in Palo Alto, held in May.
The Coit Tower restoration received the 1988 California Preservation
Foundation Design Award, commending the City and County of San Francisco and
its consultant, Interactive Resources, Inc., in their successful efforts to
halt the deterioration of the 50-year old historic concrete tower atop
Telegraph Hill.

In a separate presentation, the Art Deco Society awarded the City of San
Francisco and Interactive Resources, Inc., its 1988 Preservation Award for
refurbishing the landmark to its original, "as designed" condition. Built in
the heyday of Art Deco, Coit Tower was originally commissioned by the City in
honor of Lillie Hitchcock Coit, who bequeathed part of her estate for the
beautification of San Francisco.

                             -more-

Figure 4.4   Press release (as sent to publication).

spaced, with wide margins. If a press release involves a client, as it will if you are describing a project, *you must have the client's approval in advance.* If deadlines are tight, most clients will approve a release if you read it to them on the phone and then send a confirming copy for their files.

Be sure that someone in authority at the client's office (at least a project manager, preferably a principal, CEO, member of the legal staff, or the client's director of public relations) knows about and has approved the information. Make a record of their approval (a signature is best, but a notation on a telephone pad is probably adequate) and put it in your file. Few things get clients riled faster than reading about their project in the morning paper when they don't expect to.

Also, don't forget to get all the in-house approvals you need. The principal in charge and project manager (if it's about a project) should approve what is said. (If you are a nontechnical person, this approval process will help your credibility and show you are a team player. It also spreads the ownership for releases—and there are many—that don't get published.) Figure 4.5 shows our earlier press release (Fig. 4.4) as published in a local newspaper.

B-2 SUNDAY, JULY 31, 1988 ★ San Francisco Examiner

MetroFile

AWARD WINNER

■ THE EFFORT TO preserve Coit Tower has garnered praised from the 13th annual State Preservation Conference.

The City and its consultant, Interactive Resources Inc., were recipients of the 1988 California Preservation Foundation Design Award. The award commemorates the successful efforts to halt deterioration of the 50-year-old historic concrete tower atop Telegraph Hill.

Additionally, the Art Deco Society bestowed its 1988 Preservation Award to The City and Interactive Resources for refurbishing the landmark to its "as designed" condition. The tower was originally commissioned in honor of Lillie Hitchcock Coit, who bequeathed part of her estate for the beautification of San Francisco.

The tower and its ground-level plaza have suffered from exposure to the elements. A $1.5 million restoration program was started in 1983. The restoration was completed last April.

Figure 4.5 Press release (as published). Reprinted with permission of the *San Francisco Examiner* © 1988.

Press Packets

These are elaborate, embellished press releases and usually get sent to an editor prior to a major event, such as the ribbon cutting for a new major building or the dedication of a bridge named for a local leader. They can also be used to introduce an editor to a body of work performed by your firm, such as all your airport projects or all your work in innovative energy conservation design. Press packets usually include photos and drawings of one or more projects, along with fact sheets and other written information on the projects. For a special event they may include photos of participant celebrities.

Because they are expensive and time consuming, we strongly advise you to avoid producing them on your own unless you have a big PR budget. You can, however, contribute material and get your name included in press packets submitted by your clients (e.g., for new corporate headquarters or developer buildings).

If you do put one together, tailored press packets work best, we have found. Send a cover letter, one or more project descriptions, fact sheets, client profiles, renderings, plans, and construction photos to a specific editor to whom you have already spoken about the proposed article. Include only that information you think, from having discussed it, will appeal to the editor and meet the publication's needs.

In general, editors don't want much of the material included by eager PR people and would rather receive a few items, first, to get their attention, then meet with you or talk over the phone to arrange for more appropriate material. Unless you have a big budget and lots of high-power media contacts (in which case you already know all this), don't waste money on a mass mailing of press packets.

ADVERTISING

People in the publicity industry distinguish advertising from public relations. That is, advertising, to a journalist, is not public relations. The former is openly and obviously paid for, while the latter at least masquerades as news or a valid feature story, which generally cannot be purchased.

Advertising usually has less credibility than the same information presented in an article written by a third party, such as the magazine's editorial staff. However, you have less control over the content in an article because the editor can abbreviate, expand, or otherwise change what you have submitted. An ad must be placed exactly as you submit it.

Rate sheets tell the various sizes of ads, how much they cost, and how much less each one costs if you buy more than one. Advertising agencies get discounts on these rates; if you have a large advertising budget, you can set up an in-house division for placing ads and qualify for this price break.

Some design firms have begun advertising on television, either in a straight "plug" format or as sponsors on public television. In the latter case, all that the viewers see is the note, "sponsored by XYZ Architects, Inc.," at the end of the show, but they probably see it every week. Some advertisers have reported favorable client comment: "Hey, I saw your name on TV last night." Whether the comments are worth the several thousand dollars it costs to be seen there depends on how much the design professional wants name recognition.

Some large firms have used print advertising effectively to reach their targeted corporate clients; most employ professional agencies to help them and have large (by A/E standards) budgets for this effort. Smaller firms without the big bucks to spend should be very cautious about venturing into this medium. A corny ad or one that doesn't attract your clients can do you more harm than having none at all.

More firms, especially those with sophisticated engineering specialty services, have advertised in trade magazines read by their clients. These ads cost less—sometimes under $1000 for up to half a page—than the mass circulation magazines or newspapers and reach only those readers who are potential clients.

Among professional firms responding to a survey a few years ago, those who said they used advertising indicated that they employ the image of "experts," linking what they do to the client's need for specialists in that field and placing their ads in client publications.

A firm may actually pay more to "place" an article in the right publication than they would pay to get an ad of similar size and content in the same periodical. The higher payment is usually a fee to a professional PR consultant, who either writes the article or works with a journalist at the periodical; it does not go to the publication. If it did, it would be advertising.

DIRECT MAIL

Direct mail can refer to anything that your firm sends to its potential clients. We have found this targeted approach is often more cost effective than having an article published or buying advertising. It seems to be most successful when combined with advertising and a publicity program.

Direct mail, in fact, combines PR and direct marketing and depends heavily on the quality of your mailing list for its success. Use of word processing or computerized mailing systems have made these efforts less labor intensive and more targeted. We talk more about these systems, including mailing lists, in Chap. 5, "Sales Tools."

Let's look at some of the kinds of direct mail pieces you can develop. Many of them are "do-it-yourself" publications, things produced by your firm and designed especially to meet your marketing needs.

Brochures

If your brochure is the "image" type, intended to impress a broad spectrum of your target market segment and conveying to those potential clients your expertise in an area of interest to them, it can be a PR tool. It can also be marginally effective as a direct marketing tool when you are pursuing a particular project.

We describe in more detail how to go about planning and designing a brochure in Chap. 5, "Sales Tools," and we also define more clearly the difference between image brochures and others that address specific client issues.

Announcements

Use announcements for:

- New appointments to the firm
- Major promotions
- A new address—whether a move, an acquisition, or an expansion
- A merger or acquisition
- A new discipline or service being offered in the firm
- An award or competition recently won

The announcement can draw special attention to your firm and remind those on your mailing list that you are alive and well and prosperous enough to afford postage. It must, of course, be short, sweet, graphically appropriate (e.g., slick or low-key), but never cheap looking, unless that is the image you want to convey.

Invitations

An invitation is a special kind of announcement, which we have used as both a direct mail piece for putting our firms' names favorably in front of potential clients and also to attract attendees to a special event (Fig. 4.6).

Posters, Cards, Seasonal Greetings

These devices put your name in front of your intended clients on either a short- or long-term basis but always in a graphically impressive, pleasing manner. Posters must go on a wall in order to justify their expense; cards need only make a momentary impression but must be appropriate to the recipient. If you are marketing to other designers, for example, an engineer-

KAPLAN/McLAUGHLIN/DIAZ

WOULD LIKE YOU TO JOIN
US ON FRIDAY, DECEMBER 18TH
FOR A

CELEBRATION OF THE SEASON

FROM 5:30 TO 8:30
AT 222 VALLEJO STREET

COCKTAILS

MUSIC BY
THE SAN FRANCISCO BRASS QUINTET
AND
BROADWAY LIMITED

DANCING
FROM 8:30 TO 1:30
AT THE GREEN ROOM
VETERANS MEMORIAL BUILDING
VAN NESS & McALISTER

COCKTAILS AND LIGHT SUPPER

ROYAL SOCIETY JAZZ ORCHESTRA
AND
MAD MARTHA, THE D.J.

Figure 4.6   Party invitation.

ing firm trying to impress architects, keep in mind what impresses them: design. Don't spend the money unless you can do it right.

Client Newsletters

Probably the most abused marketing tool, especially in the A/E profession,
client newsletters are effective only if the material in them is factual, newsworthy, appealing to the targeted markets, and it arrives regularly. We have
found that newsletters involve a major commitment of budget, professional
writing, and graphic design time. We are talking here about something written primarily for a client audience, not the in-house folks. (References to a

client newsletter as an "out-house" piece are not generally appreciated by those who edit them.)

Newsletters are used as small brochures, as direct mail advertising, and for stroking the ego of the firm's leadership. We have seen them get developed without a clear sense of the marketing goals they need to serve. As a result, they often lack credibility, seem silly and self-serving, and get thrown away without being read. We have also seen design firms confuse the goals of a newsletter with those of a brochure. While both can be effective as parts of a direct mail campaign, they have specific differences which should be kept in mind.

A newsletter reports the *news* on a recurring, periodic, fairly regular basis; it goes to a broad spectrum of past, present, and potential clients as well as to the professional friends and associates of the senior staff. A small brochure (pamphlet, flyer, etc.), while physically resembling a newsletter, addresses a particular topic, usually of interest to a limited portion of your market (either geographic or by project type); it can easily be used over an extended period of time but sent only once to each recipient.

Newsletters require commitment to continued, regular publication; if you publish fewer than three issues a year, you lose the benefit of the recurring association of your firm's name with the positive message you are presenting. Also, news gets stale fast. Something is newsworthy if your readers are interested in the subject and haven't seen it all before. Analyze your current and intended client base, determine some common denominators, and include enough diversity so almost everyone will be interested in something you have to say. Remember, project descriptions seldom have news value.

For distribution to a wide audience your newsletter must present a spectrum of topics that will appeal to that readership. How do you know? Analyze what gets read the most—*The Wall Street Journal, Fortune, Forbes, The New York Times*, and other business publications in the client's own specialty. It's okay to emulate the best characteristics of those publications that are already successful with your intended audience.

To start a newsletter, assemble the following team:

- Writer (or writers)
- Editor/coordinator
- Final authority (CEO or other top executive)
- Graphic designer
- Photographer
- Printer
- Mailing person or staff (and don't forget the person responsible for correcting and updating the mailing list)

We have generally had better results in our firms if the graphic designer is an outside consultant, hired specifically for this project, with a clearly stated budget and experience in doing corporate newsletters (or better, in doing communications pieces for other clients whom you want to attract, e.g., corporate executives or health care administrators). The designer's experience is especially critical if none of the other team members has done a project like this before. Architects and environmental graphics people usually cannot check a four-color press proof with anything like the efficiency of a good graphic designer.

Develop a schedule after you have decided some basics about budget, how many pages, whether to use color, what kind of fold or binding, and what size. Then put together a rough "dummy" (Fig. 4.7) of how you want

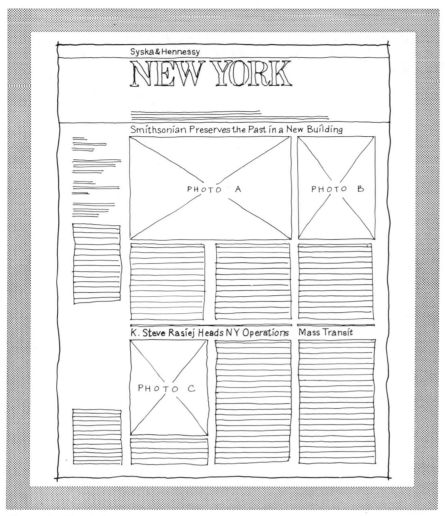

Figure 4.7 Newsletter layout.

the publication to look, with sketches and lines drawn in for text. Decide what articles you want to include, what photos or other illustrations.

As with a press release, don't write anything about a client's project without prior approval—both client and in-house—no matter how flattering you sound or how sincere you are. Make it newsworthy. Avoid self-laudatory prose; be as objective as possible. The following are some criteria for good newswriting:

- Controversial subjects
- Timely coverage
- People
- New solutions to problems your readers may be facing now

Clients, especially, will enjoy seeing themselves in your paper if the subject is appropriate and makes them look good; your own people will also appreciate friendly coverage, but they must do something worth reading about.

AWARDS PROGRAMS

Winning awards for design, energy conservation, or creative use of a particular building material can enhance a marketing program under certain conditions:

- If the award substantiates a capability you are promoting to meet your marketing goals

- If receipt of the award gets publicized and reaches your intended clients (send announcements and reprints of articles to potential clients; use reprints in proposals)

Awards programs, like other forms of PR, are difficult to analyze in terms of value to your firm. Many designers will want to enter programs to bolster their egos and their enthusiasm should not be squelched. However, awards programs are expensive in terms of material submitted (excellent photography or presentation drawings for which the client will not pay) and personnel time (those involved will want to pull out all the stops).

Through publications of interest to your firm and its clients, and through professional societies, you should know in advance (say for a year) which awards programs are worth entering. Decide ahead of time which, if any, your firm will enter, and budget time and money accordingly. Approach an award program as if it were a project you want. Make the commitment to win, follow the requirements carefully, and respond as thoroughly as possible. Those who review award submittals are looking for reasons to drop out contenders; don't give them any. Because awards programs are costly and therefore sometimes controversial, you may need to write guidelines for entry and your expectations.

DESIGN COMPETITIONS

This method of pursuing projects clearly overlaps both direct and indirect marketing. For many firms the exercise is of dubious value. However, in pursuit of a project your firm may be able to attract attention from similar potential clients, especially if the winning and runner-up commissions get published. Competitions are entered by firms:

- For whom it is a luxury in which they feel they can indulge

- Who are starving and feel they must pursue this last-gasp effort

- Who see themselves on the cutting edge of new design: the big innovators, the trend setters, or those firms who want to be seen that way

- Who want to develop a track record in a new market, often young firms, just starting to build their reputation in specific markets

Entering a competition can give you credibility in a market area in which your firm has little actual experience or in which individual firm members have backgrounds but the firm has none. In our experience the cost to receive this kind of publicity is always very high; the chances of winning are usually low. Even when reimbursed, competition costs exceed the amount offered by the client; and not all losing—or even winning—competitors receive adequate promotion. Some firms restrict staff involvement to uncompensated nights and weekends, but there will still be a real toll on billable productivity.

If you do not win, your promotion will show that, although you were a finalist, you did not get first place. Most clients will not know how good you had to be just to compete and will be more interested in the winner's work than in yours.

TRADE SHOWS AND CONVENTIONS

Architecture and engineering firms, to avoid looking like building material suppliers, have tended to shun the exhibition circuit. But, as with advertising, the old fear that self-promotion is unprofessional has begun to fade. Many firms, especially those involved in specialized markets like health care and public infrastructure regularly have booths at national and regional conventions. Before you decide to exhibit, ask such questions as:

- Will you find your market represented at the convention?
- What is your marketing objective?
- What is your budget?
- What is the theme for the show and how should you relate to it?

If you decide to go ahead:

- Attend the show first, usually a year in advance of the time you will participate with an exhibition, to get a feel for attendees, the other exhibitors, and what will be effective.
- Promote your exhibit through literature, calls, and invitations to attendees ahead of time.
- Use a professional booth-production consultant to create exactly the image you want. (Many shows have specific guidelines for booth sizes, materials, and types of exhibits.)
- Be prepared to answer questions: have knowledgeable people present.
- Plan to follow up with the contacts you make. Keep careful notes and have materials ready to send with personal letters as soon as the convention is over.

Some firms have had success combining the trade show and a hospitality suite or a cocktail party for visiting clients. Again, advance publicity and an appropriate environment can spell success for this tool. If you hold a hospitality suite and send project people to schmooz the clients, make certain they can do so in the clients' vocabulary and areas of interest.

MEMBERSHIPS

As in the old days, we still find that memberships in organizations whose members send the right kind of work our way should be encouraged. These memberships include church or synagogue, private social clubs, golf and tennis clubs, chambers of commerce, Boy and Girl Scouts, etc. But don't forget the professional organizations addressing issues of interest to your clients. Organizations such as the Urban Land Institute, International Facilities Managers Association, Building Owners and Managers Association, National Association of Industrial and Office Parks, and the National Association of Corporate Real Estate Executives, to name only a few, can be very helpful.

The more effective memberships fall into two major categories:

- Those directly related to your target markets, e.g., in the health care field, criminal justice, retail sales, food service, hotels, transportation, or electronics industries
- Those that attract senior executives from any market place who will, once they know you, refer you to their colleagues and associates—these organizations include:
  National, state and local chambers of commerce

State and local business organizations such as Kiwanis, Toastmasters, Lions

The list is endless and the point simple: join every trade association you can that attracts executives of organizations that constitute your market. Next, make sure a qualified representative of your firm is active in the association; just being a member will not raise the profile of your firm. Beware of contributing too much time, however, if no return on investment seems to be forthcoming. This warning especially applies to membership and participation in the American Institute of Architects, American Society of Civil Engineers, and similar professional organizations in the firm's own discipline. While such activities may enhance the professional development of the individual, they seldom do much for your marketing plan.

An architect we know is very active in professional organizations of interest to his clients. He considers this his most important marketing investment because of the exposure he gets for his firm and the opportunity he has to meet clients on a one-to-one basis as equals. He stresses that architects are sometimes seen as going to clients "hat in hand," looking for work, and that by working on committees with clients, they communicate as colleagues, making it much easier for him to get to know his intended clients, and they him. Developing this "collegial" level of communication practically ensures that his firm will be considered for appropriate projects. This approach also underscores an important message in third-generation marketing, that of developing strong long-term relationships with clients that lead to work as a natural outgrowth of the relationship.

SPEAKING ENGAGEMENTS

The lecture circuit is not for everyone, but if you have a natural ham in the office who can combine technical knowledge with a witty sense of delivery, send this person off to address any and all groups where potential clients may be lurking. The information this person offers must be factual but not too technical for a generally lay audience; you are striving for credibility *as* experts but not necessarily *among* experts.

Opportunities for giving lectures may include local or national universities or professional societies such as those made up of scientists, realtors, and bankers (the American Management Association is a good example). But keep the talk and the audience focused; and above all, follow up on the contacts this loquacious character will make. Get good speeches published in a relevant journal, send briefs to interested members of the audience, use questionnaires to assess the impact of the speech.

SEMINARS

Educational events sponsored by your firm can provide an effective forum for demonstrating your expertise in a given subject. A successful formula for some firms consists of combining a lecture or two given by specialists in your office with a wine-and-cheese reception or a more formal luncheon. These events can range from elaborate, very expensive affairs with overnight accommodation for guests to more casual get-togethers for lecture and discussion over 2 to 3 hours. However you approach the seminar, keep in mind why people come:

- To learn something from specialists to take back to their own firm

- To meet others in their field and exchange views
- To get away from their own workplace and get a different perspective
- To look for a job or recruit for their firm
- To have a good time

(Not necessarily in that order.)

In order to serve your seminar attendees and, in the process, serve your own marketing goals, you need to do the following:

- Put the guest list together with extreme care; some people will come because others will be there. Mix your clients and their clients if you can. Don't invite your competitors. Include some stars and spend extra effort trying to get them.

- Carefully select subjects for discussion to correspond to your marketing plan; they should be educational but not proprietary (whet their appetite, but don't give away the store). The topic should relate to the concerns of your market and to your special capabilities. Keep it focused; don't try to cover too much.

- Draft invitations appropriate to the event—formal or informal, frugal or lavish (never cheap), technical or broad brush, etc. Send invitations in plenty of time; if you're too rushed to do a good job, postpone the event.

- Allow plenty of time for invitees to respond; place a follow-up phone call to those you especially want to have attend; call them all if the list is short enough and time permits.

- Have enough members of your firm attend the seminar so that guests have someone to talk to about your work. But be sure everyone who represents you can answer questions intelligently and conducts him- or herself well around clients. Try to include some of the junior staff to show your firm's depth, but beware of someone not well versed in your firm's work.

- Have a handout relating to the talk—technical, not self-laudatory—available at the seminar.

- Prepare a follow-up piece to send in the mail.

- Keep expenses and approach appropriate to the audience. For example, if you are courting corporate executives in a fast-moving growth industry at a session on the tax advantages of research and development investment, go all out with the amenities: good food, lavish accommodations, and other comforts customary to this group of people. If, however, you are an engineering firm talking nuts and bolts issues to architects or plant maintenance people, who may care more about your overhead rates than your vintage wine, set the stage more modestly.

A seminar can cost between $200 and $100,000. Should you charge attendees to cover costs? We think charging is risky since the audience must get its money's worth. Don't charge if you can afford not to. Your return on investment is often high. How else can you have the key individual in your market sit and listen to you for up to 8 hours—or more—on the area of your choice, in which you are clearly the expert? If you really get the right people, your payback may be almost immediate and very high. However, some people believe they get only what they pay for and don't want to attend a "free lunch" for fear they will either "pay" in some way later or not get anything of value.

Make sure your audience knows what to expect before they arrive. Fulfill or exceed their expectations through use of graphics, lively and informative speakers, and stimulating question and answer sessions. We recommend a range of speakers, not just people from your office.

Allow your guests time to mingle with one another and with members of your firm. After a seminar, invite selected guests to join members of your firm for a more intimate meal to follow up on the issues raised. Make the most of this opportunity to *listen*; you have set the stage, now let your clients perform on it with you. You will all feel like stars.

ENTERTAINING AND OTHER GOOD EXCUSES TO SPEND MONEY

While the open house or party during the holiday season is usually fun, we have found the expense may be more appropriately placed under human resources than marketing. Most principals would agree that few clients are persuaded to retain their firm based on the ambience of the holiday party. However, a fun-filled gathering for staff, friends, and selected clients can increase morale and productivity.

If you do plan an open house, many of the same observations apply here as did to the seminar: Who should come? Why? What good will it do your marketing program to have them? Use some people to lure others; at least one star should be invited, (for example, a chief executive from a prestigious corporation or the mayor or a general or, if you like, a real movie star), but make sure others know this person will attend and spare no expense to be sure your guests are not disappointed by a nonshowing celebrity.

Parties help to continue a good relationship, rarely to establish one. The one-wine or two-martini lunch, on the other hand, can be of enormous help in smoothing the way into a working relationship, as can the elegant dinner at a quiet restaurant; but they must be followed with the traditional professional contacts in an office setting. We always seem to return to the clients' concern with working with people they like. But this must be within the context of professional competency.

SUMMARY

Keep accurate expense records and review your programs carefully during and at the end of each year. Remember some PR programs take longer than a year to bring results, so evaluate your progress accordingly. We have found some activities do have a positive effect, while others come off as pretentious, a waste of time and money.

Don't try to do too many PR activities at once. Focus on one or two things that work for you and make the most of them. The former journalist loves to work with editors and can produce award-winning client newsletters. The out-going former project managers enjoy design competitions, seminars, and giving lectures. Do what feels good and clients will respond to your enthusiasm.

Chapter Five

Your Bag of Tricks— Sales Tools

INTRODUCTION

The marketer's stock-in-trade is a set of tools that can be divided roughly into two categories:

- Marketing tools—those that help you get and stay organized as you pursue clients, e.g., lists of leads, tickler files, historical data, market information

- Sales tools—those that help you tell your clients how great your firm is and why specific clients should hire you

This chapter deals with the second of these—sales tools. Information on the other kinds of systems—the lead sources and filing systems—is in Chap. 2, "Getting Organized." Some tools, especially proposals, are also described in Chap. 3, "Direct Marketing." Figure 5.1 depicts the relationship between marketing (sales) tools and the direct and indirect marketing practices they serve.

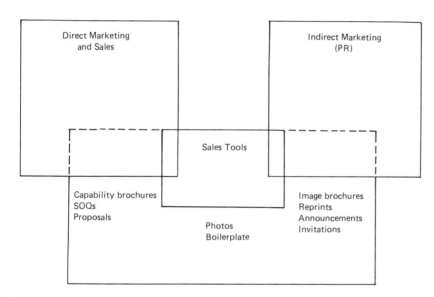

Figure 5.1   Sales tools in support of direct and indirect marketing.

You have to think in two directions simultaneously to plan your basic sales tools successfully:

- You have to put yourself inside your clients' shoes and into their heads (uncomfortable at first, but you can get used to it). What do they need to know about you? Why? What tools will be most effective in communicating with them? What are their problems and how can your firm help them?

- You must also look at how your firm can use the sales tools you are developing quickly and with minimum revision; consider how one document relates to another and how the tool you are producing today can be used in a multitude of formats to get your point across.

The tools we describe in this chapter have been subdivided into two categories:

- Building blocks—project descriptions, résumés, project photos, miscellaneous boilerplate

■ Products resulting from the building process—brochures, proposals, award submittals, press releases, presentation materials, newsletters

Tools must reflect both the firm they serve and the character of that firm's clients. An engineering firm, for example, that sells primarily to technically trained clients, may rely most on charts, graphs, and detailed project descriptions in a statement of qualifications format to show its capabilities. A design firm specializing in executive offices must rely more on photos in an elegant, sophisticated brochure.

Figure 5.2 shows a matrix (one of our favorite tricks is to make a matrix suddenly appear) to describe better how these tools interact. It helps if you understand your end product and how you will use it (shown along the top of the matrix) before developing the components (along the vertical spine).

Primary tools	Secondary tools	Proposal	Presentation	Introduction letter or visit	Image brochure	Client newsletter	Technical letter	Trade publications packet	Press release	
Project description		●	●	●	●	●	●	●	●	
Resumes		●	●	●		●			●	
Project photos prints slides transparencies		●	●		●	●	●		●	
People photos mug shots action shots			●		●	●	●	●	●	
Awards (list of)		●	●	●				●		
References (list of)		●	●	●						
Reprints		●		●	●					
Technical papers (synopses)		●	●	●		●	●	●		
Misc. graphics (site or floor plans, costing records, etc.) ● reduced 8 1/2 X 11 ● boards		●	●		●	●	●	●		

Figure 5.2 Tools matrix.

Another useful way to look at these kinds of sales tools is to divide them into three phases, each representing an aspect of client contact or communication (Figs. 5.3 and 5.4.). Phase 1 consists of creating an *overall image* of your firm in the client's mind. Your tools for this phase may include an image brochure but will also probably consist of business cards and letterhead, your office (its location and appearance), and your personnel (how they look and act when they first meet someone). You create an image—whether you mean to or not—in a few seconds—probably no more than 10–30.

Phase 2 consists of establishing *qualifications* to provide certain services. In this phase your tools tend to be more elaborate or detailed brochures and statements of qualification; your personnel who conduct phase 2 communication are those who make introductory (not project-specific) presentations and/or speak at conferences. You are establishing your firm's capability and credentials to work with a particular type of client or on a type of project and the emphasis shifts from the firm as a whole to a group or team within the firm. It may take from 30 seconds to 5 minutes in this phase to convey the essence of your qualifications as they might appear relevant to a client. Re-

Phase 1	Phase 2	Phase 3
Create an image (7-30 seconds)	State qualifications (30 seconds — a few minutes)	Specific capabilities for a particular job (30 minutes — several hours)
Business cards	Capabilities brochure	Proposals
Letterhead	SQOs	Presentations (team project)
Image brochure	Speakers and seminars	Tailored boilerplate
Personal appearance	Boilerplate	
Location and appearance of office		

Figure 5.3 Three phases of marketing communication: time and components.

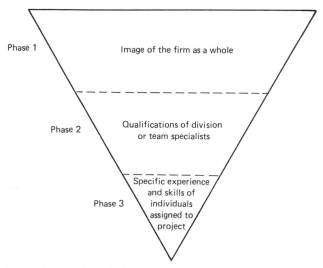

Figure 5.4 Three phases of marketing communication: focus.

member, those receiving this information, especially unsolicited material, will spend only seconds reviewing it.

Phase 3 enables you to communicate with a specific client about a particular project. Your tools are your proposal and its component parts and your project-specific presentation. The emphasis has clearly shifted from the image or qualifications of the firm as a whole to a group of individuals who must have the requisite skills and experience and also be compatible with this client. This phase may take from 30 minutes to several hours to communicate.

Ideally, a pro-active firm will have tools that correspond to each phase and use them appropriately. Phases 1 and 2 go to clients in the courtship and development stages of direct marketing, while phase 3 tools are used only after a project has been identified and defined. Many firms fail to get maximum effectiveness from their sales tools because they don't analyze their needs in terms of each phase, and they use tools inappropriate to the phase they are in with a particular client.

For example, many firms use a qualifications (or capabilities) brochure as an introduction to the firm. A document that delves into your specific capabilities tends to have too much detail and take too long to absorb. A client who is just being introduced to you may only want to get an image, an overview, a sense of what you're like and have done. Or, the same firm might use pages from that same brochure in its submittal for specific jobs. Here, those descriptions or statements of philosophy are too general, not related to the project at hand, and sound "canned." At this point the client wants only information that is relevant and specific to his or her project.

You may, actually, have a fourth phase as well, which consists of on-going communication with clients, e.g., newsletters, postcards, announcements, and press releases (sometimes sent directly to clients as well as to the news media). In this fourth phase you may be reasserting your experience or merely keeping your name in front of them.

In developing tools for your firm:

- Keep in mind how tools have been used in the past and upgrade first those that are most popular since they are most likely to be used again.

- Evaluate at the same time what your firm needs in terms of the three phases and try to develop things that can be cost effective in each.

- Introduce new tools only when you have commitment from others or the control to assure they will be used appropriately and therefore cost effectively.

WRITTEN TOOLS: WORD GAMES FOR FUN AND PROFIT

A/E professionals are often unable to express themselves in plain English. A facility planner told us once, "If I say it so others can understand it, it doesn't sound very difficult, so I can't charge much money for doing it." Well, jobs are seldom lost because proposals or brochures are too simple for the subject matter. Sometimes language does need to be technical and include the client's jargon, but keep it to a minimum. Gerre Jones has some good rules on writing in *How to Market Professional Design Services* (see "Resources").

Although the market has been flooded in recent years with literature on the subject, a basic text for anyone having to write expository prose remains the venerable *The Elements of Style* by William Strunk and E. B. White; it's short and very readable itself.

If you still feel uncomfortable about writing, if the blank page or empty computer screen causes you to break out in sweat, here are some solutions:

- Take a writing course, the more creative the better, to free yourself from both inhibitions and a tendency to split infinitives.

- Explain (or pretend to explain) to another person exactly what you are trying to say. Tape yourself. Explaining ideas aloud can help clarify them and talking may be easier than writing. And, for some, it's easier to identify gobbledy-gook when you hear it than when you see it.

- Set all your thoughts down as rigorously as possible and then hire a professional writer to polish them into great prose. It may be more cost effective in the long run to hire a specialist than to agonize over your own garbled syntax and misplaced modifiers.

Professional writers cost from around $10 per hour to 3 or 4 times that much, depending on the level of technical knowledge required and whether they are drafting specific pieces or producing a complete written program for you.

The building blocks of most *written* marketing tools can be developed from two key ingredients: project descriptions and résumés.

Project Descriptions

Project descriptions should follow a formula for best results and they should always include as a minimum:

- Name and a brief description of the client. By putting this information first you indicate that clients are important to you, that you understand something about them, and that their concerns come first in your consideration.

- Scope, scale, and location of the project—just the facts, so the reader gets a sense of its magnitude at a glance.

- A description of the problem(s)—but don't include, as one project architect did, that the client was a dimwit who couldn't make up his mind. This section is essential; too often architects and engineers describe what they did on a project as if it were an academic exercise. In fact, our work is almost always in response to a serious actual or potential problem (or there would be a problem if the project went wrong). This paragraph can convey the *value* of your work.

- Your successful solution to the problem—don't forget to describe at least the rudiments of your solution, but not just in your terms; indicate that your client's problem was met.

See Figs. 5.5 and 5.6 for examples of information sheets and a complete project description. Project descriptions may, in addition, include such information as:

- Date and cost of the project (indicate if current or old dollars)
- Status of the project (e.g., complete or in progress)
- Project team, including key personnel and consultants
- Estimated bid and actual cost (if completed)
- Design or construction schedule, planned and actual
- General contractor and major subcontractors
- Client references

Descriptions can go on for several paragraphs with considerable detail regarding your approach to the problem. Remember, what the potential client wants to know is usually only:

- Is this project similar to my project?
- Was the problem similar?
- Was it solved successfully? How?

For example, if the client's project involves a fast-track construction program, information on your fast-track experience is relevant, even though the project type is different. If not, it just clutters up a description. You may, therefore, want to develop several problem and solution descriptions for each project; you can then select or modify the most relevant. With computers, you can manipulate the information to emphasize key points, add or delete others. But, as with all other material filed on computer, keep hard copies of everything you need close at hand.

PROJECT DESCRIPTION FACT SHEET

[Information from this sheet will be used in marketing and promotional activities. Thanks for filling it out!]

Form completed by: _____

Date: _____

Project Name: _____

Location: _____
(complete address)

Client (owner): _____

Address: _____

Phone: _____

Client
Contact: _____
(Name and phone)

Estimated/actual completion date (construction) _____

Estimated/actual construction cost: _____

Description of project, e.g. size, configuration, type of
building and construction)
_____
_____
_____

PROBLEMS: (What problems did we help the client solve? This
section is the most important one on this form!!!)
_____
_____
_____
_____

Description of services: _____
_____
_____
_____

[complete on other side if needed]

PROJECT DESCRIPTION, cont.

Project Team:

Principal in Charge: _____

Project Manager: _____

Project Architect: _____

Designer: _____

Others: _____
(include name and project role)
_____

Consultant Team:

Structural: _____

Mechanical: _____

Electrical: _____

Landscape: _____

Other: _____
(include firm and discipline)
_____

Contractor/CM: _____

Our construction cost estimate: _____

Bid or GMP _____

CO Record as percent of total cost: _____

Owner-generated changes: _____

E&O: _____

References: _____
(include name, title, address, phone)
_____

Post-occupancy evaluation: _____
(indicate date scheduled or completed; report filed?)

Figure 5.5 Project description information sheet.

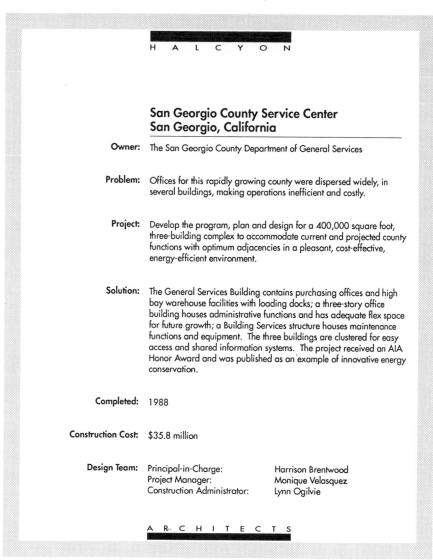

HALCYON

San Georgio County Service Center
San Georgio, California

Owner: The San Georgio County Department of General Services

Problem: Offices for this rapidly growing county were dispersed widely, in several buildings, making operations inefficient and costly.

Project: Develop the program, plan and design for a 400,000 square foot, three-building complex to accommodate current and projected county functions with optimum adjacencies in a pleasant, cost-effective, energy-efficient environment.

Solution: The General Services Building contains purchasing offices and high bay warehouse facilities with loading docks; a three-story office building houses administrative functions and has adequate flex space for future growth; a Building Services structure houses maintenance functions and equipment. The three buildings are clustered for easy access and shared information systems. The project received an AIA Honor Award and was published as an example of innovative energy conservation.

Completed: 1988

Construction Cost: $35.8 million

Design Team: Principal-in-Charge: Harrison Brentwood
Project Manager: Monique Velasquez
Construction Administrator: Lynn Ogilvie

ARCHITECTS

Figure 5.6 Project description.

Process Dictates Content

The technology for producing project descriptions has changed dramatically in the past few years. Your options may include:

- Word processing, without photos, printed on an impact, good quality dot matrix, or laser printer in-house and photocopied

- Word processing, same printing and reproduction, leaving space on the page for pasting one or more project photos in place

- Professionally printed photo-offset photographs and titles, with blank space left on each page for word processing text, modified as needed, and printed in-house

- Photo-offset photos (color or black and white) with printed text

- Color photo-reproduction of photos and text (getting better, but still not the best)

- Desktop publishing (which can combine the best of all of the above—more on this subject later)

If your descriptions are going to be printed on an offset press—as opposed to making multiples on a laser printer or making photocopies—be careful not to provide too much dated information. For example, if you state in your description that the project is *due* to be completed in May 1990, you can't use the descriptions past that date without changing the information, which is expensive and time consuming if they are typeset and printed.

We also recommend against using client references in a printed description. Everyone has a right to change his or her mind, and most people do; we've had what was a glowing recommendation one day become a grudging, "Well they did okay, but I don't think I'd hire them again," tomorrow. Don't take chances. List references only when you can check them and make necessary deletions or corrections (e.g., the *boss* may not like you this week but the project manager does).

Similarly, don't offer project costs unless you identify when they occurred and what they refer to. Don't volunteer this information unless you need to use it to provide project scale, and supply it only when you can explain how the figures are both relevant and favorable to your performance.

Project descriptions can include a rendering or photograph of the job. If the page is going to be printed, the initial cost of preparing each page will be higher because you will need to obtain a photo, prepare camera-ready art, and use a printer. The cost per page, however, may be no higher than photocopied reproductions without photos or with photos pasted in place if you print a thousand or more. Remember, printed project descriptions permit no flexibility. If you want to change the emphasis (e.g., from the fact that this project was a 100-acre master plan to the fact that it included a computer center), you can't do it by this process.

We think the ability to make changes is key to good sales documents. We keep some professionally photocopied descriptions "on the shelf" for quick retrieval, but the information is all on floppy disk for easy manipulation. It takes only minutes to massage a description and print a new version that responds precisely to the client's concerns.

Résumés

These are key pieces in your firm's selling arsenal, written or at least edited by someone involved in marketing and indicating the project experience of all members of the firm whose experience is important in terms of obtaining new work. What kind of new work do you want to get? If your key technical people have "extensive experience" (a terrible cliché; try to avoid it) in educational facilities but your marketing plan specifically identifies schools as money losers and a project type to be avoided, you must creatively translate their experience into something you want to go after—conference centers, perhaps. Or, instead of designing laboratories for high schools and colleges, you may be able to design them for industrial facilities, projects which are targeted in your marketing plan.

In other words, take the information available and use it to present a case that serves your firm's needs and interests. We never fabricate information of this sort, but we do describe experience in laboratory design as just that, rather than referring to the project as the Sophie Glutz Memorial High School's Biology Lab.

Both content and format of the résumé are important. As with a project description, the reader is primarily concerned with, "Has this bimbo ever done a project remotely like the one I've got here? If so, was it a successful project? When was it done, and did the person have a significant role on it or was he or she merely a draftsperson with little responsibility?"

Arrange the information so it can easily be absorbed by the reader. Use:

- Short sentences
- Lists rather than long paragraphs
- Indentations
- A visually appealing balance of print and white space

Former CRS-Sirrine vice president Stephen Kliment, FAIA, says:

- Limit résumés to one page.
- Identify special qualifications for the project (or project type) first (not education or marital status).
- Include education, if significant, at the end.

We suggest you don't include photos on résumés. Some clients subconsciously dislike beards, for example, which might put your team at a disadvantage.

As with project descriptions, there are two basic uses for résumés and corresponding approaches to them: statements of qualification and proposals. In the former, the information may be comprehensive and intended to appeal to a wide audience, many of whom may not have a specific project in mind at the time they first read the material. You are conveying a sense of broad competence.

Most firms, fortunately, do not include résumés in their brochures. In the proposal, however, you are responding to specific criteria identified by your potential client. Address the issues, cite examples, and demonstrate those exact capabilities needed to get you the job. Be specific and relevant. Many firms try to make one document serve both functions. In most cases we find the document does neither very well.

One engineering firm we know of keeps all the résumés they need on the word processor. For the six key personnel who are named to almost every project, at least 12 different hard-copy versions are kept on file at all times, one for every major and some minor market segments in the firm's marketing plan. Each version emphasizes experience and capabilities relevant to that market. Unpredictable situations and routine updates can be handled quickly because all information is on disk.

Obtaining Information

Writing résumés and project descriptions is one thing. Getting the information to put in them is another. Many architects, engineers, and planners, while confident they can leap tall buildings with a single bound, have little to say about their useful experience. A favorite expression is, "Oh, there's nothing special about me; I've done a little of everything, nothing special though. It's just another project."

There are two ways we obtain the needed facts: the form and the interview. For best results we use both, filling out the form while we talk to the staff member. First, to develop a form that works for you, keep your marketing objectives in mind:

- What kind of information do you most need to obtain?
- What is the emphasis?

Sometimes, we have found, you can circulate a blank form with a nice memo explaining that the information sought will be used to get more jobs for the firm in the areas best suited to the person's interests. Refrain from adding that, if they don't fill it out, you will turn their names over to the resident hit squad. But you can drop hints to this effect.

Forms alone work well in firms in which the marketing function is clearly understood and the staff can be motivated to participate. We assure you they don't do as well in other kinds of firms, and in those cases at least some personal interviews are essential. Figure 5.7 illustrates the type of form you may use to obtain information for developing résumés.

The personal approach works best in a smaller firm or in one in which a cast of thousands can be cranking out proposals and making cold calls while you have coffee and a long heart-to-heart with the head of production about how he introduced this fantastic pin-graphic system into the firm back in the Dark Ages. Those kinds of talks do make the difference between a dry, nonresponsive résumé or project description and one that sings your praises with total conviction. But, the hours involved can be devastating. We've never worked in firms in which we could spend enough time with every key technical person to really understand each one's special talent and those projects that set each person apart.

However you obtain the information, you still have to be creative in order to meet your needs. For example, high schools and laboratories—if one of your technical people says his or her experience includes high school design, and you are looking for experience in laboratory design, ask the person if the high school work included a lab. If it did, great. Figures 5.8, 5.9, and 5.10 show how you can format the information on your questionnaire to meet different résumé needs.

Other Boilerplate: What Works and How

You *must* have project descriptions and résumés. In addition, we know creative marketing people who devise all sorts of boilerplate, prepared in advance and used repeatedly. These pieces should address issues commonly raised by prospective clients, as indicated by your research. All boilerplate has one major liability—it often puts the reader to sleep. Somnolence can usually be avoided by inserting the client's name or a reference to the project. Some common boilerplate favorites deal with:

- Cost control methods and record
- Design philosophy
- Awards
- References (remember to check often, *very* often)
- Lists of completed projects by building or client type, e.g, hospitals, long-span bridges, municipal buildings
- Experience on projects with a construction manager
- Standard scope of work statement (for fee proposals)
- Schedule control record
- Typical critical path method graph
- Organization chart (project specific with client's name at the top)

Look through your recent proposals for examples of material that could be modified slightly and made into boilerplate.

Keep It Short Why emphasize brevity? Some estimates place the attention span of the average person at about 7 seconds per piece of unsolicited material (or even solicited, if there are 10 or more brochures or proposals and they all look alike). Keep your prose brief and to the point.

Most written marketing material is not read. To get your point across, rely on headlines, short paragraphs, short lines (wide margins), and illustrations with captions or other graphic devices. Ask yourself, "If I came to this page, would I want to read it?"

RESUME INFORMATION

[INFORMATION FROM THIS SHEET WILL BE USED TO HELP OUR FIRM OBTAIN NEW PROJECTS AND CLIENTS. PLEASE FILL IT OUT THOROUGHLY. THANKS!]

NAME: _____

TITLE: _____
(e.g. Vice President, Associate Partner, etc.)

PROJECT ROLE(s): _____
(e.g. Group Engineering Director, Project Manager, etc.)

EDUCATION: _____
(show school(s), degree(s), date(s)

PROFESSIONAL LICENSES: _____
(include type of registration, discipline, year rec'd)

CURRENT PROFESSIONAL ACTIVITIES AND AFFILIATIONS: _____
(e.g. AIA, ACEC, ASCE, etc.; indicate committees)

AWARDS, PUBLICATIONS, LECTURES/TEACHING POSITIONS: _____

PROFESSIONAL EXPERIENCE:

Joined Halcyon Engineers _____

List projects you have worked on since joining this firm

_____
_____
_____
_____
_____

RESUME INFORMATION, Page 2

PROFESSIONAL EXPERIENCE, cont.

List firms you have worked for previously AND
List major projects you worked on while with each firm; indicate your job title for each project.

Other firms, projects, title(s): _____
_____
_____
_____

SPECIAL INTERESTS AND OTHER COMMENTS:
(Include project types you would especially like to work on)
_____
_____
_____

Figure 5.7 Résumé information form.

Figure 5.8 Résumé—project list style.

VISUALS: LOOKING GOOD MEANS BEING GOOD

Visual material conveys a firm's capabilities graphically. Types of graphics include:

- Photos
- Renderings
- Charts
- Graphs
- Plans

The effectiveness of these aids depends on how well they fit your market objectives. For example, we know firms that have worked with a photographer or graphic designer and spent lots of money to produce images of great beauty. But the materials didn't meet the marketing needs of the firm.

Interior design firms, for example, may restrict photos of an office project to show only the executive suite with its elegant furnishings, attention to details, spaciousness, color, and image. But if a significant amount of the firm's

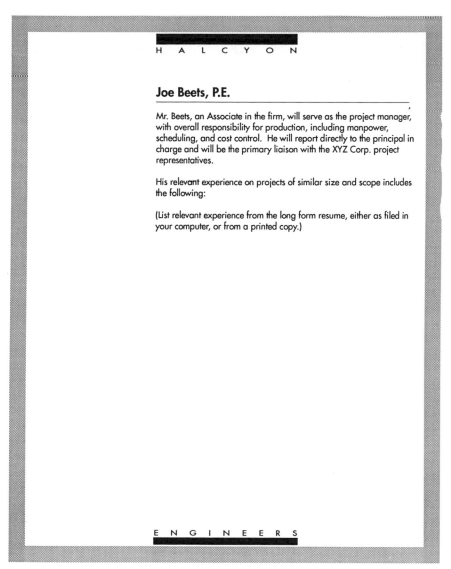

Figure 5.9 Résumé—paragraph style.

market is—or has been targeted to be—building standard tenant improvements and open-plan offices, the photos will miss a key marketing need.

Following are a few of the basic visual aids you may need.

Photography

Photography is more expensive than most other media, but it can have the greatest impact on design firm clients. Photographers cost from $250 to $2000 per day, excluding travel, expenses, and the product. Prints and slides cost extra, ranging from under $10 each for black and white prints or 35-mm slides to more than $20 for one 8- by 10-inch color print. Many photographers retain the negatives, and it is against copyright laws to obtain duplicates or extra prints by going to another source.

Architects and interior designers are more dependent on quality photos than are other consultants. If, however, as engineers or landscape architects, you find architects are your major clients, you better supply the same quality work they demand of themselves.

Most photographs are of projects—completed or in progress. But we have also used other subjects for sales tools, such as:

7. Brief resume of key persons, specialists, and individual consultants anticipated for this project.	
a. Name & Title: Joe Beets, P.E. Associate	a. Name & Title:
b. Project Assignment: Group Engineering Director	b. Project Assignment:
c. Name of Firm with which associated: Engineering Systems, Inc.	c. Name of Firm with which assoc
d. Years experience: With This Firm 5 With Other Firms 20	d. Years experience: With This Fi
e. Education: Degree(s) / Year / Specialization BSME/1958/Mechanical Engineer	e. Education: Degree(s) / Ye
f. Active Registration: Year First Registered/Discipline 1962/Mechanical Engineer	f. Active Registration: Year Firs
g. Other Experience and Qualifications relevant to the proposed project: J. Beets has the following relevant experience in management of engineering design for medical facilities: MacNeal Memorial Hospital, Berwyn, IL Dominican Santa Cruz Hospital, Santa Cruz, CA SOHIO Medical Facility & Firehouse, Prudoe Bay, AK Flowood Mississippi Hospital, Flowood, MS Detroit Osteopathic Hospital, Detroit, MI Cadillac Hospital, Richland, WA Franklin Hospital, Franklin, PA Greenville Hospital, Greenville, TN	g. Other Experience and Qualifica proposed project:

Figure 5.10 Résumé—form 255 style.

- People in the firm
- Teams of people in a typical work environment
- Stock shots of cityscapes and landscapes
- Construction shots demonstrating how something works

In any case, photographs should be exciting. Use unusual angles, lighting, expressions on faces.

Presentation boards, charts, graphs, plans, and renderings can also be photographed. And we have seen aerial photos of a proposed site that are particularly impressive to a potential client.

Debates rage between those who like to see people in project photos and those who do not. On the positive side of this argument, people:

- Bring spaces alive.
- Lend scale to them.
- Present them as they probably look in real life.

And most lay persons (clients) would rather see people (don't underestimate the importance of this preference).

On the negative side (no pun intended), we know that styles in fashion immediately date a project and may make it look foolish (pictures of miniskirted women seemed pretty absurd during the late 1970s). People also detract from the purity of the design and may defeat the marketing effect you are striving for. When shooting interiors, which generally require long exposures, people increase the difficulties because they must hold still. And, you may need model release forms.

For project photography the following rules apply:

- Before hiring a photographer, interview carefully; learn all you can about the techniques and style as well as the personality of the photographer. For example, some are better at interiors, some at exteriors, some with people.

- Your results will be in direct proportion to the quality of your communication with the photographer. Just saying "Here's the address, take a few good shots," will rarely result in what either the marketer or designer had in mind.

- Use a written contract. You (the marketing person), the designer, and the photographer should walk through or around the project together and agree on:
  How many shots?
  Which ones?
  What size format (35 mm; 4 by 5, etc.)?
  What kinds of film (print negative or slides; color transparencies, etc.)?
  What angles?
  What details?
  What kind of lighting?
  What time of day or night?
  How long will the shooting take and how can it best be organized to save you money?
  Who will assist and what added compensation, if any, will be required for extra people?

Determine also if you want to buy the negatives, if any, and what the charge will be for prints and slides. Agree under what circumstances, if any, the job will be reshot and at whose expense. Incidentally, if the photographer is not familiar with or prepared for this type of contract, beware: you are dealing with an inexperienced person. Figure 5.11 shows a sample short-form photography contract. (Beware, too, if, as we once experienced, the photographer shows up at your client's posh offices in ragged cutoffs, rubber sandals, and a mildly scatological T-shirt; this also is the mark of a nonprofessional.) You should also:

- Decide in advance what the end product should be from this shooting: for publication you will need both 8- by 10-inch black-and-white glossy prints and 4- by 5-inch positive color transparencies. Positive transparencies look like big slides but are not usually mounted. Publications such as *Progressive Architecture* require them for reproduction.

- For use in your brochure as well as for your portfolio and awards submittals, etc., you will want 4- by 5-inch black-and-white and/or color print negatives made, so you can later obtain almost any size enlargements. (Images get fuzzy when enlarged too much, so the bigger the original image, e.g., 4 by 5 instead of 35 mm, the bigger you can make the final without loss of clarity. Images get sharper when reduced, so you can make slides from a 4- by 5- negative.)

- If possible, go with the photographer to do the shooting. Be prepared to make last minute decisions regarding changes since the initial visit (e.g., the client had vivid, chintz draperies installed in the interim, or a huge delivery truck is parked in front, blocking a perfect shot through the pine trees. Even more probable, as we have found, for an interior shot some of the lights will be cool white instead of warm white fluorescent and turn green on film).

- Don't let the photo session disrupt the client's home or workplace. Even

Photography Commission

From: _____   Date: _____

To: _____

cc: Marketing Dept., Accounting, Project Manager

XYZ Architects, Inc. has agreed to engage you for photographic services as outlined below for
_____(project)_____ , _____(number)_____ , according to the following terms:

Fee rate: $_____ per _____

Assistant will/will not be used at rate of $_____ per _____

Estimated maximum fees: $_____ based on _____(time)_____ and ___(# of shots)_____

Estimated expenses: _____

Estimated total cost: _____

Purpose of shoot: _____ (interior, exterior, image)_____

Products to be provided: B/W   Color   Size
    Prints   _____   _____   _____
    Slides   _____   _____   _____
    Positive Transparencies   _____   _____   _____
    Other   _____   _____   _____

Schedules: Shoot_____   Deliver Proofs_____

Usage: All usage except consumer or trade advertisement or as noted below:

To confirm this agreement please sign and return one copy. Thank you.

Photographer's signature: _____   Date: _____

XYZ firm representative: _____   Date: _____

Figure 5.11 Sample photographer's contract.

though the design work is completed, the client may not have paid all of the bill yet; and, don't forget, clients are always potential references—good or bad. Complimentary prints or slides for the client make a nice "thank you" for their cooperation.

- Take time to do the job well; interior photography will take from 1 to 4 hours or more *per shot*. Exteriors usually take less time. The main difference, of course, is lighting. But either way, pay attention to details.

So much for projects; what about people? Photographs of people fall into three categories:

- "Mug" shots, head and shoulders, used primarily for publicity
- "Environmental" portraits, which show the full figure of a person in his or her workplace
- Groups of people, for example, surveying a site, both literally and figuratively, or of people at a ground breaking or topping off

The latter two types are more interesting to the average viewer, but you will probably want all kinds to complete your files.

Drawings

By using a drawing rather than a photo you usually admit that the project has not been built. But, if it's under construction, say so, and use the drawing. Drawings (by this we mean elevations, sections, and perspectives—isometrics and axonometrics—as well as plans, rendered plans, and concept sketches) serve two purposes:

- They give an idea of what the project will look like.
- They demonstrate that your firm has talented people who can draw.

Of course, as we move further into the age of computer-aided design and drafting (CADD), the "isos" and "axos" may demonstrate that you have computer capability. This capability can be a "plus" if your system has unusually sophisticated aspects that can benefit the client (generating color perspectives in seconds).

The most basic architectural drawing is the plan. These range from small-scale (area) site plans to specific site plans to floor plans to detailed portions of a floor area used to illustrate a point. They may include, for example:

- Phased plans to show incremental development
- Transportation plans
- Lighting plans
- Signage plans

If you are not an architect or engineer, you can offer insight into how useful the plan is (or is *not*) as a sales tool when seen by a lay audience. Designers sometimes rely too heavily on a tool with which *they* are comfortable but which may be difficult for the nontechnical person to understand. The nontechnical client will seldom bother to study a plan of someone else's project. Period.

Make sure all drawings are labeled adequately and clearly—but not excessively. Work with project designers, managers, and job captains to make sure that you have a set of prints for every project being designed that may be useful to the marketing effort. Plans done during the project's schematic phase, for example, reduced to 8 ½ by 11 inches (photostatically), often result in sharp, clear prints that can be used as sales tools. (Of course, we have had projects change dramatically between schematics and working drawings, but the first plan still looks good. Don't use the old version if doing so will anger the client.)

Know the difference in reproduction qualities of blue-line, sepia, and photostatic originals. (Your friendly local graphic reproduction firm will probably tell you more than you ever wanted to know about the subject.)

Other Visuals

Presentation boards, for use in front of a selection committee, are another important tool for some firms. These boards may consist of:

- Charts
- Graphs
- Lists of key planning or design factors
- Photos

- Renderings
- Plans of all kinds
- Project-related issues

Most boards, such as the team organization chart, are specific to a given project or client and cannot be reused. But some, such as the firm's cost-estimating record on large projects, can have almost unlimited applicability. These should be developed with standard graphics (logo, typeface, type size, style) so that, when used together, they have a common theme and you appear organized.

Other exciting visuals you can explore if your firm has the budget and inclination include videotape, movies, and canned slide shows with or without voice-over.

Video: Still the New Kid in Town

From the results of numerous surveys, more firms, but still not a majority, are investing in video to help create their image or even to serve as a proposal for a particular project. As with all tools, these must be evaluated in terms of how they will affect the targeted markets. Video, also, still depends on the basic building blocks we have just described. A/E firm marketers Barry Gaston and Doug McKay offer some comments and suggestions to the marketer considering audiovisual tools for marketing:

- "People believe what television tells them. Therefore, the potential of video as a communications tool is tremendous. Other factors, such as the portability of the show itself and its capacity for instant replay make it an important option for the design firm marketer.

- "Initial outlay will seem expensive: don't skimp. People will judge your show against broadcast quality. Don't make home movies. Plan to spend $5000 or more to get started. Basic system includes a camera, portable player/recorder, TV/monitor, a small light kit, two microphones, tripod, storage cart, cables, and adapters.

- "Make someone responsible for keeping up with constant changes in video technology by attending seminars, reading publications, and meeting with sales representatives. Don't get immersed in details; know only what you need to be effective.

- "Outside suppliers include production houses and freelance photographers and producers. Production houses offer everything, but free-lancers may be more cost effective. Talk with school systems, hospitals, cable companies, and other users for sources. Consider: rates, facilities, business practices, people, and proximity of their operation.

- "A few applications for video include:
Training for presentation rehearsals, seminars, etc.; from this step your technical people may move to more ambitious applications.
Employee communications.
Testimonials (tape your satisfied client).
Slide shows (more convenient than six carousels).
Trade shows (formal presentation or interactive use).
Project team (use for programming phase or to obtain site information)."

They emphasize, "don't overuse it; integrate video into your other tools and use it when appropriate. Proceed with caution."

Graphic Design

Unify all your marketing visuals by using a common graphic style. The same image should tie together your brochure, proposals, title slides, presentation boards, and all other material produced by the firm. Include in this group your business cards, report covers, and the title block on technical drawings.

Your slide show should have an introductory slide with the firm's logo and other key information on it. Other informational slides might include the subject matter, e.g., Educational Facilities or Master Plans or all work done for a particular client, e.g., the Corps of Engineers.

When and how should you work with a graphic designer? Some firms have such a person in-house, sometimes assigned to environmental signage and graphics. This person has other project deadlines and is not always available to meet urgent schedules. Also, graphic design, not marketing strategy, may dictate the results this person produces. (For example, Helvetica is not the only typeface in the world but for decades in-house graphics people didn't seem to know it.)

One advantage of an in-house desktop publishing system is the ability to produce and change layouts quickly. The tactful marketer can use this flexibility to nudge the in-house graphics people toward a more acceptable design.

We know some firms with excellent in-house people who work in harmony with the marketing staff. If yours is not one of these, try to work with a savvy graphics person outside your firm who will treat you like a customer, which you are, and who will produce fast, accurate results. Producing proposal covers or a new joint-venture logo and letterhead requires speed and experience. Don't compromise if you can afford not to.

Graphic designers cost from around $40 to $100 per hour, depending on experience, quality of work, and your geographic location. You can hire a graphics person for a particular project by having one or more firms submit lump sum bids based on your specifications. Many one-time projects such as brochures are done this way but should be based on selection of a designer you like and feel you can work with, as well as on fee.

Some marketers in our experience have tried to do graphics in-house without a skilled designer, as in: "I can do it." In this instance we have tried to get a good printer to bail us out. It's true that printers can specify typefaces and leading (the space between lines) and can match paper stock and pick a PMS color. But they can't usually solve design problems and will not know, even on the press proof, if the image you want is really coming across. A good printer *is* essential, but don't saddle the printer with requirements beyond his or her capability.

Brochures: Some General Comments

For a good detailed book on brochures, read David Travers' *Preparing Design Office Brochures: A Handbook.* Another good brief text is the ACEC's *Brochure on Brochures* (see "Resources").

Here are some observations on brochure planning and production from our experience. Most A/E firms have some kind of brochure. Clients expect it. And they come in several varieties, among them:

- General brochure, usually from 4 to 24 pages—sometimes larger—covering the firm's history, philosophy, scope of services, sample project work, and, usually, senior personnel; includes text and photos; may be permanently bound or looseleaf for flexibility

- Minibrochure ranging from one 8 ½ by 11 folded page to a poster-sized foldout; usually fits in a letter-size envelope for easy mailing; focuses on a specific project type or capability; includes text and photos

- Newsletter-type sent out periodically on special topics or to update the firm's experience; works best in conjunction with other material; requires text and photos; must be timely

How much flexibility do you want in your brochure? The brochure that sets the right tone for your firm at the first client contact is probably not the brochure that will successfully address specific project requirements. In effect, we have at least two approaches to brochures:

- The so-called image brochure, which sets the stage
- The capability or project brochure, which gets down to the "nitty gritty"

Your brochure is often the first impression a client has of you. It may be the only impression the client remembers for some time. This phase 1 situation calls for an image brochure. If you present the brochure after meeting with the client and talking about specific projects, you need a phase 2 brochure or statement of qualifications to address certain issues.

The Image Brochure

Here is what the image brochure can and cannot do for you. It can:

- Give an overall impression of the firm
- Introduce the kind of projects you do
- Show the quality of work you do
- Demonstrate what you think of yourself, e.g., plain or fancy, austere or elegant, traditional or state of the art
- List past projects you have done and clients you have worked for
- Show the people who work for you
- Present your philosophy
- Quote satisfied clients

It cannot:

- Tell what you will do for a particular project
- State how much your services will cost (although in general your brochure will say "expensive" or "low-priced")
- Identify who will work on a project
- Give other project-specific information

Most (but not all) image brochures are permanently bound, either by the "perfect" method (glued), saddle stitched, or by some other method at the printer's, as opposed to being done by the marketing staff in-house.

One impression you don't want to convey results from last minute assembly of loose sheets—they often end up backward or upside down. Because you will want to distribute lots of these—maybe at conventions, at an open house, or as part of a direct mail campaign—you will want to minimize the hassle in handling them, reduce the risk of having pages bound in upside down, and so on. If the printer makes a mistake, you can have it redone at no cost to you; and be sure to check *every one* when they first arrive from the bindery in their shiny new wrappers.

The SOQ or Project Brochure

The more specific, project-oriented book must be put together in response to the client's expressed concerns. This brochure becomes a targeted precursor to the proposal. It will probably be comb (wire or plastic) or velo (heat and plastic) bound, using equipment available in-house for a fairly small capital investment.

In general, the project-oriented brochure falls somewhere between the image brochure and the proposal and is less successful than either. It not only lacks the pizzazz of the slick, printed and bound brochure, but, if its pages are typeset and printed, it lacks flexibility. However, it can be a workable compromise if enough planning goes into writing and designing the brochure pages.

Minibrochures

A growing number of firms are using shorter, smaller brochures or minibrochures to combat the high cost of printing and the failure of big books to keep pace with changing markets and new personnel and services. Minibrochures may consist of a single 8 ½ by 11 page folded twice (to form a kind of triptych) or may run to eight pages stapled.

The point is to keep the message short and aimed at the intended reader. For example, minibrochures serve to:

- Introduce a new capability (e.g., interior design or expanded cost estimating)

- Further your credibility in an existing project type (e.g., HVAC design for laboratories)

- Appeal to a geographic market in support of a branch office

These small brochures are convenient to use as direct mail pieces and to hand out at conventions or even over the lunch table. They can be carried easily, and they don't take up much storage space in a briefcase or file cabinet.

Some firms we know develop more than one so that they can send several to the same current or potential client. Using the same format also reduces design costs; you don't have to reinvent the wheel.

Decisions, Decisions

Regardless of brochure type, you will have things to work out with your graphic designer or editorial consultant:

- What size (8 ½ by 11, larger, or smaller)?

- How many pages?

- Should we use colors and if so, how many? (Each color means another run through the press or use of a more expensive press.)

- Should we get fancy and use blind or colored embossing (this is expensive)?

In 1988 some estimates on brochure production costs (to produce the mechanicals and print only, not including photography, text writing, in-house or consultant coordination) indicated:

- A four-color, 16-page brochure cost approximately $50,000 to $60,000 for 5000 copies

- A four-color, eight-page brochure cost $25,000 to $30,000 for 5000 copies

- A four-color, three-fold brochure cost approximately $9000 to $12,000 for 5000 copies; in black-and-white it might cost $3000 to $5000.

These figures vary depending on the number of photographs, quality of resolution and color separation, etc.

Care and Feeding of Brochures

Some general rules to keep in mind about *all* brochures:

- They should be produced to impress your identified, targeted client types, not the firm's principals and their buddies in the AIA or ACEC. If your intended clients are corporate executives, for example, don't produce a brochure that appeals to other graphic designers but seems totally puzzling to someone accustomed to annual reports.

- Things change. Don't expect today's brochure to last a decade. Plan for early obsolescence, redesign, and republication; keep these factors in mind when you budget for your brochure, too.

- In regard to budget, remember two things: cost per copy decreases with the number printed, but, if the thing is out of date in 2 years, don't print more than you can realistically get rid of in that time. Reduce cost by eliminating color, unnecessary halftones (photos), extra pages (if you can say it in four, why go to eight, and besides, it's more likely that four will be read). In other words, you need to consider both quantity and quality.

- Use specialists whenever you can afford to: a good graphic designer can produce miracles. So can a good editor. Don't skimp here, but use the guidelines above, along with your consultant's recommendations, to reduce costs. Frequently the basic design, grid, typeface, and general appearance of the brochure can remain the same for several printings with only projects and personnel or a certain emphasis changing from one to the next. Therefore, you can amortize the cost of your designer over a longer time and more issues. That doesn't mean you should let a junior draftsperson make subsequent changes (unless the draftsperson has a degree in graphic art).

- Keep in mind at all times *why* you are producing a brochure; who will be impressed, with what, for how long, and what your return on investment should be:
  Should the brochure introduce a new service and result in new types of clients?
  Should it introduce new people to your existing clients?
  Should it indicate a change in the firm's orientation, as in national projects and practice rather than regional or toward design rather than production?
  Is it merely an addendum to your routine proposals?

Don't expect it to be read; rely heavily on visuals, no matter how technical your audience is. It should catch the reader's attention in the first 3 seconds. Get good quality printing; the medium is the message, and no firm wants to appear sleazy. Marketer Mary Findlen offers some final dos and don'ts:

- Don't underestimate the number of copies you will need. It's more expensive to reprint than to order more originally.

- Don't produce a brochure unless you are going to use it; don't keep it in the closet, and don't ask to have it returned if the recipient doesn't want it.

- Don't attempt to produce a brochure by committee; make one person responsible, give authorization, and assign a deadline. Make it stick.

- Do establish a budget and schedule for reproduction; establish a simple, clearly defined review process for approval; stick to it too.

- Don't have technical people write the text.

Coordinating and managing a brochure project can be disruptive and exasperating for the in-house team. In the worst cases, after spending many hours of expensive principal time, the brochure still doesn't get born. More firms are hiring consultants or freelancers to help get decisions made (facilitation) and manage the photo, design, and printing coordination.

Other Secondary Tools

We described proposal writing in Chap. 3, "Direct Marketing," and newsletters and other direct mail promotional tools in Chap. 4, "Indirect Marketing." Refer to the tools matrix for other secondary tools and the elements that we think go into them.

INFORMATION MANAGEMENT: WORD PROCESSING AND DATABASES

The most effective tools of the trade, especially in regard to proposals, are those that are lodged firmly in your computer. Computers, of course, provide not only word processing but data processing (for storing and sorting information) and desktop publishing (to make it look good).

Ultimately, the most effective use of either a word processor or a database program is the ability to manipulate data. For example, when you are preparing or editing a project description and want to find out what phase of the project your firm is now in, you can call up the project management file for that job on your terminal and learn that, based on time card activity, you are currently involved in design development, with a target of 4 months to get to completed contract documents and go to bid.

It is, of course, possible to get that information by tracking down the project manager—who may be out of town when you need him or her—and get the information in person. As you try to locate the right person to tell you about a project, another designer will remind you that the photographs he or she wanted have not yet come back from the lab, so you have to stop and call the lab; meantime, while trying to find the project manager, you walk past the coffee room where a principal is talking with another designer and they ask you to meet with them to go over the schedule for the new brochure—and so it goes. That's why we say it's much faster to call up this information on a computer.

Data management applies to the marketing effort in a special way. Essentially, there are two kinds of data that you need at your disposal:

- Information about your prospects that you want to have available for making marketing decisions

- Information about your firm that you want to convey to your prospects

Obtaining information about your market and deciding what to do with it is discussed in detail in Chap. 3, "Direct Marketing." Information about your firm generally falls into the categories we have explored above: projects, people, and capabilities. Of major importance is the way in which this information can be cross-referenced to build a three-dimensional picture.

For example, you should be able to use your word processing or database program to list all of an employee's project experience on a résumé and all relevant data, including the project team, on a project description. Then you can select from this information to create a tailored document when preparing a proposal and still retain your bank of information for future use. By going back and forth from project information to information about individuals, you create a holographic image that will help you execute your marketing strategies and describe your firm's capabilities.

Desktop Publishing

One of the hottest developments in the last few years has been the advent of desktop publishing. This technology can make word processed documents beautiful and can, when used judiciously, be a cheap and more flexible alternative to printing. A good desktop publishing system will allow you to:

- Make your proposals more polished
- Create minibrochures and other sales tools inexpensively
- Produce offset-quality covers
- Save time and money by allowing production of in-house, camera-ready copy for offset printing
- Have more careful quality control

Apart from making text pretty, desktop publishing systems can import images to be integrated with text. Images (photos, plans, renderings, charts, and graphs) can be imported from graphics programs, introduced via optical scanner, and, with some systems, can be imported from CAD. Some kinds of images reproduce better on desktop than others. Some systems, for example, import scanned photographs beautifully but make a mess of line drawings.

You can enhance the quality of what you produce on desktop by overprinting sheets that have been offset. For example, you can have project photos offset printed onto one portion of a sheet and then run as many of these partially printed sheets as you need through your laser printer or photocopier to place text on the remainder of the page. With this system you can alter your project descriptions for each client or submittal. (Before you have anything offset, make sure that your computer printer and/or photocopier will accommodate the paper you intend to use.)

In selecting a desktop publishing system, you should look for:

- User friendliness—marketing documents are often produced by crazed people late at night; your system must be easy to learn and should not have bizarre quirks that show up 45 minutes before deadline.

- Potential for upgrade—a desktop publishing system represents a major investment in a fast-changing technology. You should make sure that your system will be able to grow to accommodate new developments (such as color printing) and your firm's expanding publishing needs.

No matter how good your desktop publishing system is, your final product is only as good as your printer. In choosing a printer, you should ask yourself:

- What typefaces can it handle? Can it accommodate more by adding memory?

- How many paper sizes and thicknesses can it take?

- How many dots per inch does it print? Is it capable of higher quality? At what expense?

Remember, too, that desktop systems, like CAD, are not panaceas; it takes time and effort to learn to use them effectively.

MAILING LISTS

These, too, are tools and must be addressed (no pun intended). Mailing lists should be kept on a database, either in-house or at a service bureau, and should enable you to sort out key information about your clients and prospects. Ideally, the database can feed into your word processing and desktop publishing programs. At the risk of being redundant, we must add that the categories by which you sort out data about your prospects (which include current and potential clients as well as contacts that may lead to future clients) must correspond to your marketing objectives.

Some firms sort this information by client type; for example, physicians have one code, lawyers another, etc. Others sort by zip code, by size of client firm, by whether or not your firm has worked for them previously, etc.

Most database programs permit both alphabetical and numerical sorting to take place and enable you to code many information elements into the list. Another important code identifies the person in your firm whose contact it is, e.g., the marketing director's, the president's, or a project manager's. You may also divide your mailing list into different categories, with names on one list getting all mailings, for example, and others receiving only certain types of announcements (that Joe Beets was made head of production, for example), the Christmas card, or a newsletter, while others get invitations to special events. You will probably need a special code for press releases and other media purposes.

You may choose to have a mailing house handle your database and also manage the entire mailing process, from obtaining bulk rate permits to sorting and batching by zip code.

SUMMARY

We have described basic tools—project descriptions and résumés—needed by all A/E firms to describe their capabilities and also secondary tools, some of them equally essential, such as a brochure derived from the basics.

In our firms we've had to experiment to discover the best combination of slick, printed pieces that convey the right image and very flexible tools that can be quickly tailored for specific clients and projects. Our needs keep changing too, both because our markets change and because—we hope— we grow more sophisticated. What seemed just right 2 months ago needs to be rewritten tomorrow. It is tricky, but with the right tools you and we can do the job.

See Chap. 8, "The Marketing Budget," for some guidelines on what it may cost to fill and maintain your bag of tricks.

Chapter Six

What You Need— Clients

INTRODUCTION

There is one thing you will learn about marketing. No matter how sophisticated your plans are or how well you have organized your tools, you are nowhere without clients. All other aspects of marketing—the strategies, the public relations, the brochures—are within your power to control. Clients are that uncontrollable enigma that makes marketing exciting, scary, and sometimes rewarding. Your task is to help find the clients who are right for your firm and then work on developing this match between your firm and the appropriate clients.

Sallie Durham said, at the SMPS National Convention in 1980, that marketing is war, but the client is not the enemy. Marketers often use the terms "shotgunning" or "targeting" in reference to seeking clients and projects. We use these terms, too, but want to point out that a far more useful analogy comes from Jerzy Kosinsky's novel, *Being There,* in which the gardener shows us all how to plant the seeds of goodwill and nurture relationships until they bear a ripe harvest. We encourage you to consider clients in this more agrarian context—dead clients can't pay.

Unfortunately, too many professional firms develop distinct feelings of dislike for their clients. "Users" (not drug addicts, but the people who occupy or operate a facility) are usually considered by professionals in, at worst, a condescendingly benevolent manner, as in "they need our help to make their lives more fulfilling" or "...to make this project work." Clients—facility owners or developers, those who pay the bill—on the other hand, are often seen as either criminally ignorant or villainously selfish or a combination of both. We all know, however, that not all clients are evil, and an important job of the marketer is to try to steer the firm toward those clients whose education, cultural sophistication, and level of greed are not totally incompatible with those of the architects or engineers who will be working with them. Too often we get wrapped up in the effort to "get work" and lose track of the fact that the most effective marketing aims at developing the right match between client and consultant.

Clients are actually just one of four key variables to consider in deciding on a strategy to improve your business development. The others are

- Services you offer
- Types of projects you do
- Location of clients and projects

We talk about clients because what they want to buy, as well as their attitudes toward buying design services, usually dictate what the other variables will be.

To misquote Freud, "What do clients want, my God what do they want?" One of your biggest challenges as a marketer is to find out what they want and help others in your firm tailor their sales messages, and even entire marketing programs, to respond to those wants and needs (they are not always the same and both are important). The operative word here is *response,* and the firm that anticipates and responds to client needs usually succeeds in its marketing.

But, how do you know what to anticipate? Although you can't always know exactly what a particular client's hot buttons are, by researching clients by type, and by individual when you can, you will be prepared to get your people on the "anticipate/respond" wavelength. If your planning has previously concentrated on the types of projects your firm produces or the types of services you offer, you now need to spend some time with your principals and key technical people discussing and analyzing the types of clients they want to work with. This discussion will help you set the framework for client-directed marketing.

This chapter reviews the basic interests and concerns, as well as general methods for consultant selection, of typical types of clients. We also offer some insight into how you can learn more about different clients and how they can learn more about your firm.

CLIENT COMMUNICATION

The most important art to learn is communicating with clients. At a 1988 SMPS workshop on facilities management, every client representative there mentioned the consultant's ability to communicate in the client's language as *the* most important condition of developing strong working relationships. Principals in your firm often have priorities different from those of their clients, but, and this is the critical issue, the onus is on them to address their client's concerns, not to expect clients to share their concerns. Client concerns typically consist of:

- Not exceeding a budget

- Making a profit (theirs, not yours)

- Meeting or beating a schedule

- Not being embarrassed or made to "look bad" by problems on the project during or after construction

On the other hand, architects' and engineers' concerns more often consist of:

- Finding the optimum solution—technically or through design

- Creating a project that will enhance their reputations

- Having a satisfied client (often without really understanding the basis of "satisfaction")

According to presentation experts Tim Allen and Peter Loeb, clients respond to things that can benefit them. The following are some guidelines developed by Allen and Loeb for understanding and addressing clients' concerns, especially in terms of "benefits" to the clients.

We often talk about features of our firms, e.g., "we have both architecture and engineering in-house," when what clients want to know is how the features can benefit them, e.g., "our comprehensive services can help streamline communications during design and result in a more cohesive project" or, more important, how these benefits can lead to reduced risk for them, e.g., "our in-house team, through rapid, efficient communication, can keep design and coordination errors to a minimum, resulting in tight bids and potentially lower construction costs."

Because clients are responsible for spending large sums of money, they are at risk. Risk reduction—as well as obtaining maximum return—becomes uppermost in their minds. Designers, however, have the day-to-day features of what they do uppermost in their minds. To get the attention of your potential clients, reconsider your priorities in terms of the cautious consumer of your services. If you can first address the risk reducing aspects of what is being offered and satisfy the client regarding those issues, the client will be open to hearing about benefits and be more able to translate from features to benefits.

Even the most sophisticated client will more clearly appreciate the value of what you have to offer if you help with that translation. This approach will also help set you apart from your competitors. While some designers are concerned that discussing potential problems or the client's anxieties may create a negative impression, if you can point out consistently how your experience, approach, talent, etc., can help solve those problems, you will be building confidence and trust.

TYPES OF CLIENTS

When we say "types of clients," we mean categorizing in terms of the business the client is in, e.g., large-scale land developers, municipal and regional utility districts, NAVFAC, or mid-size retail chains. One reason to analyze clients by type is to know whether they will be frequent users of services like yours and therefore knowledgeable about what you do or relatively infrequent buyers and therefore unsophisticated. You need to understand, also, what their typical risks consist of, i.e., are they using their own money or that of investors or is it public funding, is the client more likely to worry about "looking bad" before his or her peers and supervisors if a project goes badly, or is the person more concerned about being fired or not being re-elected? Issues like these lie behind every decision a client makes; design firms that don't understand and empathize with these client concerns will have trouble both getting and keeping clients.

To learn about clients you need to focus both on how the client will view firms like yours and on how people in your firm view a particular type of client. When you hold meetings to review clients with whom you may want to work, encourage technical people in your firm to give their likes and dislikes about working with different clients. These attitudes are probably linked to your firm's ability to produce quality work and be profitable. This analysis can help you develop strategies for learning more about clients or determining that some clients are not right for your firm.

In Chap. 2, "Getting Organized," we discussed how to organize your marketing material. Information about markets of interest to your firm can best be organized around your firm's targeted client types, so that materials, personnel, and strategies can be geared to those clients and accessed quickly. One way to organize clients is by the following groups:

- Public sector—including federal, state, regional, and municipal agencies
- Private sector—including corporations, real estate developers, professional firms (e.g., lawyers and accountants)
- Institutional and quasi-public organizations—including hospitals and universities

Although different types of clients may have similar project requirements—laboratories or site development, for example—the process of selecting consultants may vary widely from one client type to another, as we discuss in the rest of this chapter.

PUBLIC SECTOR CLIENTS

Many public sector clients are becoming more like private ones in their concern for cost cutting, especially at the front end of a project. There are still numerous distinctions worth noting between public and private, however. If you consider the public sector as a source for work, remember that selection is almost always made in an open forum with stated project goals and parameters. There are generally prescribed methods for introducing a firm to the various agencies contracting for work, and shortcuts are not usually approved. Although who you know may be important, friendships rarely let you avoid jumping through the required hoops. Selection is almost always based primarily on the amount of experience with a very similar type of project rather than broad competence or innovation and creativity.

"Public sector" covers a broad range, including government, institutional, and quasi-public clients that depend on a government for funding; they vary greatly in what they expect of a consultant. If the public sector is a strong market for your services, start by doing the following:

- Identify all the public sector agencies and organizations in your area or for whom you want to work.

- Determine which ones develop projects already within your firm's demonstrated capabilities. (This analysis will also show you where you are not prepared to compete and where you may need to do some work on your firm's organization, structure, and marketable talents.)

- From phone calls or directories (usually in public libraries) learn the names of regional or office directors to whom proposals or requests for information should be directed.

- Visit these people, introduce your firm to them, learn about their procedures, requirements, and, if possible, their personal preferences (e.g., for CADD) and find out what upcoming projects may be of interest to you.

- Become familiar with new systems or ways of doing work, such as the growth in design-build or turn-key projects for public sector clients and the volume of joint public-private ventures.

- Review the information you collect in your research and determine which agencies and projects are worth further consideration and pursuit.

The following is a partial checklist of public sector projects:

- **Federal agencies** Any construction project sponsored by departments such as Health and Human Services, Defense (all branches of the military, including Naval Facilities Engineering Command and the Army Corps of Engineers), Transportation, Energy, EPA, and the Veterans and General Services Administrations

- **State agencies** Public office buildings, road and bridge construction, universities, hospitals, and facilities for departments such as Criminal Justice, Water Resources, Transportation, General Services, and Human Resources Development

- **Municipalities** Master-planning, city planning, community development; offices, libraries, recreational, housing, waste and water treatment facilities, roads, and schools. Many of these projects are similar to or are shared with special districts or county agencies.

Within each of these broad groupings are many subsets of agencies, review boards, special projects groups, and organizations that deal with selecting consultants for specific projects or for general qualifications. In reviewing the public sector as a source for work, remember:

- Each organization has its own prejudices and concerns regarding selecting consultants. Try to find out what their past history has been in working with firms like yours—what firms have been successful and why and what firms have failed.

- The people who make decisions regarding consultant selection for specific projects are not always closely involved in the project and do not always have much knowledge of the project type. What they do know about is their own process for selection.

- Some agency officials are trained in the same discipline as your firm and may feel (sometimes with justification) that they could do the work themselves. They may, consequently, harbor feelings toward you ranging from great respect, because they know how difficult it is to do what you do, to real animosity, because you get to do it while they only watch and monitor.

- Many selection and project management officials have seen firms like yours really botch important projects, when their heads were on the chopping block. They may have suffered because of the mistakes of firms like yours, so be wary.

Let's look at the levels of public sector work in more detail.

FEDERAL AGENCIES

The granddaddy of public sector clients, the federal government is responsible for generating billions of dollars in construction-related projects per year. This is a big pie, and it is cut into many pieces. All federal jobs over a certain size are dispensed in a public forum unless selection is made under emergency provisions. Some smaller projects are granted in a discretionary fashion. Most federal projects are advertised publicly, and submittals meeting the stated criteria are evaluated. This situation makes for stiff competition, especially in tough economic times when private sector clients are scarce. However, the federal government is prohibited, as of this writing, by legislation (the Brooks law) from selecting professional consultants by fee; selection must be based on qualifications, then a fee can be negotiated.

Background Research

The fact that government projects are open to public competition does not mean personal contacts and connections are worthless. Knowing people on a national or local level can be helpful in researching the following:

- Upcoming capital expenditures
- Where the agency will be concentrating its programs geographically
- What qualities agency staff look for in consultants, such as size of firm, minority- or women-owned firms, affirmative action programs, geographic distance from project, the importance of CADD, attitude toward joint ventures and affiliations, and basic nature of the preferred firms (e.g., high design, engineering oriented)

It helps to make regular personal contact with directors of local and regional agencies targeted in your marketing plan. This way, you can keep up to date on their future development plans and often be alerted to new projects long before they are advertised in a public forum. Even if you don't know about a public sector project before it is advertised, you can still compete for it (unlike some private clients who only invite firms they already know to submit proposals). But, having the personal contact and knowing about the project will put you in a stronger position to compete when the project is announced. You can already have a team and a strategy in place. At the end of this chapter, we provide some suggestions for getting to know these clients.

Going After a Federal Job

The energy you expend in researching and courting a specific agency should reflect your marketing plan and the degree to which you have targeted that particular agency. Each federal agency has subtle but distinct differences in consultant requirements. You may need to have different people within your firm contact separate agencies based on the individual's personality or project experience. Pay a personal call on the targeted agencies at least four times a year just to keep them aware of your interest and to stay in tune with changes in their management structure.

The Project

All federal government A/E projects over $10,000 in fee are advertised in the *Commerce Business Daily (CBD)*. A typical *CBD* announcement and guides for completing the form are given in Chap. 3, "Direct Marketing."

The SF 254 and SF 255 are used by federal agencies (and increasingly by state and local governments and even some private sector institutional clients in modified form) to compare and qualify firms for consulting services. The government uses these forms to evaluate qualifications and eliminate firms (creating a "short list") and to request more information or fee proposals from qualifying teams. As with all submittals, give yourself enough time to complete the forms properly. Two warnings about completing these forms:

- If you are assembling the material for a team of consultants, make sure to get the forms from your subconsultants ahead of the time you need them. We can remember many times waiting until the last moment to receive material from subconsultants, only to find the forms filled out improperly or that they were just plain sloppy. The result was that we burned the midnight oil patching up the forms for other firms and suggesting to our principal-in-charge that we not work with these firms until they learn how to fill out a simple form.

- If you have a computer program for completing these forms, make sure you update the information periodically so that you can quickly access the information, edit it for the particular job, and run it out efficiently. You may also want to enter information on the consultants with whom you often work so that you have the data on your team prepared ahead of time for certain types of projects. You can make last minute modifications more quickly.

Each federal agency's local representatives generally have final say over projects up to a certain size, and we have found it is best to contact the agency to see what that size is. Beyond that, higher-echelon officers in Washington, D.C., make the final selection on consultant services. Therefore, to garner projects funded by federal agencies, include in your plan a courting ritual in your own geographic area, as well as in Washington. But do not go tramping off to Washington without first meeting and interviewing the local officials to find out what you should do when you get there.

STATE AGENCIES

There are numerous state agencies contracting for design and construction. They may include the office of the state architect or the state's general services administration (projects like state office buildings and supervision of other department's building programs), and departments of corrections, justice, or courts, public health, public utilities, and transportation and highways.

Generally, state agencies will not grant projects to consultants from outside the state unless the project type is so specialized that the proper expertise cannot otherwise be found. In those cases the state will usually require (either officially or unofficially) that a certain percentage of the fee remain in the state. For this reason joint ventures and associations, using out-of-state specialized consultants and in-state firms for support, are often seen in state-sponsored work. Rapid transit and criminal justice facilities, for example, have often been handled this way in the past. However, before you consider a joint venture or association of firms, determine whether the client accepts this approach to creating a project team. What has their history been, and do they have an unstated policy against associations of this type?

In our experience state agencies are more approachable than federal agencies, in part because they are more geographically accessible and closer to their voters and taxpayers—a situation even more obvious in local agencies. However, exercise caution in nurturing relations with state agencies because:

- The politics are more apt to change with elections than those of the federal government (the bureaucracies are smaller and therefore more vulnerable).
- Your connections may prove embarrassing.
- Getting too close may raise suggestions of impropriety—a "fix."

MUNICIPAL GOVERNMENTS

Municipal governments include city, county, and special district or regional agencies. We have found that the closer the contracting agency is to the taxpayer (the source of funding), the more careful that agency tends to be in keeping the flow of dollars close to home. We have also noticed that the larger the area of interest of the contracting agency (as in a federal agency), the more emphasis the bureaucrats place on objective competence of the consultant. The smaller the area (as in a municipality), the less they require technical competence in lieu of a favorable political position (or at least that your firm pay taxes in their territory).

On a local level, at least for larger jobs, you may find it important to be visibly active in nonpartisan community affairs. However, our warning about playing politics on the state level is even more true on the local level. It is often difficult to tell what is truly a nonpartisan concern. Every political alignment and friend can become a stone around your neck. So try to walk a fine line between contributing to the development of your community and political partisanship.

PUBLIC SECTOR SUMMARY ANALYSIS

We cannot overemphasize these key points:

- Approach each agency personally, and keep each contact alive.
- Match the personality of the agency to someone in your firm with technical experience and the ability to communicate with the leaders of the agency.
- Make sure the talent and experience you are providing respond to the stated and interpreted criteria.
- Be certain that the types of projects the agency grants respond to your marketing plan and the talents of your firm.

In addition to the points listed above, here are some other issues about public sector clients:

- You can usually break into new public sector markets only after careful and consistent effort and with a fairly high investment of both time and money.

- Government clients generally pay their bills (although with government clients, contracting and billing procedures may be complex and time consuming).

- Accounting and auditing procedures can be very confining.

- The profit a firm can make on a given project may be limited by federal and/or state law and is monitored by public audits.

- Committees generally make the selection, and the process is usually open and reasonably fair. Decisions by committee tend to be safe and conservative. A committee will usually opt for the firm with truly relevant experience in the project type.

- Proven competency in the project area is usually the most important criterion for selection.

- If you want to move your firm into new markets, you probably will not do so on your own with a government project.

PRIVATE SECTOR CLIENTS

Private sector clients are not governed by the same laws or rules as are those of the public sector. However, they *are* governed by the rules of the marketplace, including demographics, consumer demand, and the desires of corporate directors and shareholders. In dealing with private sector clients you must know what drives your intended client's business.

In private sector work, it is essential to market your services prior to the notification of specific projects. In fact, knowing your client is often as important as knowing what that client's key concerns are. Experience has taught us to place emphasis on *building relationships,* rather than just going after jobs. Many clients have stated outright that what they look for in a design consultant is, "someone I like to work with." This comment refers to a subtle quality of style and personality in the match between client and consultant.

The ole boy network still serves in the private sector, and you need to understand how to get your people into that network. It is safe to say that no private sector client will hire a firm they do not know and trust. Therefore, you need to get your targeted clients familiar with your firm, through both direct contact and indirect marketing activities.

In developing your marketing strategies, look carefully at the range of private clients and the types of projects they control, then target specific clients within each type. Your market research (Chap. 3, "Direct Marketing") will tell you about the clients you want to acquire. Get to know each client in terms of:

- Their key concerns
- What you need to do to enhance your position with them
- What they look for in consultants
- What their social and political interests are
- Who the decision makers are within each organization

Private sector clients have concerns that reflect the nature of their organizations and the types of projects they develop. Primary concerns tend to include:

Here's our modest corporate statement.

- Knowing that their consultants understand their business, the pressures they are under, and the goals they need to achieve
- Costs for services and cost control of projects; the ability of the consultant to control costs (even in "prestige" projects with high budgets)
- The ability to manage and control a project's schedule
- Seeing the image they wish to convey in the work of consultants
- Political savvy

Unlike the government, private sector clients are not obligated to spread the work among different firms nor are they obligated to direct some work to smaller or minority-owned firms. Indeed, private sector clients tend to select consultants whose style and personality reflect their own. Sometimes, private sector clients will work in collaboration or assemble a joint development with a government agency. In these cases, many of the rules governing public sector work will apply to the private sector client.

We have divided private sector clients into three basic groups: real estate developers; corporations, and private institutions. Within each of these groups are specialized client types, as well as numerous types of associations between types of clients. We will also review some of them.

Real Estate Developers

Clients in this category, obviously, develop real estate for profit. Their projects are often speculative in nature but may be largely or wholly on be half of a major investor or tenant and have to produce profit through valuation of the property due to the marketing success of the project or the attraction of additional investors.

There is often a high degree of financial risk in these projects, but the rewards can also be very great. Real estate developers come in all shapes and sizes, from the very small, aggressive, highly risk-oriented developer of small office complexes, housing, and retail centers to the corporate developer who is charged with investing vast sums of money generated by a company whose primary concern is not real estate development. When other forms of pension investment become less reliable, we see more large corporations—like public utility companies—investing in speculative real estate ventures. Although these developers differ in the way they do business, in the types of projects they develop, and in the types of consultants they hire, we have yet to meet a developer who was not vitally concerned with two issues: money and time (in that order). Some, however, are more concerned with money as "return on investment," while others are more concerned with "front-end" money. The difference is critical to how you approach both the client and the project.

You need to know what types of developers are most appropriate for your firm to pursue as clients, given the nature of your past work, the goals of your marketing plan, and your capabilities as perceived by potential clients. A smaller developer may be more willing to try you out on a project for which you are not particularly well qualified if he or she has strong regard for your work and trusts that you will serve the project well, no matter what the project type. However, in pursuing work with a real estate developer, you must show your ability to work efficiently, to be responsive to changes in program, and to produce a product within strenuous budget constraints, all for a fee that is at best competitive and at worst inadequate. (Because your client is constantly adjusting to changes in the market, you must be able to make these quick adjustments as well.) You must take the pulse of your firm and be certain your firm is of the right temperament to work with these kinds of clients. We have seen many firms pursue speculative real estate developers as clients, only to regret the fact that they were successful in their pursuit.

Assuming you are interested in these clients, how do you approach them and learn about them; what do you need to know? You can learn a lot about real estate developers from the people who work with them, particularly leasing agents and land ("dirt") brokers; the former lease space to tenants for their developer clients and the latter are involved in the sale of property and projects to developers.

Before approaching a real estate developer, do some market research. You want information like:

- What types of projects has this client sponsored before?
- Where is he or she interested in developing projects?
- What types of projects will be successful? Why?
- What consultants have they worked with in the past—both successfully and not?
- Do they pay their bills?
- How do they treat their consultants?
- With whom would we be dealing?
- Are the projects they develop consistent with our marketing plan?

Because projects go through many hands and are influenced by numerous specialists and investors, it may sometimes be difficult to determine just who your client is. As an example, if your firm provides interior design services, to which of the following do you market your services:

- The developer?

- A leasing agent for the building?

- Each individual tenant—perhaps through the building's leasing agent or each tenant's agent?

You may end up selling your firm to all three clients or client representatives, but each one has different needs and concerns, sometimes in opposition to the other (tenants and developers, of course, have a give and take, with the leasing agent somewhere in the middle).

In another example, most mechanical and electrical engineers have traditionally marketed their services to architects. However, with the growing number of construction management, design-build, and turn-key projects, the M/E consultant is often hired by the contractor or CM or even directly by the client without the involvement of the architect. With the growing importance of facilities managers within developer and corporate client's companies, the trend to hire these types of consultants as primes will probably continue.

The point is, you need to know the chain of command both within a client's organization and in the process of developing a project. For example, if a residential developer works with a civil engineering firm first, does he or she rely on them to help select an architect, or has the design firm been chosen far ahead of its active participation in the project?

Corporate Clients

In the ideal world all our clients are prestigious corporations, benevolent in their treatment of consultants, with time and money to investigate all possible design alternatives, and a vital concern for creating an elegant but humanistic image while producing a landmark project without defiling the environment.

Well, there ain't no such animal. The corporate client is generally most concerned with return on their facilities' investment, which makes them somewhat like the developer client. The difference may be that the developer is more interested in making money directly from the project, whereas the corporate client may have a more wide-ranging agenda—from increasing worker productivity to creating a symbolic structure to enhance the corporate image (think of San Francisco's Transamerica Pyramid, an obvious and controversial underuse of expensive real estate but a powerful corporate image).

For purposes of this discussion, the corporate client is an owner-client, one who manages the project, generally occupies the project, and maintains ownership for use by the corporation. Corporations develop a wide range of projects, including:

- Office facilities

- Research and development facilities

- Industrial manufacturing facilities

- Retail facilities

Often these projects get developed by different divisions within the same firm. (Some giant corporations also have separate development arms, which function like the developers described in the preceding section. There are also various types of associations, discussed in "Hybrid Clients," below.)

To be considered for consulting work, you must indicate knowledge and experience in the corporation's areas of interest, be well versed regarding trends in the client's marketplace, and know a good deal about the business activities of the corporation. When one of the authors was a marketing director for a large A/E firm, we designed a number of automated manufacturing facilities, but we had no chance of getting this work until we understood not only the manufacturing process, but the reasons why certain products had to be in the market on schedule and how our work effected that schedule.

Corporate clients generally act with more caution than developers, and your marketing activities with corporate clients may include lengthy courting until they get to know your firm and feel comfortable with all the key players in your organization. Like some institutional and public sector clients, a corporate client may "test" your firm on a small project or one with less design concerns than what you would ideally want to do. Therefore, you may run the risk of being typed by the corporation as a firm capable of only certain types of projects, and these may not be the types you have keyed in your marketing plan.

Budget, schedule, and image are as important to the corporate client as they are to the developer, but often for different reasons. Unlike the real estate developer, the corporate client may not rely on the development under consideration to produce revenue. The development of a project by a corporation involves less speculative financial risk than does a venture by a developer. However, there are risks in other areas, and to market effectively to the corporation, you need to know what the risks are that they are taking. The questions they are asking themselves include:

- Will their research facility adapt to future research techniques; will their technicians like it and enjoy putting in long hours and developing new products?

- Will their new headquarters provide the appropriate image for the company, pleasing both stockholders and employees?

- Will their new plant be a good neighbor and bring support for future expansion from the community in which it is located?

- Will the new office building be a successful testing ground for divergent management philosophies for the corporation that is going through major management restructuring?

Corporate clients can usually base their budgets on producing something of lasting quality. Quality and performance are often key concerns for the corporate owner and user. Corporations can amortize first costs over the life span of a building, allowing for higher-quality materials. They will also develop projects with more specific user program data than a developer has available, so certain design decisions are more prescribed.

Time has different impacts on a corporate client than on a real estate developer. The speculative developer generally wants a project to proceed as quickly as possible. Indeed, the speculative project is often a race against time as the developer pays development fees and loan costs while aiming to hit certain "windows" in the market for the project being developed. The corporate client, on the other hand, must often fit the project into some overall plan of development within the corporation itself. Therefore, corporations usually have more time for project development and review. (They may not have anywhere near enough time, however, if the building is linked to development of a new product.)

Most design firms prefer working with corporate clients rather than speculative developers because the corporate client generally works with a more generous or at least more established budget. However, corporate clients present their own unique problems for consultants, especially in areas of:

- Internal politics
- Budget versus image concerns
- Complex criteria for selecting consultants
- Confusion in the project management and reporting and decision making hierarchy

One advantage we experienced in working with speculative developers is that they are usually quick to make decisions and because of time pressures do not usually waste their consultants' time. Corporations developing new or ground-breaking building types, especially industrial and research and development facilities, take risks in building because the product the building is developed to produce may be untested in the market. To reduce front-end risk some R&D facility users lease shell space from developers and have it furnished to fit their needs. Another example of "Who is your client?"

So far we have discussed corporate clients as a monolithic group. However, among corporate client types are the following, each with their own standards and concerns regarding consultant selection:

- Product manufacturers
- Transportation firms
- Petroleum producers
- Retail stores and chains
- Hotel operators
- Financial institutions
- Insurance firms
- Law firms, accountants, and other large professional service corporations
- Pension funds

To market effectively to any of these diverse corporate types, you need to develop a solid relationship between your firm and the client, based on your experience and understanding of their business. This relationship building may take years and cost thousands of dollars, so your targeting of particular clients should be a serious matter involving principals and key technical people in your firm. Questions you need to answer before marketing to any corporate client include:

- How strong is the client's market?
- Where does the company stand relative to its own competition?
- Is it growing, expanding geographically?
- How do its leaders select consultants?
- Who within the corporation should be contacted to initiate discussions with your firm? (Increasingly, this person is a facility manager.)
- What is the best approach to use? (Some suggestions are given at the end of this chapter.)
- Which of your competitors have they worked with, and what can you find out about that experience that will help you develop the right approach?

The answers to these questions, as well as many others, can be found in your research on targeted markets and specific clients.

Corporations often select consultants through very detailed and demanding processes involving committees. Even though you have approached the right corporation for your firm and think you have a commission "wired," you will often end up competing with other consultants with comparable skills and may find a deal "unwired" at the last minute, possibly through no fault of your own. You must know enough about the corporation to understand how decisions are made and who makes them.

INSTITUTIONAL CLIENTS

In many ways institutional clients, while privately owned by stockholders, resemble the public sector client because they are highly regulated to protect public safety. These institutional clients include:

- Hospitals
- Educational facilities
- Transportation operations (e.g., bus and rail companies)
- Power and communication utilities

As with the others, the institutional client usually looks first for consultants who are competent in a specific project type. Health care organizations rarely hire architects based on their design approach if they have no working knowledge of hospital organization and function. Proven cost control methods, ability to produce a project on time, and knowledge of the development and approval steps are essential. However, this concern for technical expertise does not discount the importance of getting to know the clients and working hard at the all-important relationship building we keep harping on.

Project managers and other representatives of institutional clients are usually sophisticated about the operations they control. Unlike the real estate developer, they may not need to understand how an architectural or engineering team really functions. They do need assurance that your team has the best answer for solving *their* complex set of problems and meeting their time pressures. Therefore, many institutional clients need education regarding how your approach can benefit them. We cannot overemphasize the delicacy of this process. In organizing meetings between your technical people and the institutional client, drill your people on listening and responding. In their response, they have the opportunity to explain how they work, but if they get too heavy about this or distract the conversation from the client's concerns, you will lose the attention and respect of that client.

You must determine whether your firm has the technical capability to be considered by the type of institution you have targeted. If you are technically weak but still want to pursue the client, you must hire the knowledge or associate with other firms to create credibility. Probably even more than with other types of clients, it is essential to identify the people in your firm who perform critical tasks and to use them in "selling" to the client.

HYBRID CLIENTS

The last client group to be discussed here is what we refer to as the hybrid client, a client that is really a combination (through joint venture, limited partnership, or association) of two different types of clients. With the rapid changes in real estate development, corporate mergers, and financing of public and institutional projects, you can expect to see a growth in both type and number of hybrid clients. Therefore the following overview cannot be seen as complete. However, the key from a marketing point of view is to get to know both types of clients comprising the hybrid and the hybrid entity as well. (Oh great, more work, more complex strategies, and more material to develop.)

Government Agencies and Private Developers

With cut-backs of many federal building programs and some communities undergoing cuts in their tax base, many public agencies in the late 1980s are seeking private parties to develop projects for them to occupy (on a lease-back basis) and/or eventually own. Generally, governments enter partnership with private developers through the auspices of a redevelopment district. Redevelopment districts often operate under their own rules and development guidelines, which may differ from those governing private development in the same community. Those guidelines often call for relaxing some of the planning regulations but strengthening requirements for such things as minority participation in the project, or they call for special features such as day care facilities, public space, art programs, and other public amenities. Redevelopment districts often develop projects such as:

- Elderly and low-income housing
- Mixed-use commercial centers
- Convention centers and sports arenas
- Large malls specializing in certain industries (like auto dealer rows) and manufacturing districts
- Port and other mixed-use waterfront property

Financial Institutions and Private Developers

We sometimes find financial institutions looking for projects in which to invest and a developer bringing his or her project management expertise to the deal. In some instances the financial institution takes title to the property. Usually the developer retains control over hiring consultants, but each project is unique and you will need to find out who calls the shots on ones you've been tracking. Sometimes, the associated firms start a new company for the sole purpose of developing a project. In this case, you need to stay close to the parent organizations since the key people in the new company will most likely be drawn from these groups.

These arrangements almost always get complicated and, although having a joint venture partner may strengthen the project, it may complicate design decision making. You need to know such things about the JV partners as:

- What about getting paid for changes not approved by the financial partner?
- Are both parties hands-on?
- Who takes responsibility for design team selection, project management, and design review?

On the bright side, a JV arrangement between a developer and a financial institution generally increases the likelihood of the A/E team's getting paid in a timely manner.

Developers and Land Owners

In this scenario, a land owner turns property over to a developer to build a project, the ownership of which will then be shared. Again, the role of the design consultant may be complicated by needs to communicate simultaneously with all parties. You need to clarify the role each party plays in decision making.

Developers and Corporate or Institutional Clients

Again, as with financial institutions and developers, the corporation is relying on the developer's expertise to build a project for the corporation's use. The developer uses the financial backing of the corporation and either maintains ownership and leases the property to the corporation or eventually sells the project to the corporation. Increasingly, corporations are hiring developers to put together projects for a negotiated fee. In these instances, the developer is never considered to be an owner. However, because the developer has the experience to build the project, your clients may be representatives of both parties or only the developer if the corporation has insufficient skill or experience in this area. Or, your client may be only the corporation if certain design needs are highly specialized and the developer is functioning as a program manager for a fee.

We know a firm now designing a major corporate headquarters facility being built by a real estate developer but to a program being developed by the consultant with the corporate client. The process is not always smooth because the design firm must respond to the corporation's programmatic needs, with a budget and basic building scope sold to the corporation by the developer. To say that these two entities are not always in agreement would be an understatement.

NONCLIENT CONTACTS

In addition to the public and private sector clients described above, we also maintain important contacts and stay in touch with professionals in related fields. Nonclient contacts are those who serve as advisers, resources, or friends to your targeted clients. We cannot overemphasize how important these "communicators" can be. Too often, A/E firm principals may see marketing as only a one-directional process—that is, the only people worth nurturing are potential clients—period. But your nonclient contacts can be critical in gaining important market intelligence and insight into specific clients, not to mention viable leads you can follow. It may fall to you to develop a network of "friends of the firm," people who are not clients but can help you win clients.

In the commercial development market, a nonclient contact may be a leasing agent who can tell you when a certain client might need your services and advise that client of your firm's capabilities. In institutional projects, a nonclient contact could be a program specialist or planner, an expert in funding for the type of institution you are selling to, a vendor of specialized equipment, or any contact whose interest in the project precedes your own and is therefore in a position to recommend your firm or advise you early as to the status of projects.

The nonclient contact could be a lawyer, banker, accountant, market analyst, or local newspaper reporter. We find that, whatever the professional role of the nonclient contact, you must determine through your market research the value of the contact and the type of ongoing maintenance the contact will need. Once the decision has been made, the nonclient contact requires the same kind of courting and maintenance as would a client.

ASSOCIATED PROFESSIONALS

Many engineering and other consulting firms market primarily to architects or other engineering firms. In targeting other professionals as sources for work, you must analyze their needs just as you would for any intended client. In general, associated professionals in the role of clients look for:

- Technical know-how to save time and money and to minimize problems

- Experience of specific project team members as well as that of the firm as a whole

- Cost control in design, both in cost for consultant services and the systems recommended

- Competitive fees, since your fee often comes out of their fees

- The ability to work well as a team

- Marketing skills to help win this project and bring in leads for additional work

- Convenient location, accessibility

The subconsultant in this marketing position must often choose between architects or other prime consultants in passing on a lead. If you are in this situation, ask yourself which firms you want to work with, as well as which firm has the best chance of getting the job. Try to avoid the situation in which you find yourself saying, "the good news is we got the job, the bad news—it's with...."

GETTING TO KNOW YOU: ACQUIRING CLIENTS

If we could tell you precisely how to acquire a particular client you have had your eyes on for years, it would be magic or a great lie. Your relationship to the client is like any long-standing professional relationship; if you work well together and learn from one another, the relationship will grow and lead to other relationships—and to repeat work as evidenced by the many clients who produce series of projects with the same design team.

Good Old Clients

Repeat work proves your success with a particular client and also reduces your marketing budget. Experts say that a firm can expect 80 percent of its projects to be repeat work, but we know this has much to do with the types of projects and clients you work with. New firms or firms entering new markets may have a lower percentage. To obtain that 80 percent repeat rate, your firm needs to do two things: produce good, professional work and conduct good, professional marketing to existing clients.

Good New Clients

The most cost-effective new clients are referrals from other satisfied clients; it will take less of your time and effort to convince them, and you should find them more amenable to a reasonable fee. Second in desirability to the direct recommendation of a past client is the potential client who comes to you as a result of your public relations campaign. Articles about your firm or awards you have won can lead a potential client to your door. It is up to your team to lead that client through that door, without disillusionment or disenchantment.

The third, less profitable but often successful way to obtain new work is through the courting and lead-finding process described in Chap. 3, "Direct Marketing." This process should never be initiated without research into the client type, as outlined in your marketing plan. The fourth method is to sit around waiting for an RFP to arrive, but that's not marketing. Following are some strategies for getting close to new clients:

- Find out which professional and industrial organizations enjoy active participation by your intended clients. Have a technical person from your firm with the proper qualifications join as an associate member and attend meetings and seminars. (Qualifications include a knowledge of client concerns in this market and the personality to interact positively with potential clients.)

- Take an active role by joining task forces or serving on committees (otherwise the membership is useless) and by enhancing the organization through your technical knowledge.

- Attend agency or public hearings and meetings at which issues relevant to your clients' interests are being discussed.

- Arrange to have your principals appointed to public or agency task force groups or committees. However, do not even consider this if they are not really interested or are unschooled in the issues under consideration or if the committee is highly political and could fall into disfavor with a turn in elections.

- Learn how pending legislation will affect your clients, know positions of politicians and candidates on development issues affecting your clients, and be able to inform your clients of issues that may affect them.

"Developing" Your Own

You may also develop a project by starting the programming and development process for a client who needs help. You can sometimes assemble an entire development team for a client and become a member of that team. When you become involved in the development process, you can provide services that, once completed, may mean the end of your involvement. We have been burned by investing time and money to get a first phase "study" of a project only to learn that the firm that does the study will be excluded from the actual (and more profitable) project. You can also do studies or act in a pro-active fashion to help get a project moving. This position can entail anything from helping find a key tenant to investing your own resources in a project.

When you join the development team, you run the risk of compromising your professional position, because your firm is concerned with other issues (such as profitability of the project) that relate directly to the professional services you provide. However, generally, the earlier your firm is involved in a project, the more chance you have of working through the entire length of the project and benefiting from this long-term commitment.

EVALUATING YOUR POTENTIAL CLIENTS

Throughout this chapter we have concentrated on what you must do to learn about and attract clients to your firm. Sometimes in our rush to "get" clients, we fail to look carefully at what getting that client will really mean. A study of clients should include their characteristics to make sure they are worth the marketing effort required. Qualifying characteristics may include having:

- A good track record—has successfully completed projects and pays bills on time. (You can check with Dun & Bradstreet financial reporting services as well as with other consultants.)

- The capacity to pay and a stable source of project financing.

- A willingness to avoid litigation.
- A clear and stable organization that can streamline negotiating, contracting, and billing.
- The potential for future work, to make it worth your investing in a long term relationship.

ENTERING NEW MARKETS

We have all confronted the problem of trying to attract new clients in areas in which we have not previously ventured. We know the difference between calling on a hotel developer and recounting a roster of hotel projects on six continents and calling on the same client if our firm has never designed a hotel.

Here is where the reference to the four key variables that we made at the beginning of this chapter comes into play. If you have identified your current services, clients, projects, and locations where you work, you can enter new markets most successfully if you change only *one* of those variables. For example, if you currently do health care facility design for nonprofit institutions in your region, you may be able to provide the same programming, planning, design, and construction administration services in the same region for proprietary (for-profit) health care providers. But, if you have never designed a hospital or never done one in the same region as your client, you have a more difficult job to sell your ability.

So, if a new market is targeted in your marketing plan (after you finish swearing at your marketing plan for making your job more difficult), establish as many connections as possible between your firm and the intended market, keeping the variables in mind:

- To change your client type, review your staff and see what credible experience you have in terms of the services you offer and the types of projects you have done.
- To change the project or service type, see what different types of projects are developed by or influenced by clients with whom you have worked successfully.
- Learn about the people in the new market (both clients and consultants with whom you would work), and begin to develop personal associations. Let them know about your relevant competence and specific related experience.
- Form associations with firms that have the right experience or connections to complement your own in this targeted market. (Be certain that the associations will appeal to potential clients.)
- Be patient; it takes time to break into a new market. Make sure principals in your firm know that and are not expecting miracles.

Keep in mind that no firm works effectively with all types of clients. You simply cannot be all things to all people and hope to be successful. That is why we emphasize setting and/or reviewing your firm's marketing goals. More importantly, understand the personal preferences and values of your firm's leaders and see that they are consistent with projects and clients for whom you can reasonably expect to work. With that understanding, you can then cultivate appropriate clients, learning as much as you can about them, including their dreams and their perceived risks.

INTRODUCTION

Hardly anyone we know has written a marketing plan that really worked. Especially if it involved more than one person. But, chances are, as a marketer, you will need to write or assist in the development of a plan sooner or later. This document, whether formal or informal, long or short, is a road map to guide the development of your firm, generally from 1 to 5 years. It outlines goals and defines tasks to meet those goals. How can anything that sounds so good go wrong?

This chapter describes how to develop a marketing plan, some things that have worked for us and others, and some trouble spots. We address three key issues:

- Why you need a plan and what a plan can do for your firm
- How to develop a plan, the process
- The contents of a plan

Even a good marketing plan will not tell you what to do in every situation, but it can establish priorities for action and help you determine the best use of your time, what types of projects should be pursued, how your firm should pursue them, and who should do it.

WHY YOU NEED A PLAN... OR DO YOU?

Effective marketing plans are basically plans of action, with the methods for achieving and monitoring results spelled out. These plans need to be put to use. Let's start by taking a look at who needs to use a plan. In most firms it will be the marketing staff (whether that includes ten people or one), as well as managing principals and project managers with marketing responsibility.

You may have to start by convincing your principals that you and they need a marketing plan in the first place. Experience has taught us some compelling reasons for having one and trying to make it work. If your principals don't agree, we also have some suggestions to help you do your own planning—in increments—which may help them buy the idea. Read also Chap. 9, "Internal Politics," which offers more insight into why a marketing plan helps the marketer and why planning is a political act.

Real Professionals Don't Eat Plans

A/E firms are frequently run by self-made people who pride themselves on their individuality and who do not like feeling confined by systems, programs, or plans. Entrepreneurs feel confident shooting from the hip, basing decisions on a healthy mix of instinct and common sense. To them (and you may be one of them) a written plan smacks of heavy-handed bureaucracy and constitutes another way to waste time when you could be improving a design or even out selling. (In fact, some consider it a dangerous document that can fall into the wrong hands—your competition for example—and weaken rather than strengthen your position in the market.)

A few things should be considered, however, no matter how well you or other entrepreneurs in your firm have done in the past:

- We all know that communication is the single most difficult aspect of management. The marketing plan is a good tool for communication because it forces people to outline their concerns and puts in writing ways to deal with critical issues.
- A plan assigns and delegates responsibilities to individuals in a way everyone can understand.

Chapter Seven

Your Road Map— The Marketing Plan

...accountability in marketing and enables management and staff to measure performance. Bonuses, raises, and/or pink slips can be tied to this measurement.

- The larger the firm, the more reliant the marketing staff will be on a detailed plan or plans.

Plans are used to:

- Specify how you will stay in touch with existing and past clients (describe who will contact whom, when)
- Define the need for new or improved sales tools (brochures, etc.)
- Build a PR program (what are the targets and how to reach them)
- Determine changes in staffing (to enter new markets or improve in current ones)
- Outline changes in the firm's markets such as shifts in volume or productivity
- Target higher (or lower) fee projections

There are some conditions under which a firm does not need a marketing plan (although even in these cases it wouldn't hurt):

- If it is a sole proprietorship and subsidized by personal wealth
- If the owner(s) is (are) nearing retirement and has (have) no interest in being bought out or transferring ownership
- (There must be a third but we haven't thought of it yet)

If you are new to marketing or have come to A/E marketing from a product marketing background, you must remember that the goals of the principals of your firm are often based on their personal aspirations, not on what the market dictates. Therefore the marketing plan will need to reflect both these goals and a realistic assessment of markets that interest your firm. It will often be your job in developing a marketing plan to help your principals turn their personal goals into realistic marketing objectives.

Business Plans versus Marketing Plans

Business plans define financial and other management goals of the firm and how they are to be achieved. Like a marketing plan, a business plan projects future growth and development and guides the firm leaders in issues of personnel development, investments and retirement plans, operating expenses, and profitability requirements for the overall practice.

Many firms operate without a business plan, but increased capitalization requirements (to purchase computers, for example) often mean acquiring loans from financial institutions which in turn means developing these plans. If the marketing plan is a road map for future growth, the business plan defines the type of vehicle you'll be driving down that road. The marketing plan must relate to the business plan in areas of profit goals and projections. If, for example, the business plan states a net profit goal of 15 percent, you must evaluate your marketing goals to see if the services, clients, and projects identified will be likely to meet that goal. (See Chap. 8, "The Marketing Budget," also.)

PLANNING—A SOCIOPOLITICAL, ECONOMIC PROCESS

Among marketers, strategic planning is right up there with sex as a favorite indoor sport. Gathering information and figuring out what to do next—as creatively as possible—is the art of marketing. And, there are many ways to go about developing a strategic plan. Here are a few scenarios we have encountered.

We know several marketers who prepare their own plans since no one else in their firms ever wanted to write or use one. Another marketer we know worked on a 300-page plan, which took 3 months to prepare, consisted of detailed market analyses and projections, and was never used. In another instance, the marketer, realizing that process is important, summarized notes from planning meetings and presented them to his colleagues for review and approval. But, because the meetings themselves did not resolve an internal power struggle, the resulting plan couldn't be implemented. In yet another setting, no firm-wide plan exists; but fee goals and objectives for each marketing segment of a large firm dictate short, frequently updated action plans. And, while strategic planning is challenging and even fun, it frequently fails in its main objective—to improve a firm's business development.

Why Plans Fail—Over and Over Again

Above all, we have learned that a major reason plans don't work—and really, we estimate they fail in one way or another in design firms over 80 percent of the time—is that, although the strategy may be excellent, the *actions* to be taken are either *not well defined* or *not well assigned* and *performance evaluations* do not relate to the plan's objectives.

Uh, excuse me, could you go over that again?

In the former case, no one really knows what to do; the plan is vague and general, full of platitudes and optimism. In the latter situation, even when tasks are clearly stated, they are often unrealistic, e.g., "Contact 10 new clients a month." If the person given that task is not a designated salesperson who loves to call on clients and whose compensation is based on meeting quotas, it probably won't happen.

From these experiences we make the following observations: success lies in choosing the right *planning process* for your firm and in keeping the plan itself *realistic*; the product, a written report, although important, will be secondary to the act of thrashing out the basic issues. Finally, implementation must be taken seriously by the managing principal or equivalent and *performance evaluations,* of technical personnel as well as marketers, must be *linked to the plan*. (Can you hear Machiavelli chuckling in the background?)

Who Prepares the Plan?

Everyone responsible for implementation should be involved in the plan's preparation and needs to endorse the final document. However, committees can't write plans. The principal(s), especially the managing principal, of your firm must feel that the plan outlines ways to take the firm in the direction he or she wants it to go. The marketers must be able to understand the plan so that they can clearly see both the route and the destination.

One person must take responsibility for organizing this effort, producing the document, and making sure the results are disseminated and put to good use. This activity will probably fall to the person most effected by the plan—a marketing principal or director whose performance will be evaluated in terms of how well the plan functions. Sometimes plans get written with the help of an outside consultant—often called a "facilitator"—who helps the principals see the advantages of planning. (Remember, you are never a prophet in your own firm.) Sometimes an outsider's endorsement can be more convincing than that of an in-house person. The consultant may help conduct a planning retreat, then organize and write the plan contents or review and recommend revisions to the product of your in-house staff.

What may happen when the outside person sells the planning concept is that marketing staff is excluded from the process. The principals meet in a retreat or in the office on Saturdays and produce goals and an action plan. Staff receives assignments and are made accountable with no involvement in "why" and no opportunity for creative review. Staff turnover and/or poor implementation often result. With a consultant's involvement, however, if the principals don't like some aspect of the plan or fail to accept some changes that the plan calls for (e.g., having to face their accountability for generating new work), they can terminate the consultant and fall back to their old, comfortable, if ineffectual, ways of doing things.

Although we understand that leaders of firms must often meet among themselves to decide major policy issues, try not to let a detailed marketing plan be developed in your firm without the full involvement of those who will have to make it work. If the plan is generated in-house with staff participation, the likelihood of success will be much higher. More people will want the plan to work.

How Do Issues Get Resolved?

A successful planning process will:

- Identify the source of power (authority) or lack of it in the firm
- Delegate responsibility and sometimes authority
- Generate consensus among leaders in the firm

In order to work, the process requires:

- Strong and visionary leadership
- Group consensus regarding major issues
- Genuine commitment by all involved to make it work (tricky)

At worst, the process points out where the weaknesses are and the need to address them. How *do* you address the real issues and bring about change? First, remember that, without the commitment of top leadership, you're wasting time with this process. And, if your leadership is committed to developing a good marketing program but is not strong enough to persuade others in the firm, you won't get your program. Also, if you attempt dramatic change (large increases in sales calls or a radically new image) without a corresponding change in personnel to execute the change, you will probably be disappointed. Let's look at a classic example.

In one architectural firm we know, the principals have worked together, with essentially equal ownership, for many years. There is an unwritten rule that no one intrudes on the turf of any other. Of the six principals, one specializes in housing projects, one in schools, another in military projects. One principal has been given the title of president and tries to function as a CEO but can't be effective because he can't tread on any toes. Another principal heads up production and another has successfully evaded being type-cast, as he calls these assignments. At least three of the principals need to function as "closer-doers," but only the president can market or sell effectively and he hasn't much time for "doing."

What a marketing plan could do in this situation—if they ever wrote one— is make some of the principals responsible for X fee dollars per year (or per quarter) in new business. Those who are not good closers must rely on the de facto marketing director/president for help but must maintain their clients and obtain add-on and repeat services from them. Those who do not bring in new work *or maintain existing clients* would find either their bonuses or actual salaries (or draw) reflecting this situation; they may also find their authority in the firm is not "as equal" as those who bring in the jobs. This plan, if implemented and enforced, would state clearly that marketing has as high a priority in the firm as design. Think they'll ever do it?

In good times, this firm has done fairly well, maintaining a high level of repeat clients and turning out very high-quality work. In recessionary times they have been hit hard: no orderly delegation of responsibility, no stated goals or objectives, and no plan to implement those goals in an organized way.

This scenario depicts the all-too-typical problem of gaining consensus and resolving issues in developing a marketing plan. How do you get around these problems or better, break through them to fruitful communication and change? It is almost impossible without someone with real power supporting that movement.

The best plans emerge from meetings in which people talk to each other in front of one another. People may argue and get angry, but if the firm is to survive, they will make concessions. The first meeting should cover no more than one or two planning items, focusing on goal setting, both for the firm and possibly for key individuals, and position analysis, assessing the firm's strengths and weaknesses in relation to those goals. This session should be used to determine where the problem areas will occur.

When and How Does It Get Written?

The marketing plan should be written annually. But when should the first plan be written? The adage about finding it hard to drain the swamp when you are up to your backside in alligators applies to the marketing plan.

In a firm with strong support for marketing at the very top, a plan will be part of start-up activities and will be updated frequently. In firms without strong support, the plan, if written at all, may be updated infrequently, if at all. In either case, the first plan should be written when the firm is ready to take marketing seriously. What this means is that once there are people with marketing responsibilities, they will need a plan around which to build their jobs and by which the effectiveness of their work can be evaluated. So if you or any one else in your firm is a "marketer," your firm needs a plan.

Writing the marketing plan soon after you assume a new position will help you build the coalitions you need to make marketing work for both you and the firm. It also helps define your role and those of others involved in marketing and gives you exposure to the key people in the firm. Developing a marketing plan brings out the real issues in planning the development of the firm and allows you to influence those issues or at least be aware of them. Several things happen during this process:

- Key people meet with you to share ideas and concerns.
- The real leader in the office or firm will emerge, and his or her pet issues will become clear (see Chap. 9, "Internal Politics").
- Others in the firm will get a better idea of what your role as a marketer is all about.
- They will also see how they can work with you, be involved in some aspect of marketing, and profit from that involvement.

If you can't begin to work on the plan immediately, keep alert for opportunities to get others involved in the planning process, for example, to help them see the importance of marketing, contribute to the effort, and better understand your role. Get approval and support for such actions as:

- Holding a goal-setting retreat
- Developing a market research report
- Undertaking an image survey to find out what clients and others think of the firm
- Assessing your sales tools and presentation techniques

Once the process begins:

- Schedule key agenda items for developing and revising the plan; circulate the schedule and discuss it with those whose involvement you need.
- Start each new plan or major revision at least 3 months before you need to start using it.
- Keep the key people involved. Make certain those in power *and* those who will work with the plan participate in its development.
- Send a detailed draft of the plan to all concerned at least 2 weeks prior to writing a final copy, with a clear indication of what information you need and when it should be returned; talk to them individually about their ideas.
- Encourage participation, but keep the ball rolling.
- The faster growing (or shrinking) the firm is, the more frequently the plan must be reviewed and revised.

Remember, if you have no plan and it hasn't been done because you are too busy with the alligators, not only will the swamp not get drained, but those cold calls may be falling on deaf ears and the proposals dropping before blind eyes because what you are selling doesn't match what the market wants. See Fig. 7.1 for a sample marketing plan agenda.

Next, let's look at some simple approaches to content. Each firm will need to produce a marketing plan unique to its own needs, the markets it pursues, and the personalities and interests of those who write and implement the

```
MARKETING PLAN AGENDA:    March 15 - May 30

March 15        Submit agenda for planned retreat to Harry; get
                revisions, modify; distribute to all attendees

March 17-19     Talk over agenda informally with attendees to get
                opinions, recommended changes

March 19        Discuss feedback to agenda with Harry; modify
                agenda as needed; redistribute.

March 21-23     Hold retreat: discuss firm's goals, strengths and
                weaknesses, competition; current markets.

March 25        Draft and distribute summary of retreat discus-
                sions to all attendees for comments, revision.


April 5         Meet with market research/image survey consultants
                to draft questionnaire, select respondents.

April 8-22      Market research and/or image survey(s) underway by
                consultants.

April 30        Meet with consultants to review findings, plan
                response.


May 5           Distribute survey findings and comments, along
                with agenda for next meeting to all retreat
                attendees.

May 7           Discuss agenda with all attendees to get comments

May 15-16       Conduct follow-up meeting to discuss survey
                results and develop strategy for responding,
                especially in terms of meeting the firm's goals.

May 18          Draft summary of meeting with strategic responses
                and outline action plan for 6 month and 12 month
                phases; distribute draft to attendees.

May 24          Discuss outline with each attendee in person (or)

                Hold half-day or whole day meeting to discuss
                action plan with all those affected by it, includ-
                ing retreat attendees.  Make revisions and get
                commitment to procede with actions.

May 30          Distribute action plans to all participants.
```

Figure 7.1   Sample marketing plan agenda.

plan. However, every marketing plan should include the following information:

- *Goals* of the firm (including target markets)
- Analysis of your firm's *strengths and weaknesses*—both technical and marketing (including your image)
- Analysis of your *competition*
- Research and analysis of the *markets* you have targeted
- A *budget* for all marketing activities (from principal's time to the cost of photography)
- Ways to *evaluate* the effectiveness of the plan and the work of those charged with implementing it
- *Action* plans (the what, who, when, and how much of the marketing plan)

Don't get hung up on the titles in your marketing plan; many are interchangeable. The ones we show and refer to are what we have used, but you can easily substitute, for example, "policy" for "strategy" or "capability" for "strengths and weaknesses."

Keep the plan short. No one in the trenches has time to read or use a lengthy volume. For best results the annual marketing plan should not exceed four to five pages per section. No one will read beyond that. Particularly try to avoid lengthy analyses of what you did in the past; you will benefit, of course, from knowing what worked and didn't work, but you are planning for the future. Issues like the specific action plans and breakdowns of budgets and staffing may require more pages but if so, need not be part of the general plan because relatively few people need to read these details.

Keep in mind that the plan should be:

- Functional, not full of useless information
- Frequently reviewed, referred to daily, like a "to do" list
- Friendly and easy to read, not boring
- Helpful, something that makes the work of marketing easier and more efficient

We have organized the remainder of this chapter according to the major plan sections, proceeding from goals to action plans. Using this sequence, by the time you are ready to take or direct action, you will know why you are taking each step and have a good idea who should do it, how much it should cost, how long it should take, and what the results of the action should be. We have illustrated part of this process in Fig. 7.2.

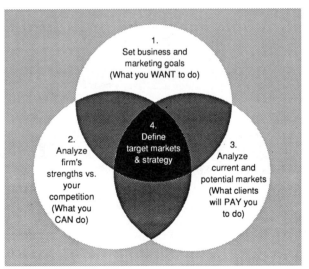

Figure 7.2 Marketing planning process.

SETTING GOALS

First, the managing principal or CEO must endorse the goal-setting efforts that form the basis of your marketing plan. The managing principal should call a meeting to discuss firm-wide goals. His or her involvement in this goal-setting process gives it the legitimacy you need in order to get the key staff to pay attention to the entire marketing planning process.

Because most design firms are motivated by what the key people in the firm want to do, unless personal and professional goals are acknowledged, the planning effort is doomed. Although many famous business schools (both institutions and "of thought") advocate that plans begin with an analysis of what markets are strong in the cold cruel world, most design professionals still base their careers on what they like to do, not how much money they will make doing it. For your marketing plan to make sense to the professionals in your firm, it must first address their dreams and fears. It may be your job later on to bring reality into this process, perhaps in the form of illustrating how the firm is perceived by the outside world or how its staff's present capabilities either support or contradict the expressed goals of the leaders. But, your first step is to draw out and acknowledge what people do and do not want to do, including marketing or sales.

Advancing Through Retreats

In many firms the first meeting takes the form of a retreat. Goals involve personal feelings, ambitions, and inhibitions. Therefore, the further away the group can get from everyday worries and the ringing phone, the easier they will find it to make some honest appraisals of where they want to go. Someone—the managing principal, marketing director, or outside consultant—must prepare an agenda for this initial goal-setting meeting. It is a good idea to develop some hypothetical goals for others to discuss, endorse, or use to prime their own goal-setting thoughts. Goals should:

- Reflect the sincere ambitions and desires of the leaders
- Stimulate clear objectives, be specific, relate to a business plan, and be obtainable within reason
- Consist of items that clearly point to a direction for the firm and by which the merit of any action can be weighed
- Avoid such generalities as "do good work" or "make money"
- Set priorities
- Include statements such as the following:
  - Types of projects desired, e.g., research laboratories, recreational facilities, airports, federal highway repair (can be listed in priority sequence and by percent of total billings they should represent)
  - Types of clients desired, e.g., private universities; new, fast-growing corporations; Department of Defense (by agency); foreign governments
  - Desired reputation for the firm, e.g., "innovative at problem solving, not high design, technologically sophisticated"
  - Desired size of firm at specified time (say 1 year out), e.g., "add four new people in design, one in administration"
  - Fee goals (gross or net—be specific) for the coming year, e.g., "$2.6 million; represents growth of 10 percent; 50 percent of fees coming from private sector clients; increase private/public sector ratio by 25 percent"
  - Geographic area of practice, e.g., "develop at least one major client in (name location) to set stage for possible branch office"
  - Changes in technical capabilities, e.g., "develop capability to provide new services and move into new markets such as tenant space planning for urban commercial developers" or "hazardous waste management for industrial and research facilities; hire new staff or train existing staff if feasible"
  - Markets to be shed, e.g., "get out of retail stores markets; fees too low, declining market"
  - Who will be responsible for what areas and activities, for example, "complete the transition from Jones' personal selling efforts to a team approach for each design studio, shared among principals and project managers"

We cannot overemphasize the importance of these goals coming from the collective mind of the principals and senior personnel, those ultimately responsible for carrying out the marketing plan. If the plan affects only a regional office or division of the firm, leaders in that office or division must contribute to these goals. Marketing people don't generally make goals, but they do help others state and clarify them. And marketers are the key elements in implementing those goals.

No Goals: No Go

Here's some advice about situations that come up too often in trying to develop a marketing plan. First, if the owners and other senior personnel can't or won't agree to meet and set goals or won't even talk about them:

- Look for a new job, because you will never get these people on the same bus.

- Engage an outside consultant to assist in bringing the group together. A specialist in organizational development or in group participation may help but only if all concerned parties participate and that participation is open and draws forth real goals for the firm and themselves.

- Resign yourself to the fact that what you may have are several independent firms and that you must develop and implement a separate marketing program for each one.

If all the principals will not agree on a set of goals for the firm, you may decide, to protect your sanity, that you need to get some semblance of a marketing plan developed, regardless. Try writing your impressions of each principal's goals, show these impressions to that individual only, and get that person to sign off on his or her stated goals, as interpreted by you. Then you can develop strategies and tools to implement plans based on these goals, taken collectively. (Chap. 9, "Internal Politics," may provide some insight to getting people to reveal their goals and to participate in planning.)

STRENGTHS AND WEAKNESSES: YOURS AND THE COMPETITION'S

This analysis of your own and your competitions's strengths and weaknesses takes some soul-searching. It can make some people uncomfortable, as they may feel, rightly or wrongly, that they are responsible for your firm's shortcomings. However, if the goal-setting went without too much bloodshed and you are able to continue meeting, next on your agenda should be to look into strengths and weaknesses, starting with your own firm, in three key areas: technical ability, project management, and marketing effectiveness.

Look in the Mirror: You Go First

There are two sides to this capabilities assessment—what your firm can actually do and what the outside world thinks you can do. The differences between these perceptions will give you some ideas where to focus marketing attention.

The person organizing this meeting should make some initial statements about his or her impressions of the firm's strengths and weaknesses and put these before the group. You may get this information from interviewing all attendees and others in the firm before the meeting. (Flip charts are good for presenting this material because you can save the sheets after the meeting and use them as notes for memos and elements of the marketing plan.) Make sure everyone present expresses his or her opinion, even if you have to poll the group to get them. Also, make sure everyone in the meeting has the same understanding of the terms being used, for example:

- Technical strengths might include innovative technical solutions and design awards.

- Technical weaknesses might be not knowing the latest code changes or lack of current information on new building materials.

- Project management strengths could consist of tight scheduling and low change order rates.

- Project management weaknesses might be poor coordination of documents resulting in high bids.

- Marketing strengths might be having good brochures, boilerplate on computer, good client relations, repeat clients, and strong personal contacts in a target market.

- Marketing weaknesses might mean not having photos of completed projects in emerging markets or a low success rate at formal interviews.

Outlining the firm's strengths and weaknesses will help you determine where to invest, both in operations and marketing—for example, in research, materials development, or adding technical staff to be better qualified in a desirable market. Unlike goal-setting, analyzing your firm's strengths and weaknesses cannot be done thoroughly within a meeting of the firm's leaders. Any in-depth analysis of your strengths and weaknesses should include information from outside sources, specifically clients. When you sense you do not have the objectivity to express the firm's strengths and weaknesses or that you cannot view the firm as potential clients might, an image survey will help.

Two kinds of image surveys serve the marketing plan: internal and external. An internal survey seeks to get employees' perceptions of the firm, their ideas of how the outside world sees them, and their views of the best image for the firm. The external image survey may help you get a better idea of how clients and others who know you perceive your firm and how they perceive your firm in comparison with others.

The internal survey can be handled by an outside consultant, through interviews or, if particularly sensitive issues are involved, through a written survey sent in confidence to the consultant for recording and tabulation. External surveys can be done by an outside consultant or by in-house marketing staff. The aim, again, is to find out if the firm's principals have the same picture of the firm as do your clients and others who may influence your clients. After all, if you want to change or maintain your image, you had better know what it is. The "emperor's clothes" syndrome can make it difficult for an in-house survey of past and potential clients to be accurate. Who wants to tell the boss that there is no one else who can see his or her imagined finery?

If you hire an outside consultant to assist you, plan to spend from $2000 to $15,000 for a survey, exclusive of your own staff time and depending on the size of your firm and the depth of information sought. Hire someone you feel comfortable with, who understands what you are trying to learn, who can act in confidence and respect privacy, who has worked with A/E firms before as well as having conducted similar surveys. Try to be certain that the consultant will not just feed back to you what he or she thinks you want to hear. Whether an internal or external survey, meet with the consultant or in-house team to develop the approach:

- What exactly do you want to find out? Make sure you and your consultant agree and get it in writing.

- Based on these goals, what questions will be asked? Put together a sample questionnaire and go through it with the consultant.

- Will the survey be "blind," i.e., those surveyed won't know the identity of your firm? Or, will you be identified and get some PR benefit from it?

- Which, if any, of your competitors will be mentioned in the survey?

- Do you want to obtain market research type of data in the same survey?

- Who do you want to have as respondents? Sometimes the consultant can help with this list, which may include past and present clients, potential and lost clients, competitors, and others in related professions.

- Set a deadline for the report and, of course, come to terms with the consultant as to the budget and quality of the results. (Be sure you are getting qualitative, not just quantitative, information; often *how* somebody responds is as important as what that person says.)

- Don't settle on a written questionnaire sent by mail; at best less than 5 percent of recipients can be expected to respond and they will not tend to elaborate or explain what they mean by terms like "quality design." Interviews by phone or face to face are best.

- If working with an in-house team, set definite time allotments for their efforts, and outline the results desired (use examples if you have them).

When the report is completed, review it carefully and distribute it to everyone involved. Discuss it at the marketing meeting and start planning how you will change or strengthen your image based on the findings.

The image study should tell you a lot about how well your firm is marketing and performing, but you need to evaluate your marketing in other ways as well. Start by evaluating how well you implemented a former marketing plan, if you have one. Look for:

- Proposal and interview hit rates

- Numbers of cold calls and follow-up contacts made by those responsible for them

- Analysis of current work by project and client type and geographic location

- Profitability for each market

- Proportion of repeat work and who these clients are

- Marketing costs compared to annual revenues *in specific markets*

- Effectiveness of support functions, such as public relations, marketing tools, and written and verbal presentation materials

For both the technical and marketing aspects, look at your firm's weaknesses in terms of what can be done about them. Your options include:

- Hiring new personnel—technical or administrative—with the special skills or experience you need in a given area

- Getting out of a market in which you are not competitive

- Developing an aggressive PR program to educate clients regarding the capabilities you do have

Weaknesses are not dead ends, and they can help you focus attention where it is needed. However you have conducted your external and internal analysis, you need to come away from the process with some understanding of what you need to do to emphasize your strengths and compensate for your weaknesses. This understanding will lead to the next phase of activity in developing a workable marketing plan.

Looking Around: Evaluating Your Competition

To complete this evaluation of your strengths relative to your goals, take each market you have identified for your firm and make a list of your competition in each market. List the strengths and weaknesses of each firm against whom you frequently compete. The type of information you should analyze about your competition includes:

- Size and gross volume of work of the leading firms
- Volume of work they have in each of the markets for which you compete
- How others in the industry perceive them
- Clients they presently serve—especially ones you identify as potentials for your firm
- How much work in each market area each of your competitors has won from you (you may also want to review how selection was made on each of these projects—was it by formal interview, informal requests for proposals, fee submittal?).

You can obtain this information from the following sources, among others:

- Your image survey
- Asking clients directly
- Interviewing potential new employees
- Asking current employees who previously worked for the competition
- Asking subconsultants and vendors who know or work for the competition.

You can also pick up this information from attending professional association meetings (AIA, ACEC, SMPS, PSMA, etc.) and listening carefully.

When you have accumulated information about your firm's strengths and weaknesses (real and perceived) and the strengths of your competition, include this information in your marketing plan. You have now completed two circles shown in Fig. 7.2; you are ready to go on to the next step.

MARKET RESEARCH AND ANALYSIS

Whereas image surveys produce information on your firm (and sometimes on your competition), market research produces information on your current and potential clients and on market trends. Remember, we noted that for the plan to succeed, principals need to state their goals based on what they want to do, not on market conditions. But, you do need to look at market conditions, too. You need to analyze the identified markets to see if they hold enough work of the appropriate kind to validate your marketing plan. If the markets do not, it may be "back to the drawing board" for the marketing plan or at least making your principals aware that some adjustments must be made.

Carol McConochie, in a seminar, identified the following things that market research will answer:

- What markets will offer the best opportunities in the next year? In the next 5 years?
- Is the firm capable and qualified to serve these markets and to compete effectively for the work?
- In the firm's present markets, what will be the volume and nature of

work in the next 12 to 20 months? Will the criteria for getting work change? Is the competition changing? How?

- What new services are being sought by clients in markets the firm presently serves?

- Will the firm need to seek new markets to maintain its work load and meet its target fee volume? What new markets would be most appropriate?

- What opportunities for work are available, with the firm's present capabilities and track record, in markets it is not now serving?

Refer to Chap. 3, "Direct Marketing," for specifics on how to conduct this research. Remember, the purpose of market research in developing your marketing plan is to find out if conditions in the real world support your firm's goals and, if not, what the firm must do in order to meet those goals. Figure 7.3 shows how you can assemble this information and use it to set priorities for decision making.

STRATEGIES FOR SUCCESS: MANAGING CHANGE

Having completed the goal setting and analysis, you are prepared to develop a strategy for achieving your *goals* that will take advantage of your *strengths,* compensate for or correct your *weaknesses* and, above all, respond to *market opportunities*. This strategy will lead to effective implementation. And, while we mentioned that this strategic phase is often a favorite one for marketers, it is also difficult and challenging and the phase most likely to go wrong. Reenter Machiavelli. Most strategies involve change. Too much change, or the wrong kind, will spell defeat for the plan and frustration for everyone involved. We don't mean to sound pessimistic, but the statistics are not in your favor. Here are some steps to help you improve the odds.

Developing Objectives

First, you may feel your goals, as stated so far, are too subjective, perhaps not very specific and therefore difficult to achieve. You may need to translate these goals into *objectives* that will start to define *what you must do to meet your goals*. For example, a goal might state: "Develop new ways for increasing work from current clients; improve relations with existing clients." Your objective might say: "Increase gross fee volume in (name of current market) by 20 percent; meet fee goal by combination of obtaining new clients (5 percent increase) and additional work from existing clients (20 percent increase)." Other examples are:

- Goal—Expand client base.

- Objective—Develop new clients through referrals from existing clients; reduce dependence on "cold calls." Improve techniques for obtaining leads. (Specific steps for doing this should be listed in the action plans that follow.)

- Goal—Develop more work with private sector clients.

- Objective—Develop better social contacts to increase access to private sector clients, especially large-scale developers and senior corporate personnel. Change image of firm to reflect more "corporate," less "institutional" interest and orientation.

- Goal—Increase billings for interior design services.

Market Segments (a)

Services the Firm Offers	Types of Clients Served	Types of Projects Resulting	Geographic Location of Work
Site selection, analysis	"Hi-tech" corporations	New R+D buildings	East Bay

Market Analysis of Each Segment (b)

Market Volume	Growth Potential	Profitability	In-house Champion	Technical Competence
2 million SF	High	Low – serves as "foot in the door"	J. R.	High – knowledge of R & D facilities needs; real estate experience

Strategic Planning (d)

Management Actions Required	Marketing Strategy	Tactics
N/A	Increase client awareness of our ability to provide this service; use this service as means of obtaining further work w/clients	Survey potential clients re: need for this service; incorporate benefits of site analysis into all marketing efforts; develop mini-brochure

Market Analysis of Each Segment (c)

Image, Market Position	Current Capture Rate	Strength of Competition	Score	Ranking/ Priority	Go/ No Go
Medium – not well recognized	Medium	High			Go

Figure 7.3 Market analysis and planning worksheet.

- Objective—Increase TI contracts by 25 percent; add one project manager to interior architecture staff; get person(s) capable of making own contacts, with experience doing this.

When you have identified all the objectives you think you can meet during the next year, review them in terms of the goals you have set and your research findings. Make sure there are no basic contradictions between objectives and goals. No one has ever failed to implement a marketing plan because it was too simple to understand. When your objectives are clear and compatible with the preceding plan elements, you can roll up your sleeves and prepare to plunge into "How the *&%#@ are we gonna do all that in 1 year?"

From Objectives to Implementation

In developing strategies, keep your objectives in mind. Strategies, in the kind of plan we are describing here, are really just amplified objectives—more detailed and specific than objectives but following logically from them and leading, equally logically, to implementation. Given the *objectives* shown above, your *strategy* for both indirect and direct marketing steps might look something like this:

- Develop newsletter to keep current and former clients informed of other projects in the office.

- Have every principal or project manager contact two clients by phone or letter every week; they must make regular reports to the principal, marketing director, or marketing committee on these contacts.

- Have every principal join one social group or become active on a new committee within an organization that will enhance our contacts with desirable clients.

- Hire graphic designer to revise current corporate graphics and recommend more sophisticated image.

- Put prospect list on computer and update it weekly to show action items and report progress.

- Look into hiring a human resources consultant or staff person to assist in recruitment and orientation (reorientation) of staff to new image.

As you move closer to developing action plans (and strategies are usually the last step before doing so), you move closer to assigning specific responsibility for taking action. This is where things can get difficult and you can lose control unless you are, or have the backing and support of, the person in charge. Remember, without this support, it is difficult to hold people responsible who may have greater longevity and higher rank than you; be realistic. (In Chap. 1, "Evolution and Structure," and in Chap. 9, "Internal Politics," we discuss responsibility for the marketing effort.)

ACTION PLANS: GETTING THE JOB DONE

We think of action plans as the heart of the marketing plan, because they define specific tasks and assign responsibility and accountability, time frames or deadlines, and budgets. Action plans bring the marketing plan into being and set parameters for evaluating its effectiveness. They need to address at least four key questions:

- What will be done? (Tasks)
- Who will do it? (Assignments and accountability)
- When will it be accomplished? (Time frames and deadlines)
- What will it cost in both labor and expenses? (Budget for planned activities)

So here it is, the to do list that goes on and on—sometimes for more than a year. You may want to divide your action plan into sections that correspond to the chapters of this book, for example:

- Indirect marketing
- Sales tools
- Direct marketing

To show examples of tasks for implementation let's go back to our list of strategies and review it, first, for those items that fall into the indirect marketing and tools development category. Starting with the first strategy, "Develop newsletter," the action items responding to it might be as follows:

- *Get client newsletter under way*
  (What will be done?)
  Appoint committee to draft goals and objectives of client newsletter. Recommend frequency of publication, target audience, annual budget, and method of approach for maximum communication effectiveness.
  (Who will do it?)
  Committee to consist of Jo Harris (principal and marketing director), Mark Smith (communications coordinator), Sarah Jones (director of interior design), Hank Peters (director of architecture and planning).
  (When will it be done?)
  Committee to report back to management committee by next meeting (show date).
  (How much will it cost?)
  Annual budget for newsletter not to exceed $12,000. Initial planning phase not to exceed $1200 in actual staff salary; one-time only cost for outside graphic design assistance, approximately $2500.

After approval of the action plan, you can further define the "whats" and costs, such as, "Board to approve or modify recommendations, authorize budget, and set date for first issue, based on feasibility."

Detailed tasks can be written similarly for every action item, based on your list of objectives. Some tasks, of course, should be left to the implementors to detail; if the people in charge know what they are doing, leave specifics to them. But, when giving assignments to those not familiar with marketing, you may need to give detailed directions.

Direct marketing (sales) plans can be written or updated weekly to correspond to your lead sheet or list of new prospects. For this exercise we can look at some sales-oriented tasks that can be identified on an annual basis.

Going back to our list of objectives, we can take from it those items that are sales related (direct marketing). Let's look at item 2 in our list of strategies—getting the principals and project managers to become more involved in client contact.

- *Increase personal contact with former clients:*
  (What will be done?)
  Develop list of former clients with whom the firm has, or should have, a good relationship.
  Indicate on the list which senior staff person should be the primary contact with that individual.
  Indicate priority sequence for contacts, e.g., who should be called first, next, etc.
  Develop graphic system (check list or chart, either manual or computerized) for recording calls or personal contacts completed or in progress.

Distribute this list of contacts to management committees (or whomever) for review, discussion, and implementation.
(Who will do it?)
Lisa MacIntosh (marketing coordinator) to develop list in consultation with Jo Harris.
(When will it be done?)
Present the list to board by next meeting (show date).
(How much will it cost?)
Staff time as needed to compile. Senior staff time to implement, minimum of 2 hours per week, maximum of 8 hours per week, depending on whether phone calling or in-person contact is more appropriate, until first pass through list is completed. Indicate minimum and maximum labor costs to implement.

Because this step—increasing principal's involvement in client contact—may be critical to your overall goals and because it is often the most difficult step to implement, the way it is structured, presented, and monitored is key to its success. Again, don't assign tasks to people who clearly won't do them (have never done them before, don't want to, don't believe they will work, and are temperamentally unsuited to doing them). When faced with a large percentage of principals who won't call clients, period—not even old friends, to say nothing of new prospects—you need to place more emphasis in your plan on indirect methods. The newsletter, frequent brochures, seminar engagements, etc., become more important. So does the direct marketing of the one person (for example) who does make client contact. Your strategy needs to maximize that person's exposure without encouraging burnout.

MONITORING THE PLAN: FACING THE MUSIC

Just because something is written in an action plan does not mean it will get done at all, to say nothing of completed on time, within the established budget, or, miracle of miracles, that it will yield the desired results. If a plan falls apart somewhere between strategy and action, monitoring is the phase in which its disintegration becomes obvious.

In order for the plan to work over time, and for it to yield the expected (or any) results, several things must happen:

- Senior management must agree that everything in the plan is worth doing and worth the time, trouble, cost, and staff commitment to do it.

- Management must be reconvinced at every milestone, whether these points consist of subcommittee reports, results of the first newsletter, or quarterly profit and loss statements. Management must be convinced that the plan is working. If not, change the plan or at least change the action items.

- There has to be some systematic method of evaluating the plan's success. Otherwise, one firm member will look at one indicator (e.g., the kinds of responses she is getting on the other end of the cold call), while another will look at the bottom line, while another measures design staff enthusiasm. What are the real measurements for your firm?

There are two ways to measure effectiveness in marketing plans:

- Did we do what we said we would do (in the action plan)?

- Did it work? Did we get the results we wanted? Why or why not?

We describe how to measure whether you succeed at the former in Chap. 2,

"Getting Organized." Measuring the latter, effectiveness, needs to be part of the plan itself, whether included as part of the action plan, listed with objectives, or in a separate section of the plan devoted solely to monitoring the system. However you do this, make sure that the criteria for performance are stated in writing and agreed upon by all whose opinions and participation are required for success.

One way to get a handle on the second kind of performance issues—did we get results?—is to establish a measurable objective when describing an action item. In our simple "newsletter" action plan, for example, we could add a note that says:

> After 1 year of publication, the client newsletter will be reviewed in terms of how many, if any, new projects resulted—to any extent—from the publication. If the publication is doing its job, at least once in the year some new or former client should call and say, "I just got your newsletter and it reminded me to give you a call about a deal I'm trying to put together...."

However, you will not always get the exact results expected, and you must work with your marketing committee to evaluate the kinds of responses your actions do bring about. Using the newsletter example, those reactions could be like the following:

- What if no calls resulted from the newsletter but it took a national award from SMPS for corporate communications and your marketing staff have been rejuvenated by the recognition and are working harder than ever?

- What if some calls came in but didn't result in any signed contracts, just nibbles?

- What if the nibbles were all in areas that didn't correspond to your marketing plan and you didn't want to chase them anyway?

Be prepared for things to go wrong, to get no reaction or one far different from that anticipated. You can use this feedback if you include a written evaluation plan for each action item, objective, and strategy. These evaluation plans can be very simple, outlining the next level of action based on anticipated results, and offering insight to using information that may not be anticipated. Try to remember that your plan, from goal-setting to action items, is a living document that must be revised to reflect changes in both the firm's thinking and the conditions and reactions of the market.

There is no one right way to develop a marketing plan. You are more likely to succeed if you:

- Involve those who will be responsible for making it happen
- Respond to the directives of the person ultimately in charge
- Develop specific, realistic strategies for implementation and evaluation

You need to know who is ultimately responsible for getting the plan developed and accepted (it may be you), because this person is also going to be responsible for getting the key people to implement it.

Weld Coxe, years ago in the *A/E Marketing Journal,* said "it is perfectly okay not to have an organized marketing plan in a successful design firm. And there are lots of marketing jobs to do in such firms that do not have to be failures." He adds that "In a service firm... the clients have as much or more to do with the goals of the practice as any principal architect or engineer. If a prospective client walks in and asks, 'Can you do ———?' and the design professionals say, 'You bet!' who has set the goals?"

Actually, we think the principals still set them, since an unwritten goal appears to be, "Stay loose, be open to opportunities, take what comes."

Coxe continues, "It is... possible for a marketer to have a very rewarding career—and exciting day-to-day work life—helping pursue the targets of opportunity that become the goals of a wholly reactive firm." In conclusion, if things are going well for you and your firm, don't feel you have to have a written plan. We have found it helpful to have them in our firms, and we still recommend you do one, but don't depend on it to solve all your marketing problems.

INTRODUCTION

Despite some statistics in the *1988 SMPS Salary Survey* to the contrary, we believe that few firms, especially smaller ones, really budget for marketing. Budgets require planning and most firms lack time, information, and incentive to conduct this rigorous exercise. Even if they do budget, cash flow and opportunities still dictate how much will actually be spent. But, as marketers seek to demonstrate the value of what they do, they are getting more sophisticated about analyzing where the money goes and how to calculate return on investment. These calculations, which reflect past expenditures, make it easier to generate budgets, which are predictions for the future.

In Chap. 7, "The Marketing Plan," we discussed the "why" and "how to" of the marketing plan. Plans call for committing time and money to reach agreed upon goals. Some people say that the most important part of the marketing plan is the budget because it means "putting your money where your mouth is." This chapter describes how you develop budgets and guidelines for spending money on marketing. We will walk through the steps you take to make the most of your marketing dollars, including:

- Establishing how much to spend
- Deciding where to spend it
- Calculating return on investment
- Determining fair compensation for marketers

ESTABLISHING HOW MUCH TO SPEND

People always want to know how much they should spend on marketing. Industry-wide statistics have been hard to obtain and harder to rely on because accounting methods for measuring overhead, especially marketing expenses, have been highly individual. For example, many firms don't keep accurate track of costs such as support staff time; some charge to nonbillable project costs what others call project-specific marketing, etc. Still others disagree as to whether to charge personnel costs at direct labor rates or at direct personnel expense including a multiplier, and if the latter, at which multiplier.

In the absence of standardization, all the figures used in this chapter are approximate. If your marketing costs seem much lower than those shown here, it may be in part because you are not including all the costs you should in marketing; if yours seem very high, you may be charging senior personnel time with a multiplier or putting some expenses into marketing that could or should be in human resources, professional development, nonbillable project costs, or other overhead areas. Or, it could just be that you're spending a lot less, or more, and have good reasons to do so.

Even if accounting procedures were standardized, the answer to how much to spend would still be that the total amount spent on marketing, even as a percentage of gross revenue, will differ from firm to firm. In the early 1980s it appeared that a higher percentage of fees was spent by small firms, say from 5 to 9 percent of gross revenue (gross revenue generally means total revenue, less consultants' or pass through fees). Recently, the *Report on AIA Marketing Architectural Services* survey shows that larger firms are spending more. Architects tend to spend more than engineers. Maintaining a high percentage of repeat clients will cost less than developing new clients or pursuing new types of projects. The majority of the budget for firms of all sizes goes to personnel, usually in direct marketing, but smaller, high design and specialized firms spend a relatively high percentage on indirect marketing and sales tools.

Throughout this chapter we describe what the marketer without financial training can do to plan expenditures in his or her department. We are not

Chapter Eight

Your Money Game— The Marketing Budget

financial analysts or even bookkeepers and frequently have trouble with our checking accounts, so this chapter will not impress your accountant. Both the language and concepts are aimed at the marketer, and tend toward the "quick and dirty" method of analysis.

One way of looking at marketing budgets is to divide them into planned and unplanned expenses. In a third-generation or "directed" marketing organization (Chap. 1, "Your Overview") you will have more planned and less unplanned expenses. In the more second-generation, reactive or "managed" organization, you will need to allow a larger percentage for unplanned activities. A comprehensive budget in either type of firm, obviously, has to account for both types of expenditures. And you need different techniques to predict planned and unplanned expenses with any kind of accuracy. Both types are influenced by factors such as:

- Who does the marketing (and how expensive are they)?
- How expensive are your sales tools (brochures, photography)?
- Is your firm entering new markets or developing new clients?
- How much do you spend on PR and advertising?
- How fast do you want to grow?
- Is your competition increasing?

Figure 8.1 shows approximate percentages for planned and unplanned marketing for different kinds of firms. If you decide to create some marketing expense guidelines for your firm, here—in lay-person's language—are three ways to develop a budget:

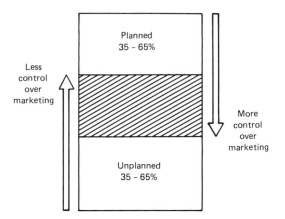

Figure 8.1 Planned versus unplanned marketing expense.

- **Comparison method**   Analyze what you spent for all marketing activities during the past year and estimate a percentage increase or decrease by category; this method doesn't work very well if you don't have at least 9 months of cost data to work with or if your data are not broken down by market or by marketing categories (e.g., "brochures" and "entertainment" as well as the cost to obtain specific projects). This method works best for determining what the *unplanned* expenses are likely to be in each market; it doesn't do much to help you plan this year's activities or set priorities for possible future budget cuts.

- **Top-down method**   Take a percentage of your anticipated gross annual revenue—somewhere between 5 and 15 percent, depending on how aggressive you want to be in marketing, your planned rate of growth, and the number of new markets you plan to enter. This approach is quick and dirty and gives you only the most general ballpark figure to work from. The only way to monitor this budget is by percentage of the calendar, i.e., at the end of the first quarter you can see if you have spent 25 percent of your budget, etc.

- A more sophisticated and useful variation on this method is to assign a percentage to your projected gross *for each target market,* e.g., 6 percent for schools, 9 percent for multifamily developments, 3 percent for single family projects. The percentages can be based on what you guess it will cost to meet your fee goals in each market, compared to your comparative strength in each. Monitoring these figures quarterly will be a little more useful.

- **Bottom-up method** Start with zero dollars and develop estimates for all expenses (indirect labor, printing, photography, entertainment, public relations, etc.) for the coming year. For best results, take these estimates from your *marketing plan* by costing out your *action items.* Base these cost estimates on past history if possible, and obtain estimates where you can (for big projects like brochures, for example) and calculate how much targeted growth you will need to pay for (e.g., increase billings by 15 percent).

- Again, a more sophisticated and probably more accurate variation consists of developing the same budget categories for both firm-wide and specific market expenses. By spelling out the costs for each activity, by market, you get a good idea where your dollars will be spent, which will help you make intelligent cuts when you need to. And in some markets it will cost more than 15 percent more in marketing to increase billings 15 percent; in some markets it should cost less.

- The main benefit of this method is that it enables you to plan while you budget and vice versa. Action items in your marketing plan get assigned a cost—labor or expense; by anticipating that cost, you have made some commitment to do that marketing activity. This method, alone, does not help you determine your unplanned marketing costs, but in your quarterly assessment, if your unplanned expenses exceed expectation, you can decide which planned expenses may have to be deferred.

The best way to prepare a budget is to use a combination of all three methods. Start with the bottom-up method to plan and cost-out your marketing activities; then use the comparison method to get a handle on prior years' unplanned expenses (especially travel and entertainment, for example, to make out-of-town presentations); take your bottom line from these two analyses and compare it to your projected gross revenue (top-down) to get the total percentage (by market and firm-wide). Use your list of itemized expenditures to see where expenses must be cut or reduced. Figure 8.2 illustrates a sample one-page marketing budget summary that uses all three methods of calculation.

Depending on where you fall on the planned-unplanned continuum, you will need to reserve a contingency of 15 to 65 percent for unplanned, special opportunities. If you are well planned, you may still need it for that special person whose time you need on an important proposal, or you may need to hire some PR help or a market research consultant before you plunge into that new market identified in your long-range plan. You don't have to spend the contingency but you probably will if your cash flow permits. If you are largely unplanned, even more of your "budget" will end up in this category (no longer a contingency, but a way of life). However, you can still plan for the balance.

```
MARKETING BUDGET SUMMARY SHEET

Gross Income from Fees        Actual              Projected
                              last year           this year

                              $2.1 M              $2.5 M
Marketing Costs

Personnel

    Partners  Hunter 60%   $39,000
              Markus 40%    26,000
              Grover 10%     6,500
              Webber  5%     3,250

          Subtotal                    $75,000

    Jr. Partners/Technical
              Beets   10%    2,000
              Goodman  5%    4,000
              3 PAs    5% each 5,000
              Knotts   3%    1,200

          Subtotal                    $12,200

    Marketing Coordinator   $22,000

                                      $22,000
    Secretary               $15,000

                                      $15,000

              Total Personnel         $124,000

Expenses

        Brochure            $3,630
        Direct Mail          2,020
        Photography          2,500
        Travel & Entertainment 5,600
        Expenses and supplies  1,100
        Books, periodicals     350
        Graphic design, repro 5,000

          Subtotal                    $20,200

    Total Marketing Budget            $144,400


Marketing costs as percentage of gross fees:  6.8%

Personnel costs as percentage of total marketing budget:  86%

Expenses as percentage of total marketing budget:  14%
```

Figure 8.2 Sample marketing budget.

DETERMINING WHERE TO SPEND IT

In Chap. 7, "The Marketing Plan," we talked about conducting market research and analysis and then developing strategies and actions for direct marketing, sales tools, and public relations. These things cost money. You may also need to allocate some dollars for time spent planning and monitoring your marketing program. We divide our budget discussion into these areas—direct and indirect marketing and tools—however, you need to develop categories and labels that make sense to your own program.

We include the costs of research under direct marketing. Some tools such as proposals and brochures usually fall into direct marketing, but other tools—image brochures, announcements, and reprints, for example—can be assigned to indirect marketing, depending on how you use them. Within each category—direct and indirect—you will want to budget for both labor (in-house personnel) and nonlabor (including consultant) expenses.

We can also look at labor and nonlabor categories for marketing as a whole. Figure 8.3 gives an approximate picture of how total marketing dollars are spent, both in terms of labor versus nonlabor and in terms of direct marketing versus indirect marketing.

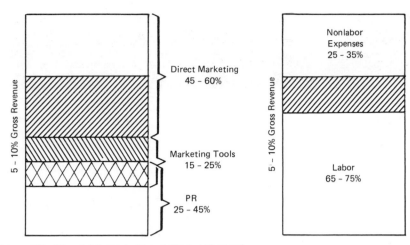

Figure 8.3   How total marketing dollars get spent.

In general, approximately two-thirds of total marketing costs go to direct labor and one-third to nonlabor expenses. Approximately 45 to 60 percent should be spent on direct marketing, 25 to 45 percent will go to indirect marketing, and the balance to sales tools.

Figure 8.4 shows how personnel or labor are typically charged to marketing. Principals and senior technical personnel tend to account for one-half of the salary expenses, with the marketing staff (including part-time word processing and secretarial) accounting for one-third, and the remainder going to technical and production staff who contribute to the marketing effort occasionally by attending presentations or researching new markets. Large firms with full-time sales representatives may spend from one-quarter to one-third of their budgets on these roles.

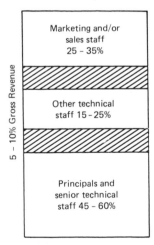

Figure 8.4   Personnel and labor charged to marketing.

Figure 8.5 illustrates nonpersonnel firm-wide marketing expenses and includes travel and entertainment, photography, printing, graphic design, and other outside consultants.

Direct Marketing

As shown in Fig. 8.3, we estimate that you will want to budget between 45 and 60 percent of your total marketing budget (firm-wide or per market) to

Non-Personnel Marketing Expenses				
Expense	Per Example		Standard Range & Amount	
	%	$	%	$
Photography	10	4,000	(5-15%)	$2,000-6,000
Brochures (Consulting & printing)	15	6,000	(10-20%)	$4,000-8,000
Reprints	3.5	1,400	(2-5%)	$800-2,000
Travel & Entertainment	15	6,000	(10-20%)	$4,000-8,000
Advertising	12	4,800	(0-25%)	$0-10,000
Direct Mail (Graphics, printing & postage)	25	10,000	(15-30%)	$6,000-12,000
Memberships & Conferences (SMPS & client organizations only)	7.5	3,000	(5-10%)	$2,000-4,000
Consulting & Facilitation	12	4,800	(10-15%)	$4,000-6,000
Total	100%	$40,000		

Figure 8.5 Nonpersonnel marketing expense(s) (firm-wide or by specific market). (Assume a firm grossing $2 million in fees—net consultants—spending 10 percent of that gross on marketing. Total marketing budget is $200,000, of which 20 percent, or $40,000, is allocated to nonpersonnel expenses.)

direct marketing (see Chap. 3, "Direct Marketing"). Where you fall in that range depends on how willing the principals and others in your firm are to make contact with clients, especially in the courtship phase, prior to receiving an RFP. In the direct marketing category you need to budget for personnel time—both principals and senior technical people and a dedicated sales staff if you have one—to make contact with clients—former, current, and prospective. You can calculate this time (at straight salary rates, without a multiplier) as a number of hours per billing period or per month, or you can do it for a fixed percentage of time per month, e.g., 10 percent of a principal's time at her salary, not her billing rate. What's important is to budget a fixed amount of time for planned client contact and also allow room in the budget for unplanned time to be spent preparing proposals and making presentations. Remember, these percentages will vary depending on whether most of your client development takes place before or after you get an RFP.

In direct marketing you will also want to budget travel and entertainment expenses for client courtship and possibly for lead finding services, market research, or an image survey, if you do not have the resources in-house to accomplish them. However, at least 70 percent of direct marketing costs should be personnel time.

Although only about 20 percent of firms establish budgets for obtaining specific projects (according to the *1988 SMPS Salary Survey*), we estimate that the average architecture or engineering firm spends approximately 5 percent of its annual gross revenue pursuing individual projects. (This figure can account for your entire marketing budget if you are highly "reactive.") As much as one-half of that 5 percent is spent on lead finding, developing relationships, and selling. In general, the other 2.5 percent of the gross revenue is spent on submittals, proposals, presentations, and job-specific negotiations. If you include negotiations under marketing (where else?), we suggest you reserve 0.5 to 1 percent of your annual gross for negotiating scope and fee. With government clients it is not uncommon to spend as many hours negotiating the contract as you spent getting the job. Remember also that jobs are sometimes lost during negotiations.

How do you know how much to spend on any given project? As we are fond of saying, "it depends." Some firms try to hold spending to a specific percentage of the potential fee. Others calculate a percentage of anticipated profit. But in many cases you won't know the full scope and fee potential until you sit down to negotiate or even after you get into the job. And profit, of course, depends on so many variables we won't even list them. From a marketing standpoint, how much you should spend will depend on answers to questions like:

- Will this project help us enter a new market?
- Is it with a potential repeat client?
- Do we have a high probability of winning it? (Spend more as your odds of selection increase.)

Remember, not every project can be that all-important one for which you pull out all the plugs to win. But some will be. Do not make the mistake of planning to spend very little (say, 1 percent of your projected fee) on a competitive project. Spending less never increases your probability of winning. However, you will want to minimize your spending if you know you will lose and are using the exercise merely as a means to get to know a prospective client better. (But, it may be more cost effective not to pursue the project at all and find another way to court the client.)

Indirect Marketing

In public relations, costs will again depend on whether you have an aggressive, client-centered firm or one that would rather not ever call on a client. PR—including getting published and participating in professional or civic events—can constitute between 25 and 45 percent of your total marketing budget. Remember, if you're not calling on clients, you need to get their attention somehow. Labor might represent from 25 to 85 percent of the cost, depending on whether you hire an outside agency or consultant or implement your PR program in-house.

Public relations is one of the most misunderstood areas of a marketing budget because there is little direct return on investment. However, for many firms (especially those trying to change their image or develop a new position) PR can be a critical marketing activity.

Most firms never have enough money to implement all their indirect marketing ideas, at least not in 1 year. Even so, you can make up a PR wish list as elaborated in Chap. 4, "Indirect Marketing," and assign percentages of your indirect marketing budget to it. Even if you can't carry out all your PR tasks in 1 year, the list will help you determine where to spend money now and what tasks can wait. Following is a sample list with costs shown as a percentage of the total indirect marketing budget of, say $10,000.

Category	Percentage	Amount ($)
Advertising	15	1500
Awards programs	5	500
Conventions/trade shows	10	1000
Design competitions	15	1500*
Memberships	5	500
Placing articles	10	1000
Public speaking	15	1500
Seminars/open house	25	2500

*This figure might represent only the direct expenses, without any labor costs, to engage in a modest competition.

Note that this list is not a recommendation. The percentages and amounts need to respond to your own strategic plan, but you may want to consider using these elements in planning your budget.

Communication Tools

These tools, as described in Chap. 5, "Sales Tools," include proposals, statements of qualifications, reprints, brochures, and newsletters. They serve to support both direct and indirect marketing activities. They also have both labor and nonlabor expense components. To calculate labor in this category, anticipate a target number of tools to be generated in-house each year (by market if possible) and estimate how many hours your current staff will need to spend on each type of tool. By adding up the hours you can get an annual number.

You can estimate these costs by hour at an hourly rate or by a percentage of time, e.g., 25 percent of the marketing coordinator's total time will be spent on tools development; the marketing principal will spend 15 percent of her time; other principals will spend 10 percent each (times an annual salary).

The nonlabor expenses for marketing tools often amount to a hefty annual cost because printing is expensive, and, the better you want it to look, the more it will cost. With the advent of desktop publishing these costs have shifted somewhat, since software and hardware tend not to be charged to marketing and the biggest expense becomes labor to run them. Nevertheless, sales tools should not consume more than 30 percent of your total annual marketing budget (with brochures amortized over 2 years) and personnel costs taking up 30 to 50 percent of that amount.

The cost of photography is often either forgotten or underestimated. You probably need to set aside at least 5 percent of your sales tools expense budget for professional photography even if you are an engineering firm and don't think you need it. You will always want some good visuals for your marketing tools. If you keep up to date with photography, rather than waiting until you need project photos for a brochure, you will not have to add the cost of the photography to the cost of designing and producing the brochure. If your firm is a small, high-design architectural firm, you might plan on setting aside as much as 35 percent of your marketing tools budget, because illustrations of your work will be one of your most effective means of communication.

In budgeting for your marketing tools, go back to your marketing plan, if you have one; if you don't, you can use this list in lieu of a plan:

- Identify or review your goals.
- List which tools will best help you meet those goals.
- Obtain accurate estimates of costs to develop those tools by consulting with graphic designers, editorial assistants, word processors, printers, and other professionals.
- Amortize your costs over the anticipated time of usage, particularly for brochures (usually 2 to 3 years).
- Review your estimated cost to support each goal relative to the importance of your other goals, e.g., if it will cost $4000 to develop a new brochure to enter the hazardous waste market with a potential first year revenue of $100,000, versus $20,000 for a new brochure on your work in site civil for the developer market, with potential annual revenue of $500,000 in fees, you need to look at more than the figures.

CALCULATING RETURN ON INVESTMENT

Marketing people are increasingly concerned with return on investment, partly to justify their own positions and also to direct the firm's efforts. Measuring return on investment can help tell you what to spend money on next year, in other words, what goes into the budget.

Oh boy, this is the year we get to do what I want!

The first challenge in this exercise is to begin thinking of expenses for marketing as "investments." Or you may find that the thinking in your firm begins to change as a result of this exercise. You can start by asking several questions, among them:

- Do I know how much I am spending on marketing?
- Is the expense justified in terms of jobs brought in or enhancement of the firm's reputation?
- Are there other measurements to apply or benefits to evaluate?

This analysis gets complicated when the firm has no clear goals and objectives or when you are not in control—when various principals and project managers can commit the firm's resources and chalk it up to marketing without clearing it with you (or even let you know what they are doing). You will probably need to meet with the firm's bookkeeper or accounting department to develop systems and the kinds of reports you need to find out what kind of numbers have been charged to marketing in both labor and expenses. You will need to see time card records to determine who has charged time and expense records to see what has been bought. Of course, the accounting people may have far more detailed or far less specific information than you need. You may find that too much money has already been spent without your knowledge and your projections are way off as a result. When this happens, marketing people often ask to have some role in approving charges that will be made against the marketing budget before they occur. Having actual figures of expenses to point to will help support your case for needing this review or approval.

Because a majority of your budget is in personnel expenses, you will want to review people's performance in contributing to the marketing effort. In analyzing performance you may need to work closely with a principal because often the technical people assigned to marketing are more senior than you or have longevity over you. You don't want to butt heads with a valuable technical person, even if they fall short of expectations in marketing. Better to put down in black and white what they've spent and what they've accomplished and let the principals draw their own conclusions. However, you should be prepared to offer advice on how to improve the situation, either through training or providing better support, research data, or tools.

Some Problem Areas

Some aspects of marketing expenditures are more difficult than others in terms of calculating their benefit to the firm. The following categories are often difficult to justify because the returns are not quantifiable within a period of time generally covered in return on investment analysis:

- What people charge to marketing
- Results of market research
- Benefits of public relations

Personnel Charged to Marketing

Let's look at how budgeting problems arise for both technical people who are assigned to help the firm achieve its marketing goals and for marketing support and sales personnel.

With regard to the former, as a result of your strengths and weaknesses analysis, your firm may decide to invest in high-level, technical "experts" to help achieve agreed-upon marketing goals. Because they are hired to help you get work you don't already have, they may not be billable initially. But they may be responsible for marketing and sales in their areas of specialization. Therefore, a percentage of their salary will come from the marketing budget. In this case, you need to outline ahead of time what percentage of the technical experts' salaries will come from marketing and what the marketing objectives are for them. Senior technical people with sales responsibilities often also demand costly support from your department in terms of tools and public relations.

Your marketing and/or sales staff represents overhead to your firm, and you should be prepared to justify this expense in terms that make sense to others in management. We remember working 60-hour weeks for months on end until we confronted a firm principal and demanded assistance. We were suffering burn-out and the principal's reaction was to request an accounting of what the marketing department (which consisted of one and a half people) was accomplishing for the firm and how the assistance requested could improve this service and the firm's ability to get work or reduce the amount of time highly paid technical people spent on marketing. This was a rational reaction and after ten deep breaths and a walk around the block, we were able to outline the tasks a person in an x-salary position could undertake and how these tasks could save time and money in other areas.

When you consider adding staff or getting assistance, analyze the impact and expected results. See if you can use someone already on the payroll on a part-time basis. This approach opens the possibility to provide someone with a career opportunity as well as lessening the immediate financial impact on the firm.

Market Research as Investment

Market research is misunderstood because many firms don't know what it is or how it can serve their firm, especially if the firm is entrenched in certain markets and considering branching out into new ones. These firms need market research to determine if the new markets are right for them and if work is available. Because most firm leaders feel they already know their markets well or because they are good professionals and therefore don't really depend on "the market," the prospect of analyzing new markets seems like a costly, time consuming process.

However, as with personnel expense, you need to illustrate how the research will benefit your firm by helping to make your marketing effort more efficient, use technical people more efficiently, or help develop better sales tools. If you try to relate market research to sales, develop specific objectives regarding what information you want and how it will be used. To justify using outside consultants, calculate how much of your time will be spent on this effort and what will not get done in the interim because of the extra work. And don't expect results to show in terms of actual new projects for at least a year.

Public Relations Pays Off

Public relations is probably the most difficult to measure in terms of return on investment. Public relations activities are best measured in qualitative, not quantitative results, such as:

- Some favorable comments on your publicity should be received from target clients within 6 months after your program is initiated.

- Third-party referrals should start to pay off in 1 to 3 years.

- When your technical personnel call on potential clients, the firm's name and reputation should precede them.

Because your PR effort probably will not bring in new work directly, how can you know whether or not it has helped bring more, or perhaps better, clients to your door? If getting published inspires your top designer to work harder or maintain stronger relations with his or her clients, can you relate that change directly to marketing gains? Generally, you cannot. In these indirect marketing areas, we suggest alternative methods of evaluating your marketing effectiveness:

- Measure the return on investment over a period of time greater than the annual reporting period. (In fact, many PR activities can succeed only if carried over from year to year.)

- Alter your spending habits in successive years to see if there is a comparable change in sales, e.g., from using more print advertising to more direct mail.

- Set some specific goals for your market research and PR—discuss those goals with management and come to agreement that if certain goals are met, it is worth x dollars to the firm.

- If possible, invest in a "baseline" survey of your clients and intended clients before undertaking a major direct mail or advertising campaign;

conduct a follow-up survey after 1 year or 18 months to see if you have achieved the results you wanted.

With brochures, direct mail, competitions, and seminars, don't expect to get a return on your investment in less than 1 year. In fact, you might plan on amortizing these expenses over 2 to 5 years, depending on the anticipated life expectancy of the particular tool.

Overall, for all categories, when you have completed your first year of working with a budget, review the year's results and analyze them against expenses. You may want to develop a chart (see Fig. 8.6) showing activities, costs, and results, keeping in mind that these last may be subjective and open to interpretation. Review the activities to see how many of them were planned, either as budget items or as part of your intended marketing program. How many were unplanned? Check the results of both and review what is working (or who is working) and what (or who) is not.

You probably don't need a lot of detail in this analysis. For example, it shouldn't be necessary to show when a junior drafter was dragged off a project for a day to draw an organization chart for a proposal. However, you

```
CALCULATING RETURN ON INVESTMENT - BOTH LABOR AND EXPENSE

(Assume a firm grossing $1 million (net consultants) and spending $75,000 for marketing.)

Activity                   Annual Cost      Measurable Results        Return
(from marketing plan)

1. Generate one press       $1,400          4 small mentions in pubs  5-6 phone calls
   release per month                        1 feature article in      from past/current
                                            Sunday RE section         clients

2. Develop brochure         $20,000*(total) Produce 6 pg. brochure    Technical people
   Labor                    7,500           Sent out 65 by mail;      like to hand it out;
   Expense                  12,000          handed out 32 at inter-   4-5 positive client
                                            views                     notes

3. Produce proposals        $12,500 (total) Submit 25 proposals       Make 17 shortlists;
   Labor                    9,000                                     Won 6 jobs w/total
   Expense                  3,500                                     fees of $1.4 million**
                                                                      Hit rate = 68% of
                                                                      short-lists; 24% of
                                                                      wins

4. Locate and track         $ 5,600 (total) Identified 32 leads from  See above
   leads***                 3,750           phone calls, meetings,
   Labor                    1,850           other contacts; 25 resulted
   Expense                                  in proposals; 17 in short-
                                            lists; 6 in jobs

5. Make presentations       $20,000 (total) Made 17 presentations, won See above
   Labor                    17,650          six
   Expense                  2,350

6. Client development***     $ 6,000 (total) Developing contacts and   Potential fee of
   Labor                    4,500           relations with approx. 12 of $27,000
   Expense                  1,500           clients; obtained RFPs from (short-term)
                                            3 in past year; shortlisted
                                            for one project

7. Attend/give seminars     $ 4,500         Gave 1 lunch-time program Too soon to tell
   Labor                    2,000           in-house; sat on 2 other
                                            panels; made 14 new pros-
                                            pects, got 3 RFPs

8. Photograph projects      $ 1,500 (total) Used in brochure, proposals
   Expense                  1,500           proposals; potitive client
                                            reaction

9. Misc./contingency (5%)   $ 3,500

   TOTAL                    $75,000


*    Amortized: $10,000/year
**   Gross receipts of $1 million with $400,000 to be billed in the next year
***  Divisions between lead tracking and client development are somewhat arbitrary
```

Figure 8.6 Calculating return on investment.

might show in total how much technical support time you used on proposals for the year, compared to what you anticipated using. You will also want to know:

- Did you get the job for which you pulled out all the stops?
- Did the nationally renowned lab designer you hired improve your ability to compete in this market? How do you know?
- Did your new brochure bring positive feedback and renewed interest in your firm from targeted markets? How?

In other words, what were the results of your marketing investment—both quantifiable (the lab job with the $125,000 fee) and qualifiable (national coverage of a major project)?

Finally, in analyzing your marketing expenses, you need to know what motivates your principals and why they do what they do. Making money is not the primary reason for most A/E firms' existence. Therefore, you may need to be careful not to be too "bottom line" oriented in analyzing your expenses. Even though you should aim toward efficiency and return on investment, some marketing costs are justified when they serve to infuse firm leaders with renewed energy or boost the morale of the technical or marketing staff.

Be careful. You will always hear from the sales staff, "The money I spent this year won't generate sales or revenue until next year." That may be true, but patterns will emerge. And you need to keep the reporting system as simple as possible so the hotshots with calculators don't manipulate the numbers. Furthermore, over 2 years the cost-versus-results ratio will average out.

In budgeting, always try to be cognizant of cash flow. Try to stabilize your marketing program so that you know when major planned expenditures, such as photography or printing for a brochure, will occur. Doing this will make your accounting department very happy. And, as we say in Chap. 9, "Internal Politics," the accountants are very important allies to have.

COMPENSATION: WHAT ARE YOU WORTH?

Marketing compensation—that is, the salary or salaries paid to marketing staff—is, of course, a major budget item. More important, this amount tends to reflect the relative importance of marketing in the firm. If marketers make significantly less than others in the firm, the message is clear.

Despite the obvious correlation between salary and value, most marketing people have difficulty determining how much they should be worth to their firm. As their salary constitutes overhead, the costs can be passed on to clients only indirectly. And, since landing a job is usually a team effort, commissions are not usually practical for marketers (although more than 10 percent of A/E firms say they offer commissions—we'll discuss this subject later).

As you already know what the marketing budget is, you have some idea how important marketing is to the firm, as reflected by the percentage of revenue devoted to it. Now, you may want to analyze your role relative to the firm's overall compensation levels.

To determine if your own compensation is commensurate with that of others in your region who are at your level, you can use surveys like the national one published by SMPS or local surveys done by consultants or other professional organizations. For engineers, two references published annually will help you determine the value of your basic salary and overall compensation program by comparing you to other professionals in the industry:

- *NSPE Professional Engineers Income and Salary Survey,* National Society of Professional Engineers, 2029 K Street, NW, Washington, DC 20006

- *Executive Engineering Compensation Survey,* D. Dietrich Associates, Inc., P.O. Box 511, Phoenixville, PA 19460 (Actually, Dietrich Associates publishes a number of salary surveys for architects, engineers, designers, and drafters.)

In addition, you will want to compare your salary with those of the technical and administrative people in your firm. If you have access to this information, you will need to look at both the level of responsibility you have and the potential for growth in comparing your income to that of others. Several variables seem to influence what is "fair" compensation for marketers, including the following:

- Your amount of client contact—some firms pay more to marketers who spend at least part of their time outside the firm dealing directly with potential clients.

- Your management ability—you may be paid more because you have experience and confidence leading a team of people, as well as planning, budgeting, and monitoring results. You may be paid less if you are more of a "doer" who feels more comfortable taking direction from others.

Consider your professional goals and what the firm's expectations are. If you want to deal directly with potential clients and the firm places an emphasis on that but only allows technical people this questionable privilege, you are probably in the wrong firm to realize your income potential.

In summary, your basic salary will be related to:

- The tasks you do
- The decisions you make or for which you are responsible
- The size of your firm or branch office
- The volume of sales for which you are accountable

To Commission or Not?

Should a commission be part of your compensation? While product sales people are often paid by commission, those who sell professional services are generally seen as part of a larger team effort, making commissions for individuals more difficult to assign. Moreover, an important distinction must be made between marketing, largely a planning and monitoring function, and sales, the direct client contact portion of the marketing effort. Most marketing people have sales as only part of their responsibilities.

However, in A/E firms of all sizes, sales staffs are compensated at least in part by commissions related directly to the value of the projects brought in. While we usually say, "Never pay a commission," the *SMPS 1988 Salary Survey* indicates that approximately 15 percent of A/E firms offer commissions, especially small (under 25 people) and very large (over 500 people) firms. We don't know what people do in those firms to receive the commission and assume they are mostly in sales, not marketing. (We think SMPS survey respondents may, as a group, be more sales-oriented than the A/E profession as a whole.)

There are usually good reasons for not paying a commission; they include:

- It's hard to identify who was really responsible for obtaining the work; it is often a team effort that includes the lead finder, sales representative, proposal manager, project manager, and the principal, as well as the reputation of the firm built over years by this and other teams.

- It may be hard to prevent the sales representative from selling the job at any cost (even if it is a loser to the firm) to obtain a commission.

- It may be difficult to prevent the sales representative from pressuring your potential client to close the one-time sale, thus jeopardizing a relationship for future work.

- It isn't fair to punish the sales representative if the "closers" lose the sale, either in the proposal or at the interview.

Determining how much commission to pay is also tricky. You need to decide:

- How much is the job worth to your firm?

- How much, as a percentage of fee, would you have to spend to get the project using any other methods?

- If it ordinarily costs you 2 percent to sell a job, is it worth that much of a commission to pay an agent? Or will you have to spend another 1 percent to close the job and negotiate the fee?

- If you are going to invest 10 percent of projected revenue to generate sales in a new market, is it reasonable to pay 5 percent to the agent who found and qualified the lead?

As a final comment on commissions, some firms work with outside agents who uncover and qualify leads, often introducing the firm's closer-doers to the prospective client with an imminent project. If you do work with these types of agents, put your commission agreement in writing and have your attorney review the agreement. Remember two things about these agreements:

- You don't want an implied contract based on some misunderstanding.

- You can expect something to go wrong, because it probably will, and you don't want to find yourself in a dogfight with your agent, your client, and your staff.

Other Incentives

If your firm employs sales representatives or lead marketers who bring in projects but do not get involved in projects once they're in the door, you may consider using commissions. However, we recommend that, instead, you offer these people an incentive compensation program of a basic salary plus a bonus based on performance. We also recommend that the total compensation package recognize the value of perquisites, e.g., a company car, professional memberships, attendance at conferences and seminars, a personal secretary. We say more on written job descriptions and compensation agreements in Chap. 9, "Internal Politics."

Bonuses can also be related to meeting performance objectives by others on your marketing team, for example:

- How many hot leads were generated against a target goal? How many of the leads turned into projects?

- What percentage of qualification statements made short lists? What percentage of proposals made presentations? What percentage of presentations made selections?

- Did your marketing manager meet or exceed his or her sales target? What percentage of sales were marketing costs?

In order to reward performance on the basis of targets, you must mutually agree to defined responsibilities. Furthermore, if you offer a bonus based on a performance formula, you must be able to deliver; otherwise, you will lose your sales staff.

From our experience, the best systems of compensation are those that reward people for work well done while underscoring the importance of the team effort. Incentive compensation does that and we offer some options for providing incentive compensation below:

- Develop a formula based on the analyses we presented under salary or commission. The bonus might be a certain percentage of sales for which an individual was responsible. You might also divide the bonus among all the responsible people. We are betting that engineers will love this formula and architects will shy away from it.

- Determine the worth of everyone on your marketing team and award each a bonus as a percentage of salary, depending on the firm's profits for the year. This approach allows you to reward those people who really work to help the firm get jobs. Although your star closer-doers may bring in handsome salaries, your secretaries and support staff probably do not. Here's your chance to acknowledge them for the late night proposal production and sprints to the Federal Express drop.

- Award one bonus to the closer-doer or marketing manager of a particular studio or division with the stipulation that they distribute the bonus among the team players who assisted in the sale. This method attempts to motivate support personnel to work hardest for the individuals they like most.

- Award bonuses at the whim of a managing principal. This method will depend totally on the phase of the moon on any given day.

We suggest that A/E firms consider awarding bonuses in the form of stock or ownership in the firm in lieu of cash. This method is particularly relevant to marketers because it is a benefit that fosters the concept of long-range planning and the development of relationships. This type of bonus system can be developed for marketers much as it is for technical professionals, thus helping to underscore the importance of marketing in relation to the technical interests of the firm. A more extensive discussion on incentive compensation and ownership in A/E firms can be found in Weld Coxe's *Managing Architectural and Engineering Practice* (see "Resources").

Suppose you have negotiated your salary or raise but have walked away with less than you wanted. It is time to reflect on why you do what you do for a living. We have learned that compensation is always related to success. True success depends on motivating others around you to individual achievements that lead to a common goal. As marketing people, we help define that common goal in our firms.

We must recognize what it takes to motivate ourselves as well as those around us whose support we need and that not everyone can receive the salary of a principal. We must also remember that overhead must be minimized so that profit can be maximized. If profit is maximized, presumably, it will be shared with those who caused it to happen, a custom in many architecture and engineering firms.

If you do not buy that, understand that different kinds of people respond to different kinds of rewards and motivation. Following are some of the common motivators found in business:

- Recognition
- Power

- Risk taking
- Teamwork
- Money
- Leisure time
- Enjoyment of tasks

It is your job to help combine the talents of the different people in your firm so that you can reach mutually defined, successful goals. Inevitably, meeting them will result in a combination of firm profit, growth, and individual rewards, including fun.

Now, read Chap. 9, "Internal Politics," for more on how to make this all happen.

INTRODUCTION

Other books, and some excellent ones, have been written on how to make marketing succeed or how to make your firm succeed through marketing. This book is about how to make marketers succeed in an environment that essentially sees marketing as a necessary evil. Of course, the marketer's success is linked directly to the success of the program and the success of the firm. But, what is very special about marketing in a professional service firm (as opposed to other service or product firms) is that almost always the marketing function is in no way integral to the practice itself. Marketing is "what we do to get work" or "when we run out of work"; it's "the other hat" and "what we do if we have to but we hate it." It is almost always misunderstood and mistaken for sales. And it is never the essence of the practice.

Generally not everyone in a firm will feel what we have just described, but many, indeed most of the senior professionals will, whether they admit it or not. If you are the marketer, dealing with this often subtle, sometimes overtly hostile attitude to your role can be depressing, debilitating and, at its worst, defeating. All of this book, and this chapter in particular, provide insight and techniques for handling the toughest marketing job—marketing in-house.

We began this book with an overview of the evolution of marketing in A/E firms and comments on how the concept of marketing and successful marketing techniques still represent change for the majority of firms. Now we conclude the book with some comments on how to be successful personally by using these changes to your advantage.

First of all, you need to consider very carefully what it takes for you to be successful. For some individuals it means transcending marketing to become the chief administrative, operations, or executive officer. For others it may be finding an opportunity to influence the quality of the built environment. For many it means earning a living in a stimulating job that demands multiple talents. For many marketers, success means recognition and acknowledgment in the form of at least partial ownership of the business.

If success to you means either senior management or ownership, you need to be in a firm with strong, market-driven growth goals and/or be prepared to buy your way in. If these are your goals but your firm is driven more by technology or design, you will probably not succeed in a marketing role. But, if your sights are set on mastering the marketing position, not necessarily becoming CEO or an owner, you can have a very satisfactory career in such a firm.

To help you win, no matter what your situation, this chapter gives you tools to assess the power structure of a firm, its political networks, its style, and whether or not you can be effective within these. We look at the following issues:

- Who is really in charge of the firm?
- Are there different points of view on how the firm is to be run?
- How does power flow within the firm?
- What is the management style of the firm?
- Do you really fit in?
- Can you succeed?

Now let's discuss selling in-house, otherwise known as politics.

Politics

What is politics? One definition says it is the art or science of influencing policy; another says it's the art of compromise.

You must understand internal politics to succeed in your firm. What you do to influence policy will generally be outside your job description. If you succeed in influencing policy—which is also a form of marketing yourself—inside your firm, you will have passed the best training course for marketing your firm to the outside world.

The person who specializes in marketing does something different from what the majority of people do in engineering and design firms. For example, much of marketing tends to be an intangible process as opposed to the more tangible products that architects and engineers work with daily. In addition, marketing expenses are overhead as opposed to being billable or "productive." Finally, marketers tend to be extroverted and therefore look and behave differently from the more introverted technical professionals. For all these reasons, marketers must work extra hard to develop a support base among their colleagues and to "sell" the value of what they do.

Where Do You Come From?

If you just started your job as a marketer for your firm, you probably come from one of the following three situations:

- You have been in the firm in an administrative position.
- You have been in the firm in a technical position (i.e., architect, engineer, or planner).
- You have worked in another firm in a similar marketing position.

In the first case you probably have an excellent understanding of the politics and power structure of the firm. You will have to overcome the stigma of having been a lower-echelon person if you are going to influence policy. You may have to combat the jealousy of your former peers. On the other hand, you can use these two obstacles to your advantage. You will want to pay particular attention to what we say later about informal networks.

In the second case your most difficult challenge may be avoiding project-related work in order to concentrate on marketing. Your technical colleagues may demand your attention for "just a couple of hours" to help bail out a project. This, too, is something you can turn around and use to your advantage. Pay particular attention to our discussion of the power structure later in this chapter.

In the last case you are the new kid on the block and you know very little about the politics of this firm. You will probably be respected as a marketing "professional," but you will be tested and tried in every way possible. Use this entire chapter as your checklist for success.

Regardless of your situation, start by clarifying expectations, establish the written rules, and then position yourself to expect the unexpected.

RULES OF THE GAME

If you forget everything else, remember one thing: success depends on showing results. Results can be either real or perceived. They can get measured as they are stated in your marketing plan and by both written and unwritten rules. But, which results, measured by whom, and how soon or often—these are the questions.

Written Rules

Here are some rules you should have agreed to in writing before you started your job. Your *job description* should be as detailed as necessary, yet as succinct as possible. It should:

- Cover a general area of responsibility

- Define not only the obvious, but also the vague activities that will be required of you

- Describe your tasks in priority sequence and by the approximate percentage of your time to be spent on them

- Be reviewed by all those who will be working with you

Above all, if you don't get a description, write it yourself; don't wait for someone to hand it to you.

Performance criteria for your job form the basis on which your results will be evaluated. They should be measurable, product or event oriented (not just based on style), and establish a review policy within a definite period of time.

The chain of command defines to whom you report and who reports to you. It is part of the "official" organization chart, which we will address in detail later.

Your *basis of compensation* includes the salary you will be paid, whether you are eligible for incentive compensation, bonuses, or commissions, and on what criteria that additional compensation will be awarded. This directive should also state when and how often your compensation will be reviewed.

Hours of employment may seem obvious. You come to work at 8 and leave at 5, right? Wrong. Not in marketing. Marketers work crazy hours. They spend weekends writing proposals, evenings entertaining clients, lunch hours over a quick sandwich with staff and/or consultants. Specify the following:

- Do you get compensatory time?

- Do you get overtime? On what basis will overtime be paid?

- What constitutes working hours? Is breakfast with a client, evenings at a trade association, or spending an afternoon working with a committee of a professional or civic organization an acceptable charge of time?

Negotiate your *perquisites* in advance. Do you have a budget for attending professional development seminars, conventions, and professional or civic organization meetings? Will your firm pay your dues for clubs and professional or civic organizations? Will you have a company car? If not, will you be compensated for the use of your personal automobile? At what rate? Will you receive parking privileges?

Now let's face it. These items were probably not made clear. We know no one who has obtained a thorough, written description and understanding of what his or her job is supposed to be in advance. Start by honing in on three items that are most important to you. Then get some kind of agreement to review your job, formally or informally, within a definite period of time—say, 3 or 6 months. Continue to push for that kind of review, periodically, until all the rules that structure your job and compensation are understood.

While most firms review technical and administrative staff only yearly (at best), we argue that because marketing is unlike any other role in the firm, it needs more frequent review, especially for a new position. In reviewing your job and performance, keep in mind that negotiating over too many specifics may give the impression that you are a narrow person interested primarily in details. Good marketers are also interested in the big picture. If you have been hired as a marketing coordinator, you may want to illustrate your ability to take care of every detail. On the other hand, if you have been hired as a marketing director, you want to illustrate your flexibility and negotiating talents. The marketing manager needs to show a little of each.

If you want growth opportunities, do not let a detailed agreement bog you down. Remember, a good job is based on mutual understanding. If you have to develop a 20-page contract to protect your interests, you will not have the kind of working relationship that will foster trust and mutual respect. If you feel you need this protection, you are in the wrong firm.

Unwritten Rules

Whenever a new person comes in to marketing, there are expectations that may not get articulated. If spoken, they would sound like, "Bring in the work." Marketing exists solely to improve the quality and/or volume of business. Even if you are not directly responsible for sales, you must be able to show that your work has helped meet the business development goals of the firm. Effective marketing should *reduce, not increase, the firm's overhead* in relation to income. In addition, the marketer should *help the firm become more profitable.* Eventually, if not right away, you will want to be able to show the profit potential of each new project you have worked on before the contract is signed.

Principals often have a number of subconscious reasons to bring people in to do a particular marketing job. They may do so in order to change their marketing approach, their staff, or their leadership. Be careful of the following scenarios:

- A principal is unable to close contracts, and, to cover that deficiency, a marketing person is asked to take on the responsibility without being given the authority.

- Two or more principals cannot agree on the firm's direction and they hire a marketer (read: mediator) to help them communicate. Each principal hopes the marketer will sway the others to his or her position.

- Principals reorganize to strengthen ineffective management. Here the line is "we recently changed our structure to take advantage of our strengths and move us into the next decade." That may be true, but it may also mean, "we changed our structure to avoid some issues we didn't want to talk about, and we're really in for some bloody fights ahead."

- There really is no central management and several studios operate as independent firms. Some market effectively but most don't.

- No one has authority and at least one principal is fed up with carrying more than his or her share of the load.

In any of these scenarios the firm hiring or promoting a new person in marketing is often looking for a magician who will solve all their impossible problems. We suggest that you help them confront the situation and work with them to solve the problems. You can't do it for them, but you can (sometimes) do it with them.

Marketer as Ombudsperson

Partly in response to the kinds of scenarios described above, and partly, we think, because marketers tend to be friendly and supportive individuals, as well as being organized and business-like, many firms use the marketer as the unofficial ombudsperson. In this role the person supports the firm's human resources and other organizational needs by providing an ear and often serving as a conduit for communication, particularly between technical staff and senior management, as well as between managers themselves.

This person may, through this unofficial capacity, influence changes in policy and implementation. Most often the marketer filling this role institutes staff meetings and other sanctioned forums for more open exchange of ideas and concerns, brings about an enlightened (frequent and objective) employee evaluation program, and may even be influential in generating ownership transition plans and hiring consultants needed to undertake these changes with a minimum of risk.

We think you will be successful if you can:

- Have lines of communication with all the principals
- Prove your ability to maintain confidentiality
- Illustrate your dependability in your work
- Show no favoritism
- Take the initiative to help those who need your help

Breaking the Rules

Sometimes, in order to get things done, and done quickly enough for the results to matter, as in producing a proposal, we have had to step on some toes or at least go around people who, if involved or involved fully, would cause costly, even ruinous delays. (We sometimes call this pragmatic approach "guerrilla marketing.") But, when breaking the rules, be careful. There is really only one you should never break: Don't challenge a strong principal. Some people must be sold, not told.

You may step on the toes of less powerful principals, but do not make a mistake in your analysis of who is a powerful principal. You may not be given a chance to make that mistake twice. And remember, it serves no purpose to attack anybody. Use tact, good judgment, and courtesy if, in order to get things done, you have to work around the weaknesses of others.

THE POWER STRUCTURE

Being a good leader, or even a successful follower, means you need to know the structure of your organization. In Chap. 1, "Evolution and Structure," we mentioned various organizational structures for accomplishing the marketing effort. Try the following exercise to determine who is running your firm and in charge of the marketing effort. In many A/E firms it is not the CEO or managing principal who really runs the firm, and it is not the marketing director who is in charge of the marketing effort.

Who Is in Charge?

To determine who's in charge, draw the official organization chart of the firm. If your firm does not have an official chart—many do not—draw one based on assigned titles and your knowledge of the chain of command and recognized lines of authority. Take your organization chart and mark all the informal lines of communication. Place an asterisk next to all those who need little or no advice to make decisions. Be careful. Sometimes decision makers seek advice to obtain consensus, not to obtain authority or permission; they will make their decisions, regardless.

The person with an asterisk highest on the chart and with the most informal lines reporting to him or her is definitely in charge. Analyze your chart in a similar manner to determine who is in charge of marketing decisions.

There are a couple of other things you need to know about the power structure besides who's in charge. These relate to understanding the management hierarchy and the responsibilities of those who control the firm.

- Where does the marketing decision maker fit in this hierarchy?
- Where do those responsible for design, production, finance, and administration fit?
- Who owns the firm? Is the majority of the ownership held by a few senior partners or key stockholders?
- Who are the "yes" people? To whom do they owe their allegiance? Why?

After you have studied the power structure of the firm, draw the structure of your marketing organization. If it agrees with the "official" marketing organization, you are in good shape. You have common ground and a mutual sense of purpose. If your chart does not agree, you've got problems. Now is the time either to get out or to decide that you will need plenty of patience and time to sell others in your organization on the merits of effective marketing.

Who Is Your Boss?

Assuming you are not the managing principal and therefore you are not your own boss, your boss is your most important ally. He or she must pick you up when you're down and stand up for your success when you've been having nothing but failures. You must do the same for your boss. The person you work for must understand marketing, not just sales, and support the need to spend more on marketing when business is down and the pressure to reduce overhead is up. Make it easy for your boss to support you. For example, don't disagree in public, complete your tasks when and how they are supposed to be done, get credit from others for your successes, and share that credit with your boss. Take the time to stroke his or her ego.

If there are many levels between you and the leadership of your firm, how well you succeed may depend on the relationship your boss has with the person in charge. Here are some indicators to help you determine whether you can succeed in this firm and whether you will have to develop your own power base to do so.

- Is your boss well liked?
- Are his or her ideas well received by the firm's directors?
- What will be your boss's next position in the firm?

You say you don't report to a single boss. You report to two or more people or maybe even a committee. Go back to your power chart. Of all the people you report to, who has the most informal lines of communication drawn to him or her, and who has an asterisk highest on the list? That's who you really report to. Treat that person as your boss. Above all, help that person build a coalition that will enable him or her to be decisive and in charge.

Your Own Power Base

Your own power depends on three things:

- Your access to the person in charge
- Your powers of persuasion
- Your ability to assemble political networks

Let's look at two situations, either of which may apply to you. In the first case your boss is the person in charge. As long as this person is satisfied with your actions *and* business is good, you are in great shape. Locate your office or work station near that of your boss. Stay in very close contact with this person, talking over your progress daily or at least two or three times a week. Even if this person travels a lot, stay in touch. If he or she is a memo-reader, keep 'em coming; if this person is always on the phone or tied up with projects, make frequent lunch or breakfast meetings. You must keep talking to each other!

If you can do it without threatening your boss, start drawing lines of informal communication to you. You need not be the decision maker, just the funnel for communication. Because "knowledge is power," this arrangement will give you the power you need to improve your position. Remember, if you accept the responsibility to make decisions, you must receive corresponding authority and should concurrently receive appropriate compensation.

In the second case your boss is not the person in charge. Look at your power chart and determine how your boss's reports chain to the person in charge. All the people in this reporting chain are important to you. You must recognize that they all have needs and all are trying to please the person in charge. In a sense, they are your most important clients. Give them a benefit such as information—about clients, your competition, or available talent, for example—so that they can use it to benefit someone else. We call this our "little fish" theory. In the sea, little fish get eaten by big fish, which in turn get eaten by bigger fish, which, of course, get eaten by great big fish. Maybe you have heard of the geotechnical engineer who has the structural engineer as a client who has the architect as a client who has the developer as a client who has the banker as a client. We like to be in the position of the geotechnical engineer who has the banker as a cousin; it has a way of making things happen. What this means to you is that you must take care of this network. The lines of communication run both ways, and you need to take care of the little fish who report to the big fish, as well as taking care of the big fish. The "little fish" theory applies inside the firm as well as outside the firm and information dispensing is a way of feeding the fish.

Who Does What to Whom

We have developed the charts in Fig. 9.1 to help you analyze all the essential marketing tasks in terms of who does what, how much time he or she spends doing it, and how well the job is being done.

Although it may appear that we are addressing only large firms, the small architectural or engineering practice with two partners may be just as complicated. For example, there may be a managing principal relying on the other principal for marketing, who, in turn, counts on some hotshot project architect, who leans on the marketing coordinator, who technically reports to the managing principal, and in turn, "dumps" on an assistant. Sound confusing? Nobody said marketing was easy.

Regardless of the size or complexity of your firm, you develop personal power based on your charisma and your ability to persuade others. Good marketers have tremendous personal power because they can articulate the needs of clients as well as the abilities of technical professionals. Have you ever wondered why:

- The best marketer in the firm usually turns out to be the one in charge.

- Whoever gets the work runs the firm.

- You can't be successful selling on the outside if you're not first successful in convincing those on the inside of your value.

- If you can't sell yourself, you can't sell your firm.

Okay, so you have some personal powers of persuasion. (If you don't feel comfortable with that, you had better consider some other career or resign yourself to the fact that your career in marketing will most likely remain administrative in nature.) And you recognize that, if you don't have direct ac-

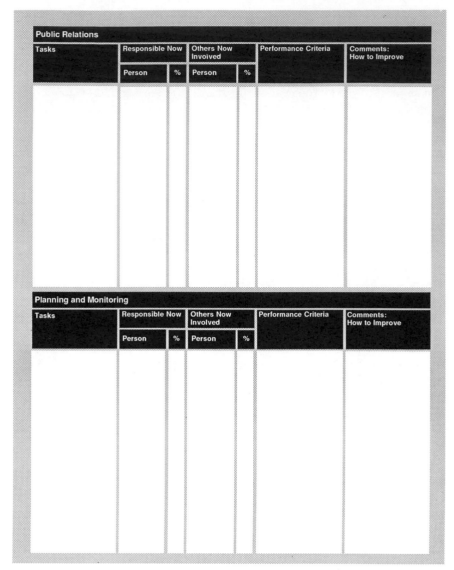

Public Relations						
Tasks	Responsible Now		Others Now Involved		Performance Criteria	Comments: How to Improve
	Person	%	Person	%		

Planning and Monitoring						
Tasks	Responsible Now		Others Now Involved		Performance Criteria	Comments: How to Improve
	Person	%	Person	%		

Figure 9.1   Marketing staffing and performance analysis.

cess to the person in charge, you do have a path of communication to him or her; and if you don't have a clear path, you at least understand the path to the person in charge. (You've got to figure how to get there sooner or later.)

Your next step is to assemble your own political network. Your power comes from above but it also depends on your ability to draw from below. You must be in a position to produce results. Your results may depend on the following:

- The timely support of those who provide typing, graphics, and printing
- A steady supply of accurate information
- Having your product (i.e., proposal, brochure, newsletter) be "on time" and "within budget"

The term "team building" applies here and is not just a cliché. In many marketing jobs a team is the most important product you have to deliver. Whether it means motivating engineers to rehearse for a presentation or getting designers to call former clients or, as is most often the case, cajole the word processor into working overtime, you spend much of your time building a team to support your marketing efforts (but team building won't show up on your job description). Sound familiar? Now you begin to understand why we say internal marketing jobs make good training grounds for those who will eventually do external marketing.

Wow, it's great to be on this team . . . I think.

In one case where a new marketer in a design firm could not get a word processing support person to produce adequate quality documents on time, she finally complained often enough to the person's supervisor and he was fired. In his exit interview the word processor complained that the marketer had failed to provide good directions and motivation. The marketer's boss sat down with her to talk about it. "You hired me to produce a lot of material on tight schedules and he was making my job impossible," she explained. Her boss, realizing he had allowed a basic misperception to occur, pointed out that her real job was as a leader and "team builder" to expedite the marketing effort, not just a producer of documents. They discussed ways she could have handled the situation differently in light of this distinction, which should, of course, have been part of her job description and performance criteria from the start.

The Regional versus the Corporate Game

If your firm has multiple offices, a new cast of characters enters the political game. You may be either in a regional, branch, or division office or in a corporate or headquarters office.

If you are in a regional office, you must deal not only with the power structure of the regional office but also with the power structure of the corporate office and how the regional players relate to those in corporate. Often you will have two bosses, for example, your regional director and your corporate marketing director. Regardless of what the organization chart says, you need to understand to whom you really report and who calls the shots.

If you are in the corporate office, you may think you are isolated from the politics of the regional offices. Not so. If you have any kind of responsibility to increase business firm-wide, you must gain the support of your regional managers and their marketing people. Remember three things here:

- Teamwork works.

- Regional managers are probably higher on the power chart than are corporate staff members.

- Regional managers are almost always closer to real markets and real clients than are the corporate paper pushers.

Regardless of which office you are in, you have the problem of the multiheaded "client," in this case your own firm. Be very careful in analyzing the relationships in your power chart, and be sensitive not to offend the important people.

In the regional versus corporate game two scenarios appear frequently:

- The regional marketing team accuses the corporate marketing team of not being sensitive to regional issues; it doesn't :
  - Provide an adequate budget
  - Provide marketing tools that apply to regional conditions
  - Provide corporate people to support regional sales
- The corporate marketing people, on the other hand, accuse the regional marketing team of wasting money. Especially, they:
  - Spend too much time planning and talking about what they should do and not enough time selling
  - Use corporate graphics improperly and, in some cases, not at all
  - Ignore the market research provided by corporate staff
  - Disregard the corporate marketing plan

Both teams are often right in their accusations. It is your job not to be more right but to be more effective in showing—you guessed it—results.

The regional versus corporate game is an obstacle that must be overcome. As with all political obstacles, the game can be turned to your advantage if you use your informal networks properly. It is just a little more complicated than the single office firm; but, then again, the potential for compensation and other rewards is often greater.

INFORMAL NETWORKS

You derive power from informal networks. Remember that the power chart is often different from the organizational chart. Informal networks direct the flow of power. They generally fall into two categories, communication and operational networks.

Communication Networks

You get the information on which to base your power from the communication network inside the firm. The kind you can get informally includes:

- Who's in charge?
- Who owns the most stock?
- Who are the "yes men or women"?
- Who are the weak principals?
- What are the firm's weak points?
- Who doesn't talk to whom?
- Who is the next person to be "canned"?
- Where are the firm's skeletons hidden?

These are generally negative questions, the kind that none of the bosses wants to answer. Generally there are three good sources for this information:

- Support staff
- Insecure executives
- Old-timers

Secretaries and other administrators are close to the people in power. They often handle or have access to confidential information. Although it is improper to ask an administrator to violate confidentially, it is not difficult to pose questions or to gain trust so as to have this person volunteer information. This can be done in many places: in the restroom, over lunch or a drink, playing golf or racquetball, sailing, etc.

Insecure executives may be a misnomer. Actually, what we mean is those executives who hold some title or own stock in the firm but who are really never going to make it to the top, and they know it. They get a sense of power from leaking information such as which principal had too much to drink at the partners' meeting and why the managing principal refuses to sell his or her share of the business and why the marketing principal is a jerk and other little bits and pieces that help you piece the power puzzle together.

Old-timers are the folks who were around when the firm comprised only 5 or 10 people and, now that the firm is 30 or 200 people, have seen all those who failed or succeeded. They have begun to put together the puzzle themselves. And what is better, because they have been around so long, they are generally trusted by the principals, who have been around as long as they have. An old timer may be the "office mother" or the "chief draftsman" in the back room. Neither will ever make it into the inner power circle. But they get satisfaction from having information and helping those they like and hurting those they dislike. They have been around long enough to know that "one hand washes the other," and that is how they get their power.

Operational Networks

The operational network consists of the people you count on to get things done. This is the crux of team building. You need to "stroke" people ahead of the time you need them to save the day for you, e.g., to stay at the office all night to complete a proposal. In a good relationship they will give up their lunch hour and work overtime for you. They may even "bump" their other assignments to give you first priority. When they do all that for you, don't forget to repay the favors. They collect chips, too. Mortgage your life to these people; you can't succeed without them. Above all, treat them with respect and courtesy.

If you are a marketer who has risen through the clerical ranks or a younger woman in a firm of older men, you may find yourself stereotyped and treated condescendingly. This situation may make it hard for you not to treat those who support you with the same attitude, especially when these same support persons challenge your authority and question your capability. Your success depends on selling teamwork to them, day in and day out.

Who are these people? You probably already recognize them. Generally they fall into three categories:

- Support services
- Operating managers
- The accounting department

Support services account for the following activities:
Word processing
Graphics
Production
Mailing

In the small firm all these things are probably accomplished by one person, you or your marketing assistant. If it is you, you had better be collecting chips for all those lunch hours, nights, and weekends you are giving up. We suggest you cash the chips in for support by either borrowing other staff members to help you when you need it or hiring outside subcontractors who can do any or all of those things. But, most of all, you must learn to ask for help when you need it, and manage that help effectively.

In a large firm you may have entire departments to deal with each service. In this case you must not only "stroke" the department manager but you must be on the good side of a majority of employees of each department. If they decide they don't like you, they'll "sandbag" you, and it won't matter what their department manager says. These relationships, of course, are a problem of scale which only you can put in perspective for your size firm.

Remember, too, that even in a small firm you must know how to short-circuit the system. You need to know some guerrilla tactics, for two reasons:

- First, there are times when the existing staff is so overworked that they cannot accomplish your proposal or qualifications statement in the time needed, and you have no alternative but to get it done some other way.

- Second, if you illustrate to your support staff that you can accomplish their job in some other way, they will recognize your power and their dispensability. This awareness will assist in creating a more cooperative working environment for future jobs.

Operating managers are the ones who control people and projects. They may be project managers or department heads. They can authorize technical staff to assist you in writing proposals. They are best able to get the information you need right away for ongoing or past projects, e.g., the scope-of-services statement, construction cost, completion date, unique aspects of the project, or client name and address.

Operating managers are also the people who tell you how to schedule and estimate the cost of a project. If they help you, you have an obligation to help them obtain the fees and schedules that will make it easy for them to look good by accomplishing the project successfully and making a profit.

The accounting department may, in a small firm, be a part-time book-keeper. Whereas the operating managers give you data on projects in progress, the accounting department is usually the resource for data on past projects, i.e., what was the original scope and fee; how much did it actually cost to do the project; and, the bottom line, what was the profit? In many firms the bookkeeper/accounting department keeps all the summary data on past projects. If your firm operates this way, ask these people if you can add information to their system.

You need the accounting department for one other very important resource—your own personal expense account. Marketing people tend to run up expense accounts, and your relationship with the person who writes the checks may well determine how quickly you will be reimbursed.

We have noted how you need the accounting department. But, what can you do for them? This, too, depends on the size of your firm and on your resourcefulness. It may be that you can share in their overhead expenses; you may be able to support them in data processing and filing, or you may have nothing to give but your own personal friendship and support. In any case, you cannot afford not to have them as allies. They'll kill you if they don't like you, particularly when it comes to reporting overhead.

MANAGEMENT STYLES

The Firm's Personality

Earlier we discussed the person in charge whose personality creates the "culture" of the firm. There is a serious side and a light side to the management style of a firm. (In marketing you've got to have a light side to everything.)

On the serious side, A/E firms have one of four basic management styles. That is, firms are basically oriented toward one of the following:

- Design or technical solutions
- Production
- Marketing
- Bottom-line

Note that these styles parallel what many call the four functions of management in an A/E firm: design, production, marketing, and finance/administration. As an aside, note that these four functions are really no different from the three traditional divisions of any business:

- Marketing
- Operations (A/E's lump both design and production into this category)
- Finance

Recently, large businesses have begun to separate a new division from finance/administration, which they call human resources (personnel). Most of the larger planning and design firms are paying more attention to human resources now than in the past for a rather obvious reason—people provide the firm's services to clients. It has been said that the next wave of enlightenment for design firms will be that of human resources development. Was marketing a wave of enlightenment?

Let's go back to the person-in-charge. You need to determine the following:

- What is that individual's personal style?
- Where does your firm place its management emphasis?
- Are the two the same?
- If your firm has many principals, which principal is in charge of which management function?

Now go back to your power chart. Place the principals in order of their position on it. (When it comes to power, remember there is no such thing as equal principals. Everything else may be equal, but one always has some advantage in power over the other, often the ability to communicate effectively.) If you should understand where your firm places its emphasis, you know where to place your priorities when conflicts over certain types of projects arise. You need this kind of analysis to determine whether or not you have a valid marketing plan and to tell if your principals are putting up smoke screens with regard to the goals, issues, and directions of the firm.

Sometimes a regional office will differ in management style from its corporate "parent." Several things may happen in this situation:

- The head of the regional office may be replaced by someone more compatible with corporate management.

- The office may close.

- The office may spin off from the firm and become an independent entity.

- The regional management may work out ad hoc compromises over every issue and continue to function; this is most likely to happen as long as the regional office remains profitable.

On the lighter side, take a look at the personality profile of the person in charge:

- How does that individual get along with people?

- What kind of clothes does he or she wear?

- Aside from business, what does that person talk about?

- Does the person in charge like to work with the staff?

- Is he or she a participatory manager?

- Does that individual like to meet with clients?

- Is he or she good at delegating responsibility?

Now take a further look at the other principals (or owners or stockholders) of the firm:

- Do they have the same traits as the person in charge?

- Do they complement that individual? Or do they conflict?

If the principals have similar traits, the firm is probably a happy one with a singleness of purpose; it will succeed on the merits of the person in charge. If the principals have seriously conflicting personality traits, pay particular attention to whether or not those conflicts are indicative of the firm's disorganization.

Remember, successful partnerships are like good marriages. The principals must be happy together. They must have some things in common. They must complement each other's strengths and weaknesses. Working together in a firm requires hard work, long hours together, and results in demands being made of each other. You had better accept the way the principals part their hair and wear their ties if your firm is to succeed. Singleness in purpose is a key to success.

How Do You Fit?

Every individual has his or her own style. You need to analyze your own personality traits to find out how you fit into the firm's personality. Ask yourself the following:

- How important is the bottom line to you? Compared to them?

- What are your priorities on design, production, marketing, and the bottom line? Are your priorities the same as those of the principals?

- What color shirts do you wear? How do you style your hair? Is it the same as those in charge?

- Do you enjoy the same sports as those in charge?

- Do you generally have the same political views as they do?

If you are compatible with the owners of your firm, you have great potential for succeeding where you are. If you are not, analyze why not in each category before you pack your bags and start looking for a new job. Maybe you complement those in charge. And, if they believe it and you like working together, you are on your way to a successful partnership.

Remember, in Chap. 3, "Direct Marketing," we discussed that in courting a client it is necessary to match the people in your firm to your client. We also discussed earlier that marketing inside the firm is the training ground for marketing the firm on the outside. You have to learn to size up and match people. Start with yourself, and continue to analyze, mold, and shape until you find a proper fit.

YOUR PERSONAL PLAN

Looking Ahead

Well, you've finally figured yourself out. You have been on the job as marketing coordinator or marketing director for a while. Now what do you want to do?

Maybe you don't want to do anything different. You like your job and you like the people you work for. In this case, if you are reasonably successful, the only thing you need to do is obtain more compensation to keep up and, we hope, stay ahead of inflation.

You always have the opportunity, if you are unhappy, to leave the firm. You may need to do this if you want to advance and there is no path in your existing firm. Before you change firms, however, remember that the grass is almost never greener on the other side. Most A/E firms have similar problems. SMPS came into being to help solve problems commonly found among marketers in the planning and design business. Remember that the A/E profession is a small world. There is a limit to how many times you can change firms because you had a "basic disagreement in philosophy with the principals."

Before you change jobs, we suggest that you create a need and fill it within your own firm. (Here we go again—internal marketing provides a training ground for external marketers.) Find your path by creating the circumstances that will allow you to move into a better position. Of course, you must first decide which position you want next.

Once you decide which position you want, you may realize that there is a small problem: it is occupied by an individual who is doing a perfectly competent job. What should you do? Find that person a new job. (No, not in a different firm; in your firm.) Create an alliance with, let's say, your boss to find an opportunity in which he or she can grow and be even more successful.

Actually, it is not all that easy. Before you move out of your job, you must find someone to replace you in your current job. You want to be ready when you hear your boss say, "I'd love to have you take over my marketing director's job, but who is going to do all that work that you do as marketing manager?" Nobody said marketing is easy. (But it can be fun.) Not only do you have to do your boss's job, you have to do your job, and your assistant's job as well. You must take the initiative yourself; you cannot expect anybody else to do it for you.

Being Successful

Earlier in this chapter we discussed building a power base and creating a position for yourself on the power chart. We discussed how important it is to have a support staff that you can count on. In building your power base, you might remember a couple of key points.

You need supporters, at all levels in the firm. People will support you only when they understand the benefit to themselves in doing so. They will not go out of their way to find this benefit; you must make it easy for them to see a benefit, help them get this idea and "own" it. Benefits can range from getting a raise or bonus to getting recognition in print for an excellent project or just getting an exciting project to work on.

If you are going to be successful in marketing, you must show results. In marketing that means that your work must result in "bringing in the work." Don't ever lose sight of that goal.

Pitfalls

Let's assume you are being successful. You have created a path to your next position. All of a sudden the bottom starts to fall out from under you. There are at least three pitfalls that will kill you in your firm.

- **Making enemies** Somewhere along the line, you stepped on someone's toes, perhaps by being too aggressive. They perceived you as malicious. Years later the person remembers and has built a coalition to defeat your promotion or a pet project. It may not be too late to patch things up (by finding a benefit for others in the coalition to support you) but it may cost you enormous time and energy to do so.
- **Losing money** You lose money by causing the overhead to be too high or being affiliated with a project that loses money. Cover yourself. Know when this situation is happening and what can be done to change it quickly.
- **Being different** You insist on wearing a different color shirt or having different political views than your boss does. You can't win. If the boss owns the firm and he or she doesn't like your face, it's his or her prerogative to refuse to promote you. All you can do is know about the conflict well in advance and understand your options.

SUMMARY

You will be successful if:

- You know your own goals.
- You know your firm's goals.
- You know the powerful players of your firm.
- You know your compatibility with the firm and potential areas of conflict.
- You have a personal plan to expect the unexpected.
- You work hard and as a team player.

- You are realistic and do not get discouraged.

- You show results.

It's okay to make mistakes—not often, not too big. Remember what Machiavelli said about starting a new venture. Marketing is always a new venture, involving change, even for the very experienced.

ORGANIZATIONS AND PUBLISHERS

The following organizations publish materials on marketing for A/E firms and will send lists for mail order selection:

American Consulting Engineers Council (ACEC), 1015 15th Street, NW, Suite 802, Washington, DC 20005 202/347-7474. Publications include:

The Brochure on Brochures, 1983.

Public Relations Guide for Consulting Engineers, 1982.

Industrial Market for Consulting Engineers, 1983. American Institute of Architects (AIA), 1735 New York Avenue, NW, Washington, DC 20006 202/626-7357.

Publications include:

Architects' Handbook of Professional Practice, Chapter B-8, "Marketing Architectural Services," and B-9, "The Architect's Communications," 1986. Society for Marketing Professional Services, 801 North Fairfax Street, Suite 215, Alexandria, VA 22314 703/549-6117.

Publications include:

Marketing Information Reports.

Senior Roundtables.

Annual Marketing Salary and Expense Survey.

Practice Management Associates, 10 Midland Avenue, Newton, MA 02158 617/965-0055.

Publications include:

The A/E Marketing Book of Forms, by Carol McConochie, 1986.

The Design and Building Industry's Publicity Directory, by Steve Kliment, October 1986.

A/E MARKETING BOOKS AND MANUALS

The following publications are recommended for *every* A/E marketer's bookshelf; they focus on our special profession.

Burden, Ernest, AIA, *Design Communication: Developing Promotional Material for Design Professionals.* New York: McGraw-Hill, 1987.

———*Design Presentation: Techniques for Marketing and Project Proposals.* New York: McGraw-Hill, 1984.

Coxe, Weld, *Marketing Architectural and Engineering Services.* New York: Van Nostrand Reinhold, 1983 (2d ed.).

———*Managing Architectural and Engineering Practice.* New York: John Wiley & Sons, 1980.

Friedman, Warren, *Construction Marketing and Strategic Planning.* New York: McGraw-Hill, 1984.

Gerwick, Ben C., Jr., and Woolery, John C., *Construction and Engineering Marketing for Major Project Services.* New York: John Wiley & Sons, 1983.

Jones, Gerre, *How to Market Professional Design Services.* New York: McGraw-Hill, 1983 (2d ed.).

———*Public Relations for the Design Professional.* New York: McGraw-Hill, 1980.

Kliment, Stephen A., *Creative Communications for a Successful Design Practice.* New York: Whitney Library of Design, 1977.

Stitt, Fred A., (ed.), *Design Office Management Handbook.* Santa Monica, CA: Arts & Architecture Press, 1986.

Thomsen, Charles B., *CM: Developing, Marketing and Delivering Construction Management Services.* New York: McGraw-Hill, 1982.

Travers, David, *Preparing Design Office Brochures: A Handbook.* Santa Monica, CA: Arts and Architecture Press, 1982.

A/E MARKETING PERIODICALS

A/E Marketing Journal, 10 Midland Avenue, Newton, MA 02158; $119/yr, monthly.

The Guidelines Letter, P.O. Box 456, Orinda, CA 94563; $56/year, monthly.

Professional Marketing Report, Gerre Jones Associates, Inc., P.O. Box 14302, Albuquerque, NM 87191; $90/year, monthly.

SMPSnews, SMPS, 801 North Fairfax Street, #215, Alexandria, VA 22314; free to members only, monthly.

SEMINARS/WORKSHOPS/CONFERENCES

The following organizations sponsor programs specifically for A/E marketers. Check with them for topics, dates, locations, and fees.

ACEC—202/347-7474

AIA—202/626-7357

SMPS—703/549-6117; national convention is in September

The Coxe Group—215/561-2020

Practice Management Associates—61/-965-0055

University of Wisconsin, Madison—608/263-3372

DIRECTORIES

Archimedia, *Profile—Official Directory of the AIA* Topeka, KS, 1989, 913/267-5433.

ACEC, *ACEC Directory,* Washington, DC, 202/347-7474.

Bellsouth National Publishers, *NSPE, Professional Engineering Directory,* Atlanta, GA, 800/222-1207.

OTHER BOOKS ON MARKETING

Of the hundreds available, the following books not specific to the A/E market have been useful to A/E marketers.

Albrecht, Karl, and Zemke, Ron, *Service America! Doing Business in the New Economy.* Homewood, IL: Dow Jones-Irwin, 1985.

Connor, Richard A., Jr., and Davidson, Jeffrey P., *Marketing Your Consulting and Professional Services.* New York: John Wiley & Sons, 1987.

————*Getting New Clients.* New York: John Wiley & Sons, 1987.

Holtz, Herman, and Schmidt, Terry, *The Winning Proposal.* New York: McGraw-Hill, 1981.

Kotler, Philip, and Bloom, Paul N., *Marketing Professional Services.* Englewood Cliffs, NJ: Prentice-Hall, 1984.

Levitt, Theodore, *The Marketing Imagination.* New York: The Free Press, 1983.

Loring, Roy J., and Kerzner, Harold, *Proposal Preparation and Management Handbook.* New York: Van Nostrand Reinhold, 1982.

Lovelock, Christopher H., *Services Marketing.* Englewood Cliffs, NJ: Prentice-Hall, 1984.

Ogilvy, David, *Ogilvy on Advertising.* New York: Vintage Books, 1985.

Pace, Patricia Ewing, and Culbertson, Jo, (comp.), *Successful Public Relations for the Professions.* Edwardsville, KS: Professional Publishing, 1982.

Ries, Al, and Trout, Jack, *Positioning: The Battle for Your Mind.* New York: Warner Books, 1981.

Wilson, Aubrey, *The Marketing of Professional Services.* London: McGraw-Hill Book Company, Ltd., 1972.

BACKGROUND ON A/E PROFESSIONS

For the new marketer with no technical background, these offer some insight into our professions. For architecture (in addition to the current design press):

Blau, Judith R., *Architects and Firms: A Sociological Perspective on Architectural Practice.* Cambridge, MA: MIT Press, 1984.

Gutman, Robert, *Architectural Practice: A Critical View.* Princeton, NJ: Princeton Architectural Press, 1988.

Kostof, Spiro (ed.), *The Architect: Chapters in the History of the Profession.* New York: Oxford University Press, 1977.

Lewis, Roger K., *Architect? A Candid Guide to the Profession.* Cambridge, MA: MIT Press, 1987.

Saint, Andrew, *The Image of the Architect.* New Haven, CT: Yale University Press, 1983.

For engineering (again, the current periodicals, especially *Consulting Engineer* and *ENR,* offer the best all-round background):

Stanley, C. Maxwell, *The Consulting Engineer.* New York: John Wiley & Sons, 1982 (2d ed.).

AUDIO AND AUDIO-VIDEO TAPES

ACEC Marketing Series of audio tapes (contact ACEC). Professional Development Resources, Inc., 1000 Connecticut Avenue NW, Suite 9, Washington, DC 20036.

PSMJ video tapes on presentations, video and sales techniques (contact PSMJ, c/o Practice Management Associates).

AIA and SMPS also have audio tapes of major seminars and convention speeches available. Contact their national headquarters for current lists of tapes.

INDEX

ABOUT THE AUTHORS

Margaret Spaulding heads her own consulting firm, MS Associates, specializing in marketing architectural and engineering services. She is coauthor of *The A/E Marketing Handbook*.

William J. D'Elia is marketing director of CBT/Childs, Bertram, Tseckares, & Casendino, Inc. He is also coauthor of *The A/E Marketing Handbook*.

MORE STORIES TO SOLVE

FIFTEEN FOLKTALES FROM AROUND THE WORLD

TOLD BY

GEORGE SHANNON

ILLUSTRATED BY

PETER SIS

GREENWILLOW BOOKS
NEW YORK

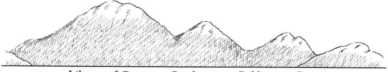

Library of Congress Cataloging-in-Publication Data

Shannon, George.
More stories to solve:
fifteen folktales from around the world/
told by George Shannon: pictures by Peter Sis.
p.   cm.
Summary: Fifteen brief folktales
in which there is a mystery or problem
that the reader is invited to solve
before the resolution is presented.
ISBN 0-688-09161-X
1. Tales [1. Folklore.
2. Literary re-creations.]
I. Sis, Peter, ill. II. Title.
PZ8.1.S49Mo 1990
398.2—dc20 [E] 89-7413   CIP   AC

TO ALL WHO SMILED
AND ASKED FOR MORE

CONTENTS

INTRODUCTION

Stories and mysteries have existed for as long as there have been people to tell them. And for just as long, there have been heroes who succeed through their ability to solve puzzles. These characters, who often have no rights, no power, no money, and no physical strength, are able to solve their dilemmas by finding fresh ways of looking at a situation. If they cannot see the solutions themselves, they are wise enough to accept advice from those who can. Like these quiet heroes, the reader can solve the following stories by careful listening or reading and by exploring different approaches to finding the answers.

1.

THE SNOWMAN

*O*nce, when it began to snow, three brothers decided they would make the biggest snowman their village had ever seen. All three rolled their snowballs bigger and bigger, and bigger still. When each ball got too big for one to push, two pushed, then all three together. When they couldn't move the biggest of the three balls anymore, they stopped.

The brothers tried to lift and stack the second ball on top of the first, but they could not. They had done such a good job of making them big that they were too heavy to lift. They were beginning to scrape the snowballs down to make them smaller when their grandfather came home.

"Aren't you doing that backward?" he asked.

When they explained their problem, their grandfather said, "You don't need less. You need more." And he told them what to do.

By the time their supper was ready, the boys had finished making the biggest snowman their village had ever seen. It was as tall as all three boys sitting on one another's shoulders. How could they have done this?

HOW IT WAS DONE

The "more" their grandfather told them about was to pack a ramp of snow against the biggest ball of snow. Their second snowball was too heavy to lift, but not too heavy to roll uphill. After building the snow ramp higher and rolling up the third snowball, they simply dug away the ramp and left their snowman standing.

2.
THE NEW PRINCE

King Leopard needed an heir to take his place when he died, but he had no sons. It was decided that a contest would be held and the winner would become prince.

"This spear will be the test," announced King Leopard. "Whoever can throw it up in the air while dancing and count to ten before catching it will be named my son and prince."

Of course, all the animals were eager to try. It seemed an easy test. Elephant insisted on being first. His dance was clumsy, and he had counted only to four when the spear fell to the ground. Ox was next. His dance was somewhat better, and he threw the spear a little higher; but it still hit the ground before he'd counted to five. Ape was next, and others followed. None of them could count to ten before the spear hit the ground beside them.

12

When the little deer said he wanted to try, everyone laughed.

"Rules are rules," said the king. "Everyone here may have his chance."

The little deer picked up the spear and danced a lovely light-footed dance. As he danced, he threw up the spear and easily counted to ten before catching it again. That very day he was crowned prince. How did the little deer succeed when the larger, stronger animals had failed?

13

HOW IT WAS DONE

He counted to ten by fives (five, ten).
The king hadn't said *how* they were to count to ten.

14

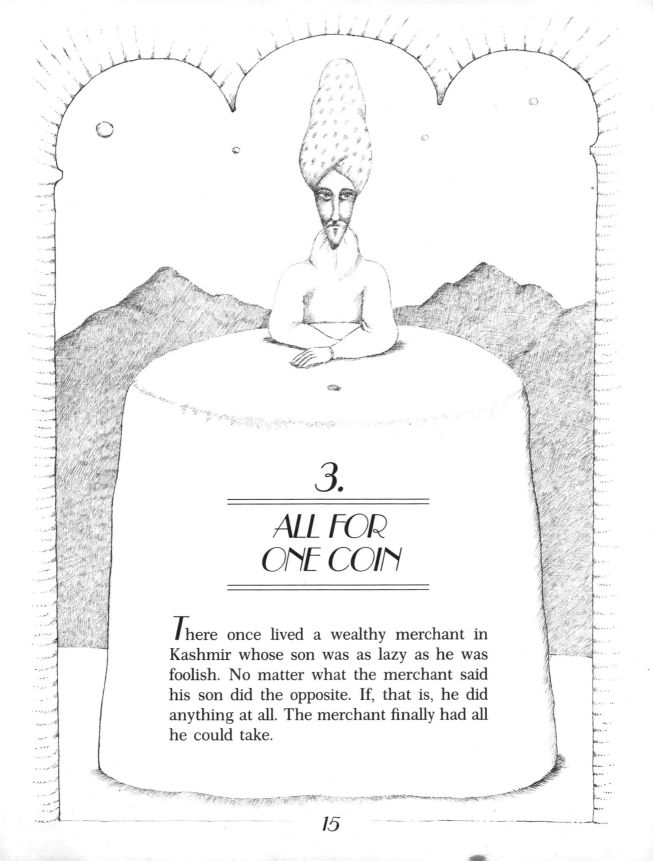

3.

ALL FOR
ONE COIN

*T*here once lived a wealthy merchant in Kashmir whose son was as lazy as he was foolish. No matter what the merchant said his son did the opposite. If, that is, he did anything at all. The merchant finally had all he could take.

"I want you to go to the marketplace," he told his son, "and buy something for us to eat, something for us to drink, something for the cow to eat, and something for us to plant in the garden. *And* you may spend only this one small coin. If you can do it, come back home. If you can't, don't come home."

As the boy walked toward the marketplace, he began to cry. He could not think of any way to buy all those things with the coin his father had given him. He'd never be able to go home. He was crying

so loudly a girl working in the field heard him and asked what was wrong. When he told her about his father's orders and all he had to buy with one small coin, the girl shook her head and told him not to worry. She said he could easily do what his father wanted and told him how.

That night the boy went home with a smile on his face as well as something to eat, something to drink, something to feed the cow, and something to plant in the garden. His father was very surprised *and* very impressed. How did the boy do it?

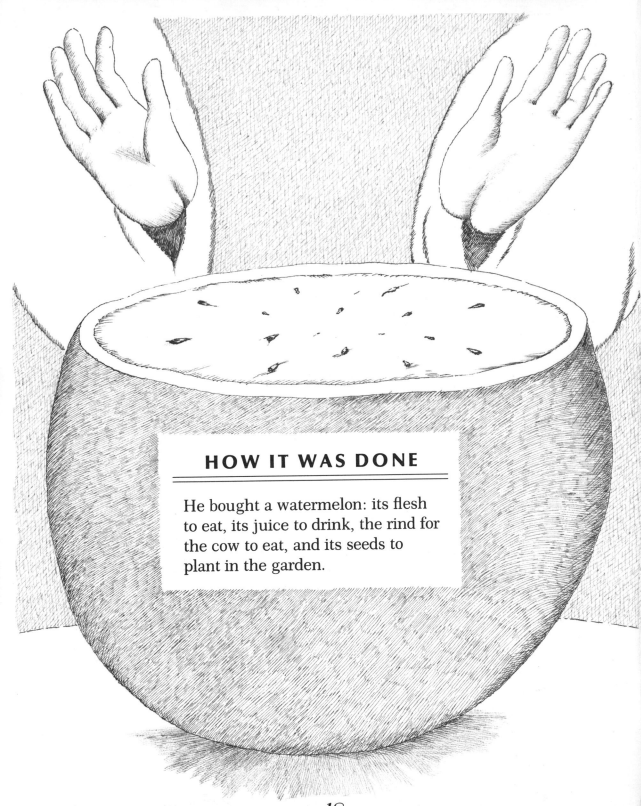

HOW IT WAS DONE

He bought a watermelon: its flesh
to eat, its juice to drink, the rind for
the cow to eat, and its seeds to
plant in the garden.

4.

FIREFLY AND THE APES

*O*ne night in the jungle Firefly was flashing his light and flying circles around Ape's head.

"Go home!" yelled Ape, and laughed. "You shouldn't be out at night if you're afraid of the dark."

Firefly said he wasn't, but Ape argued back.

"You're so afraid of the dark you always have to have a light with you."

Firefly tried to explain that every firefly has a flashing light, but Ape said that just meant that all fireflies were afraid of the dark.

"I'll prove I'm not afraid of anything," said Firefly. "Come to my house tomorrow night, and we'll have a contest—a fight!"

The idea of a contest with tiny Firefly made Ape laugh even louder.

"I can squash you with two fingers. You'd better bring all your friends and relatives because you're going to need all the help you can get."

"Maybe you're the one who'd better bring friends," challenged Firefly. "That is, if you're not afraid to come."

News of the contest quickly spread. The next evening everyone was waiting by Firefly's house.

When Ape arrived, he smiled and said, "I'm all ready to squash you flat." He had a big wooden club over his shoulder. "And I did what you said. I brought a few friends in case I need help fighting little you!"

When Ape motioned, ninety-nine more apes came down the path, and each one carried a big wooden club. Now it was one hundred apes with one hundred clubs against one little firefly. A bird called, "One . . . two . . . three . . . start!" and all one hundred apes raised their clubs and began to walk toward Firefly.

The fight was fast and furious, but by the end of the evening every one of the apes was lying on the ground and Firefly was the winner. How could this have happened?

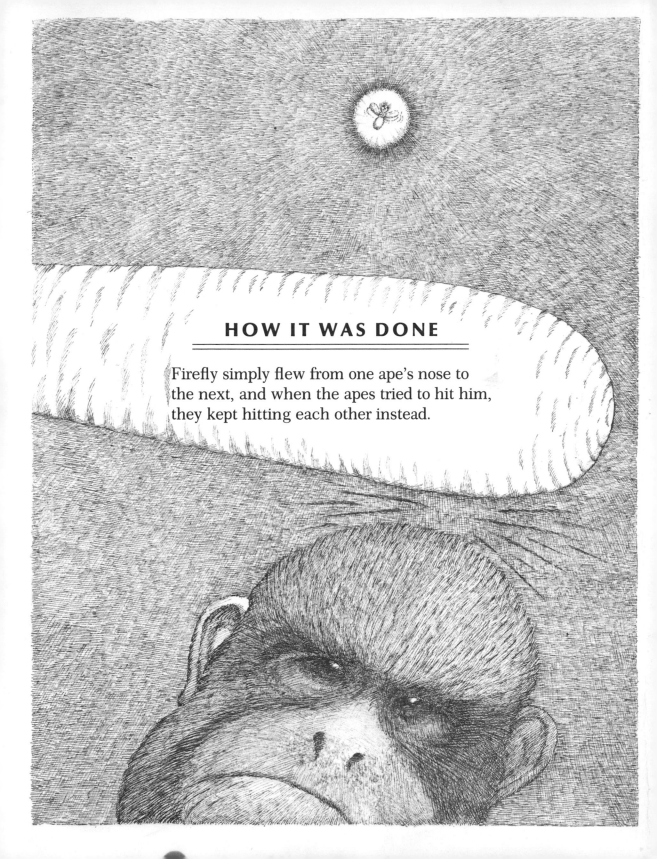

HOW IT WAS DONE

Firefly simply flew from one ape's nose to the next, and when the apes tried to hit him, they kept hitting each other instead.

5.

THE FROG

Once long ago on a summer day, a frog out looking for adventure found a wooden bucket filled with fresh cream. He smiled to himself, then jumped right in! It felt wonderful, all cool and silky against his skin. He played and splashed and swam to the left and then to the right.

After a while he was ready to go home and tell everyone about what he'd done. He was ready to go, but he couldn't get out. The bucket was too deep for him to touch the bottom and push out

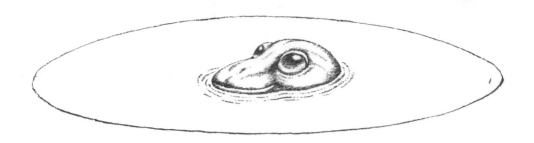

through the cream. There were no rocks or logs like the ones in his pond. And the sides of the bucket were too slippery to climb. He was trapped. His only choice was to keep swimming or drown.

The frog couldn't bear the thought of drowning, especially in cream. He swam to the left and then to the right, around and around till his arms and legs were too tired to move.

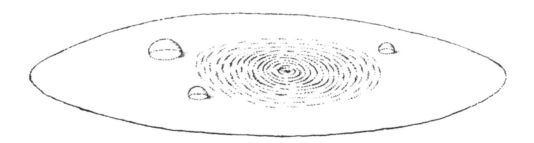

It's no use, he told himself. The end is the end. I might as well get it over with.

He swam to the center of the bucket and began to sink. But as soon as the cream covered his mouth, he sputtered out, "*No*," and started swimming again.

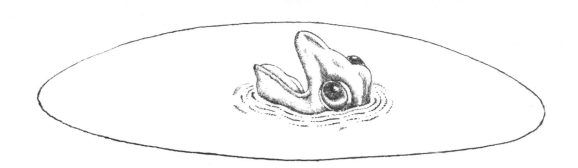

After a while his arms and legs again grew too tired to move. Again he swam to the center and began to sink. And once again, when the cream began to cover his face, he sputtered out, *"No,"* and started swimming.

But the fifth time this happened he sank only a little bit before he felt something beneath his feet. It was soft and slippery, but still solid enough to hold him.

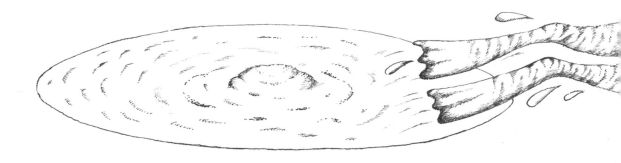

The frog pushed down and hopped out of the bucket and back to his friends as fast as he could go. When he told them what happened, they all wanted to know how he finally got out. But the frog didn't know. Do you know how?

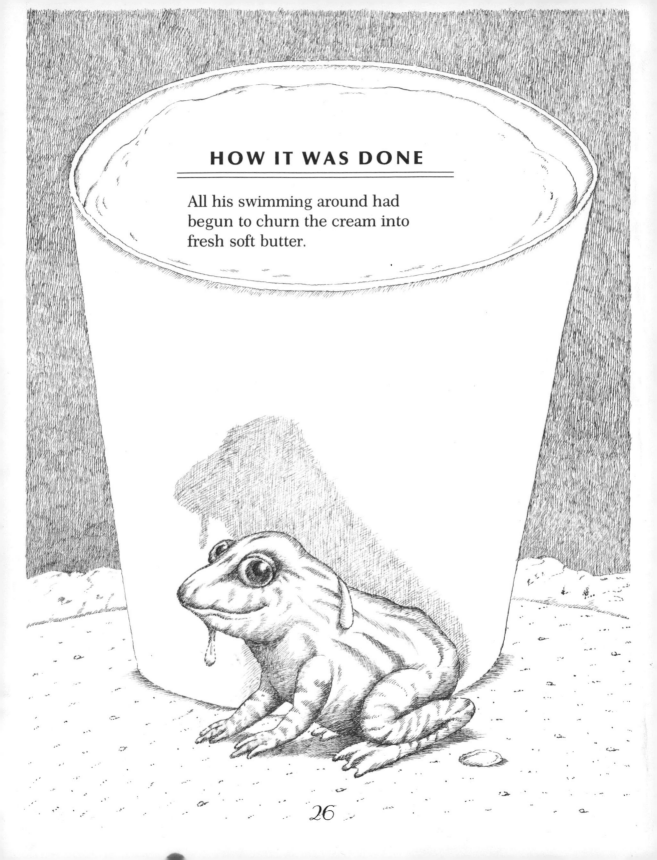

HOW IT WAS DONE

All his swimming around had
begun to churn the cream into
fresh soft butter.

26

6.

THE LAWYER AND THE DEVIL

Once there was a man in Ireland who said he would do anything to get money to send his three sons to school. When the devil heard this, he proposed a trade. The devil would pay for the boys' education in exchange for their father's soul.

Seven years later the devil returned to claim the boys' father.

Neither the father himself nor his sons wanted
him to die. The eldest son, who had in the meantime become a priest, begged the devil to let
their father live just a few more years. Finally
the devil agreed. The next time the devil came,
the second son, who had become a doctor, also
begged the devil to let their father live just a few
years longer. Finally the devil agreed again.
When the devil came a third time, it was the
third son, who had become a lawyer, who
pleaded with him.

"I know you've already delayed taking our father two times, and you can't be expected to do it again," he said to the devil. "But please, could you just let him live as long as that little stub of a candle on the table lasts? Surely you'll grant us time to say good-bye."

The devil looked at the little stub of a candle burning on the table and agreed. The old man didn't have to die that day and was assured that the devil could never take his soul. Why?

HOW IT WAS DONE

The lawyer walked over and blew out
the candle, making sure it would last
forever. He had said "as long as that
little stub of a candle lasts," not "as long
as the candle burns."

30

7.

CROWING KETTLES

Once years ago a traveling preacher stopped for the night at an inn in the country. Not long after the preacher had fallen asleep, other folks came to the inn to gamble and drink. Before long, some money was missing, and they all were arguing at the top of their lungs. When the preacher heard the ruckus, he got up to see what the trouble was.

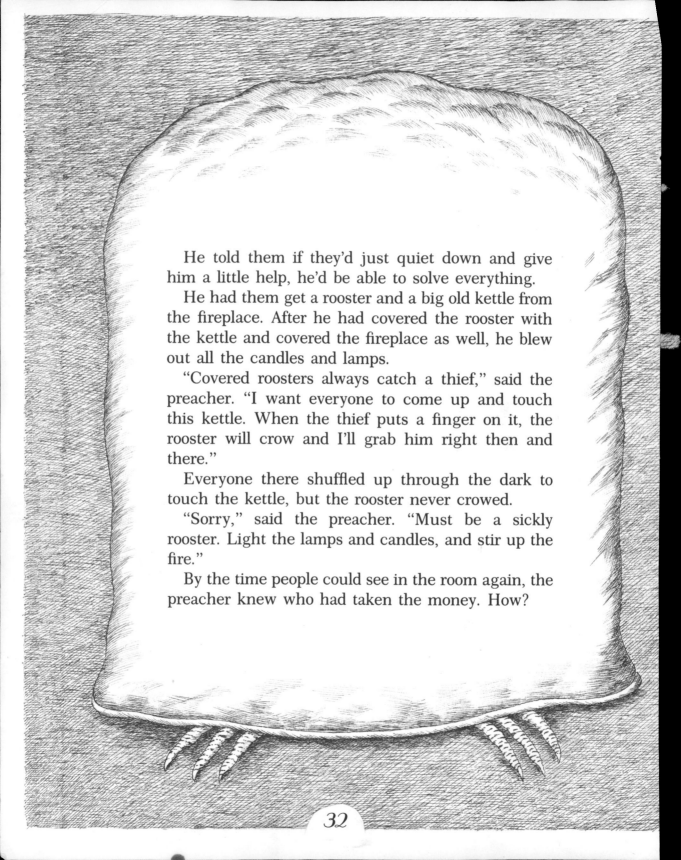

He told them if they'd just quiet down and give him a little help, he'd be able to solve everything.

He had them get a rooster and a big old kettle from the fireplace. After he had covered the rooster with the kettle and covered the fireplace as well, he blew out all the candles and lamps.

"Covered roosters always catch a thief," said the preacher. "I want everyone to come up and touch this kettle. When the thief puts a finger on it, the rooster will crow and I'll grab him right then and there."

Everyone there shuffled up through the dark to touch the kettle, but the rooster never crowed.

"Sorry," said the preacher. "Must be a sickly rooster. Light the lamps and candles, and stir up the fire."

By the time people could see in the room again, the preacher knew who had taken the money. How?

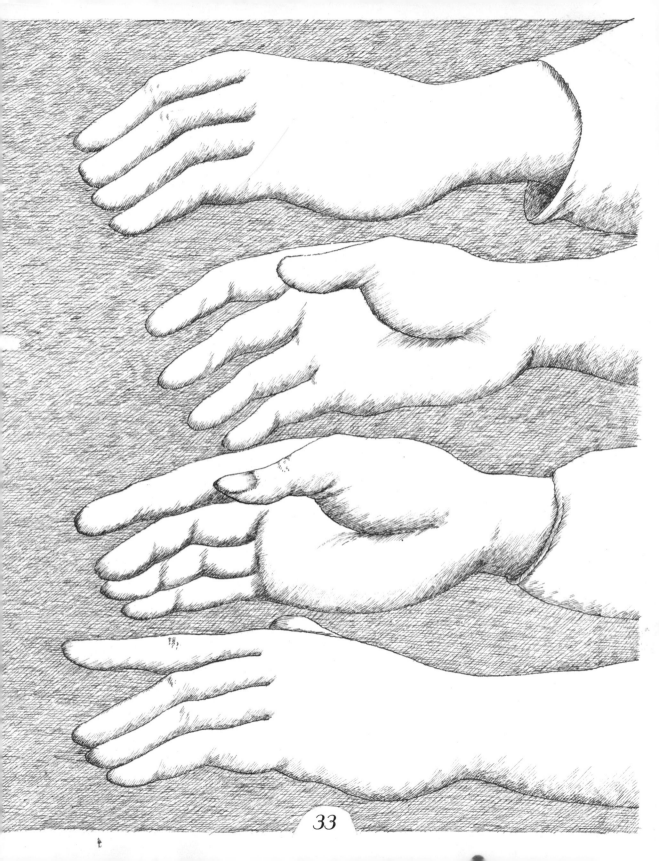

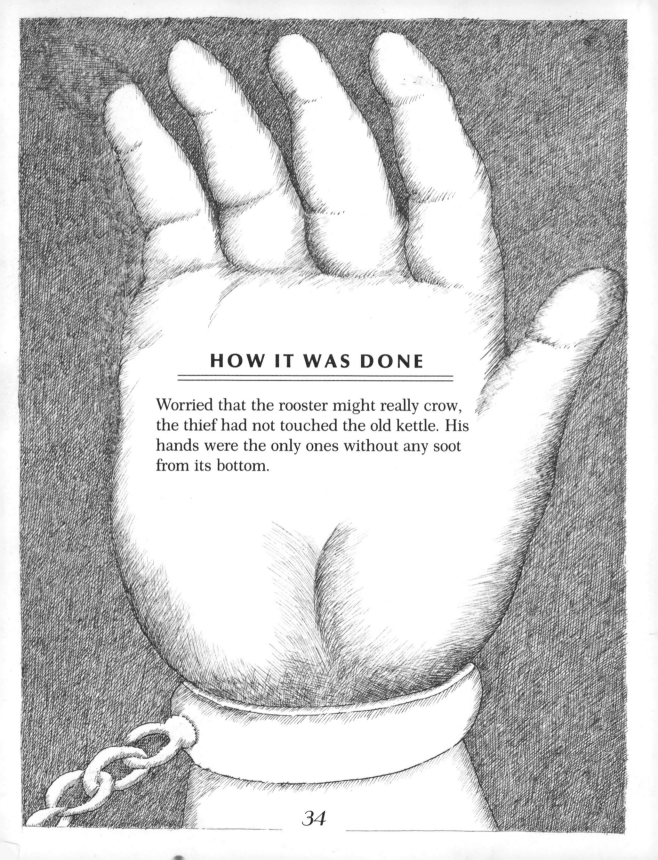

HOW IT WAS DONE

Worried that the rooster might really crow, the thief had not touched the old kettle. His hands were the only ones without any soot from its bottom.

8.

NEVER SEEN, NEVER HEARD

*I*n ancient times many kings competed with riddles instead of fighting wars. After solving the riddle the Egyptian king Nactanabo had sent him, King Lycurgus of Babylon wanted to send him a challenge in return. To make sure everything would go in his

favor, King Lycurgus sent the cleverest man he knew, Aesop, storyteller and former slave.

Aesop quickly outwitted King Nactanabo, but the king would not let Aesop leave. King Nactanabo hoped to disgrace Aesop and send him home in defeat rather than with a tribute to his king. He tested Aesop with riddle after riddle, but Aesop easily solved each one. Finally King Nactanabo came up with an impossible task for Aesop.

"If you can bring me something that I've never seen or heard about," the king told Aesop, "I'll send one thousand dollars as a tribute to your king. If you fail, you must leave and admit both your and your king's defeat."

Aesop begged to have three days to find something so rare that the king would never have seen it or even heard of it. King Nactanabo agreed. He knew that no matter what Aesop brought or told him, all he had to

do was say he'd already seen it. His advisers were ordered to say the same thing.

When Aesop returned, he handed King Nactanabo a small piece of paper. Just as planned, the king and his advisers all said, "We've seen this before. We know all about it. You have failed."

"That's good," said Aesop. "Now I'll take the one thousand dollars for my king."

"No!" said King Nactanabo. "I've never seen this paper before."

"Good," said Aesop. "I've passed your test and will accept the one-thousand-dollar tribute for my king."

There was nothing King Nactanabo or his advisers could do or say. If the king said he *had* seen the paper, he had to pay King Lycurgus one thousand dollars. And if he said he *had not* seen the paper, he had to pay King Lycurgus one thousand dollars. What words had Aesop written on the paper?

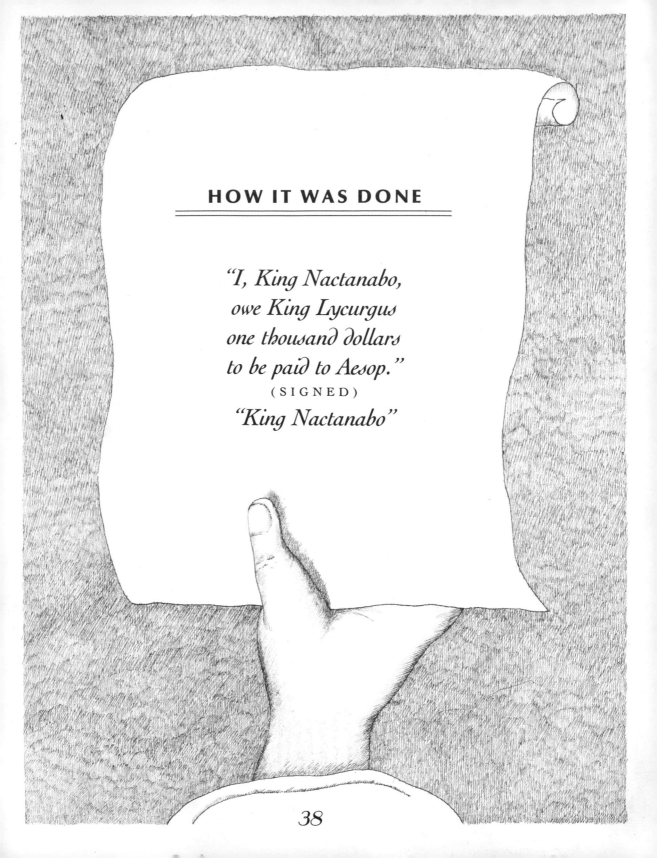

HOW IT WAS DONE

"I, King Nactanabo,
owe King Lycurgus
one thousand dollars
to be paid to Aesop."
(SIGNED)
"King Nactanabo"

9.

THE BRAHMAN
AND
THE BANKER

A Brahman and his wife once decided to go on a religious pilgrimage. To make certain that the small amount of money they had—seven hundred rupees—remained safe, they asked a banker friend to keep it for them. Because the banker declined several times before agreeing to keep it, the Brahman thought it would be an insult to ask him for a receipt.

Their trip went well. But when they got back home and went to get their money, the banker said they had never given him any to keep. Day after day the Brahman asked the banker for his money, and day after day the banker denied ever having received the Brahman's seven hundred rupees.

One day, while the Brahman was walking home from the banker's, a wealthy merchant's wife heard him crying. When she learned his problem, she quickly thought of a plan to get his money back. She told the Brahman to return to the banker's the next day at a specific time and ask for his money again. She said that she would be there, too, but that he must pretend not to know her.

40

The following day the woman went to the banker's a few minutes before the Brahman was to arrive. She told the banker she would like him to keep her many jewels while she was away. She was going to search for her husband, who was several weeks late coming home from a business trip. This time, when the Brahman came and asked for his money, the banker quickly gave it to him. A few moments later the woman's maid came to announce that the woman's husband had just returned. Since she no longer needed to travel, the woman kept her jewels and the Brahman went home with his money. How did the woman's plan suddenly make the banker change his ways?

HOW IT WAS DONE

Eager to get his hands on the woman's jewels, the banker didn't want to frighten her away by appearing to have cheated a Brahman out of such a small sum of money.

10.

A LAST REQUEST

*I*n Chile there once lived a young ruler who thought cleverness was the most important thing of all. He was forever outwitting his advisers and often played jokes on others by asking them riddles that were impossibly difficult to answer. When it came time for him to marry, the young man said he would not

marry anyone who was not as clever as he was. And so, everywhere he went, the young ruler asked the same riddle: "If you care for a basil plant tenderly, how many leaves will it grow?"

In village after village the young women ran away, embarrassed at not knowing the answer. That is, until he asked Carmelita. She looked into his eyes and said, "I will tell you, but only after you tell me how many fish now swim in the sea."

This time it was the young ruler who had no answer and left embarrassed. But he was also impressed. The next week, when Carmelita outwitted him again, he decided she was clever enough to be his wife. Carmelita agreed to marry him, but only on

the condition that he grant her one last request when it came her time to die. He agreed, and her request was written on paper, signed, and sealed.

Carmelita was soon loved by everyone in the country. She helped the people solve their problems, and when her husband made an unjust decision, she told them how to make him change his mind. Usually the young ruler was proud of her cleverness, but one day, when she proved him wrong, he became furious.

"How dare you make everyone laugh at me! Your punishment is death."

Carmelita didn't argue, but she reminded him of his promise to grant her last request. It was only one sentence long, but it assured Carmelita that her husband would pardon her. In fact, he laughed and hugged her in appreciation of her cleverness. What was Carmelita's last request?

HOW IT WAS DONE

Carmelita said, "My last request is that my beloved husband die when I do."

11.

OUTWITTING THE KING

*I*n ancient Ethiopia the men studying to be priests and village teachers were among the poorest and the cleverest. They were not allowed to own anything

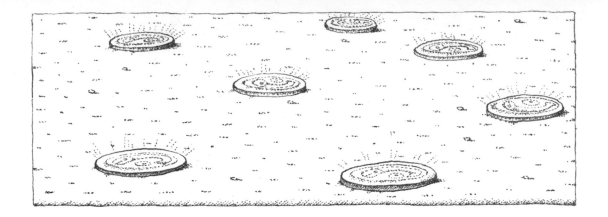

and so lived by their wits as they traveled around the country to study with monks.

Once a king decided he would catch not only every thief in his country but every potential thief as well. Knowing that the men studying to be village teachers were always in need of money, the king called them all to the palace. His plan was to scatter gold coins in the courtyard. The next morning, when the students passed through, he would arrest anyone who picked up a coin. The coins were scattered, and the students passed through the courtyard. No one bent down to pick up a coin, yet all the coins were gone when the students left.

Determined to catch the one who had taken the coins, the king invited all the students to a banquet

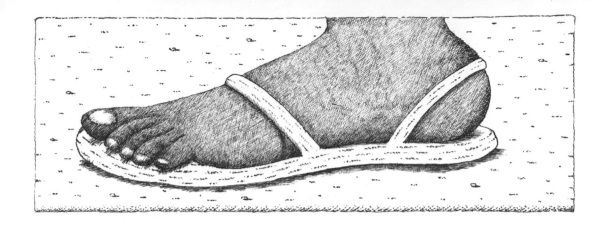

and to spend the night. There was lots of food and wine, and the king's spies were everywhere. If any of the spies heard a student bragging about stealing the coins, he was to make a secret mark on that student's arm while he slept. Then, when the students left the next morning, the king would look at their arms as they passed by and grab the thief himself.

One of the spies did hear a student boast how he'd picked up the gold coins by rubbing wax on the bottom of his shoes, and the spy made the secret mark on that student's arm. The next morning, as they all walked past, the king saw the secret mark, but he still could not figure out who had taken the coins. Why?

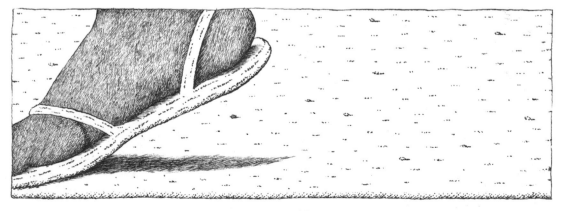

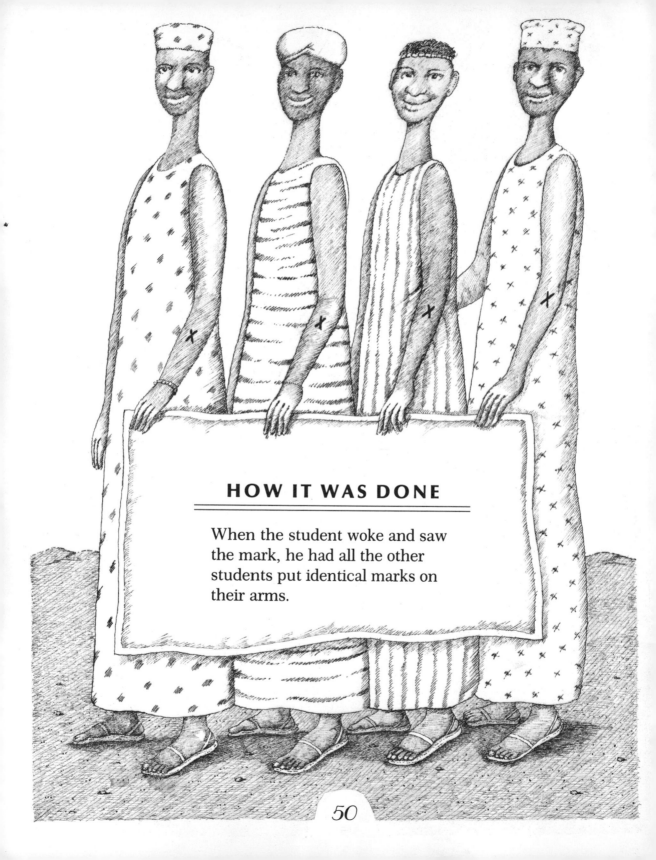

HOW IT WAS DONE

When the student woke and saw the mark, he had all the other students put identical marks on their arms.

12.

SUNRISE

*O*ne night long ago in Mexico, a frog and a deer had an argument. They decided to settle their differences with a bet.

"Twenty-five flies for the one who can see the first rays of the sun," said Frog.

Deer laughed and quickly agreed. "I will look to the east." He knew the sun always rises in the east. "You must look some other place."

Frog agreed. He quietly sat watching the highest mountain peak in the west while deer stared into the darkness of the eastern plain. After hours and hours of waiting and watching, Frog suddenly yelled, "Look! *I* see the first rays of the sun. I win."

When Deer turned to look west, he had to agree that Frog had been the first to see the rays of the sun *and* Frog had seen them by looking away from the sun.

How could this be?

HOW IT WAS DONE

Frog saw the sunlight reflecting off the peak of the mountain in the west while deer was watching the lower plain in the east. Mountains, being higher, always catch the sun's rays first as the earth turns to face the sun.

13.

THE TALLEST TALE

*T*here once lived four men in Burma who loved to tell tall tales and impossible stories. One day a well-dressed stranger came to their village. They wanted his fine clothes and thought of a plan to get them. After visiting with him for a while, one of the men said, "Since we've all been travelers, why don't we each tell about our most wonderful adventure? But if anyone thinks a story isn't true, he must become the servant of the teller and do whatever he's ordered to do."

The traveler agreed, and the four men smiled. They were certain he wouldn't believe their impossible tales and thus be forced to become their servant.

The first man told how before he was born, he had climbed a tree too tall for his father to climb to pick some plums for his mother. The men waited for the traveler to say, "Impossible," but he only smiled in admiration.

The second man told how he'd gotten stuck in the top of a tree when he was only one week old and, when no one would help him, had gone to the village and gotten a ladder so he could climb down from the tree. Again the four men waited for the traveler to say, "Impossible," but he only nodded and smiled.

The traveler even believed the third man's story about catching a tiger and breaking it in two when he was only one year old, and the fourth man's tale of swimming for three days to the bottom of the sea, where he caught a mountain-size fish with his bare hands.

The four men were disappointed that the traveler believed them. Now they could not make him their

servant and order him to give them his clothes. On the other hand, all they had to do was say they believed his story no matter how impossible it turned out to be, and they, too, would be safe.

"Your turn," they told the traveler. "Tell us your best adventure."

He did, and when he had finished, the four men had to give up their clothes despite the fact that they said they believed him. How did this happen?

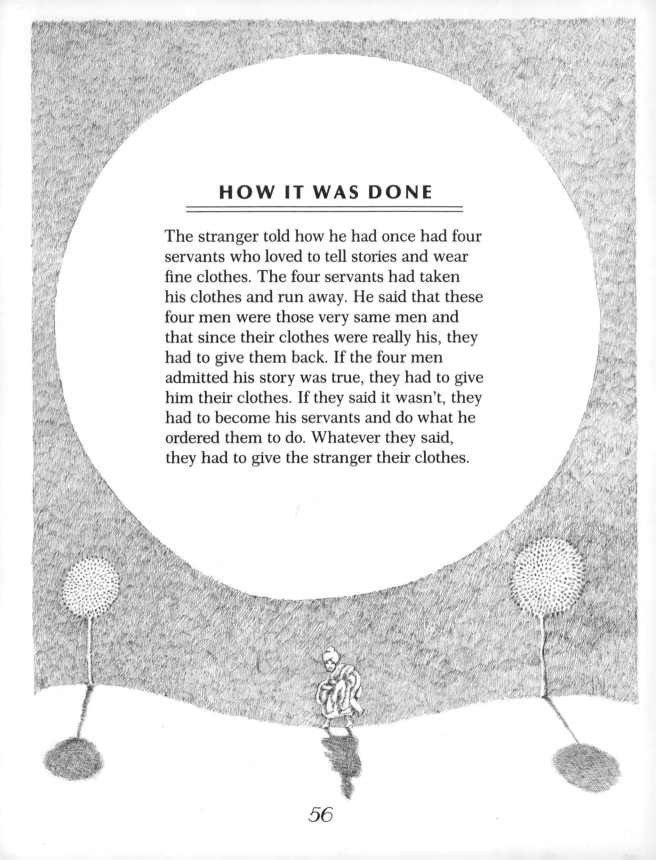

HOW IT WAS DONE

The stranger told how he had once had four
servants who loved to tell stories and wear
fine clothes. The four servants had taken
his clothes and run away. He said that these
four men were those very same men and
that since their clothes were really his, they
had to give them back. If the four men
admitted his story was true, they had to give
him their clothes. If they said it wasn't, they
had to become his servants and do what he
ordered them to do. Whatever they said,
they had to give the stranger their clothes.

14.

THE BET

*I*n the old South when people claimed they could own other people, there lived a slave, named John, who could outsmart anybody for miles around. He was always making bets, and he never made a bet he didn't win. This only made people more eager to bet with him. Everyone, including Colonel Blake, wanted to say that he'd been the first to outsmart John.

"I'll bet you," John said to him one day, "that I can stand at one end of your parlor and throw a raw egg all the way across the room and onto the fireplace mantel without breaking the egg. I'll bet you fifty dollars, all the money I have."

The colonel quickly agreed to the bet. He was certain nobody could throw a raw egg without having it break.

"I'll even give you a dozen tries," he told John.

The first egg John threw smashed on the edge of the mantel. The second hit the candlestick sitting on top. The third egg smashed and smeared the painting above the mantel, but the colonel just laughed. He was happy because he was going to be able to say he was the first to outsmart John on a bet. John threw all twelve eggs, but not one landed without breaking.

"Looks as if I won the bet," said Colonel Blake with a bragging smile.

"Yes," said John. "Sure looks that way."

He paid him the fifty dollars, but when John went to bed that night, he still had fifty dollars from winning a bet. Where did it come from?

HOW IT WAS DONE

John had also made a bet for a hundred
dollars with the neighboring plantation
owner. He bet he could throw eggs all over
Colonel Blake's parlor and that the colonel
would only watch and laugh. By losing the
first bet on purpose, John had managed to
outsmart both men at the same time.

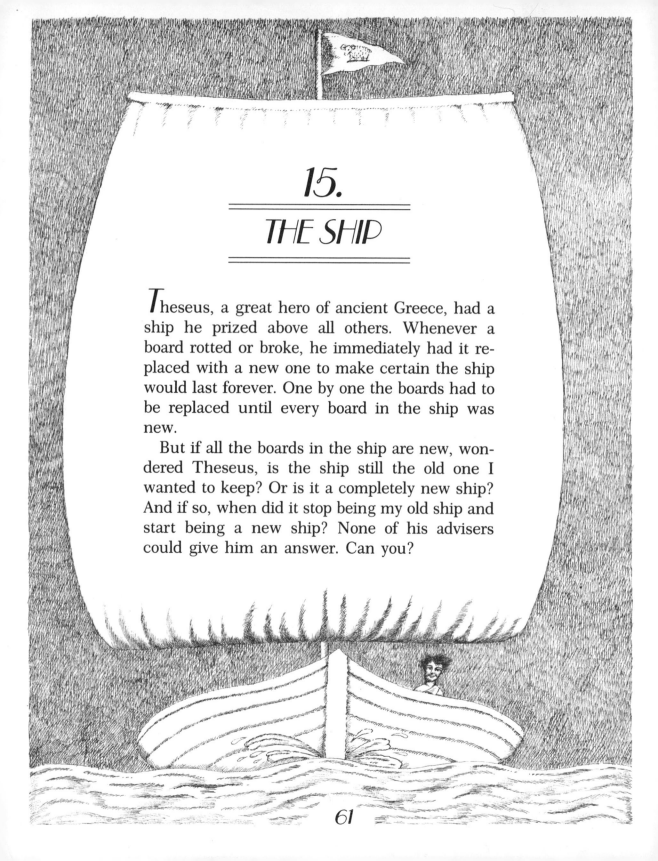

15.

THE SHIP

Theseus, a great hero of ancient Greece, had a ship he prized above all others. Whenever a board rotted or broke, he immediately had it replaced with a new one to make certain the ship would last forever. One by one the boards had to be replaced until every board in the ship was new.

But if all the boards in the ship are new, wondered Theseus, is the ship still the old one I wanted to keep? Or is it a completely new ship? And if so, when did it stop being my old ship and start being a new ship? None of his advisers could give him an answer. Can you?

HOW IT WAS DONE

No one yet has been able to find an answer.
Sometimes the wisest answer may be
that there is no answer.

NOTES

1. I first encountered the basic plot of THE SNOWMAN more than ten years ago in a thin, dilapidated book of Korean folktales. I have not been able to find that book again or any other version of the story. In the version I read so long ago the story took place on a beach with large stones rather than snow.

2. THE NEW PRINCE is a Liberian folktale retold from *African Wonder Tales,* edited by Frances Carpenter (Doubleday, 1963). It can also be found in *With a Deep Sea Smile,* edited by Virginia Tashjian (Little, Brown, 1974).

3. ALL FOR ONE COIN is a folktale from Kashmir retold from *Folk-Tales of Kashmir,* collected by J. Hinton Knowles (Kegan Paul, 1893).

4. FIREFLY AND THE APES is a Visayan folktale from the Philippines retold from "Arnomongo and Iput-Iput," collected by Berton L. Maxfield and W. H. Millington in *The Journal of American Folklore* 20 (1907): 314–315. Variants are told by peoples of the Western Pacific and Southeast Asia, including the Hmong, recent immigrants to the United States. A German variant can be found in *The Complete Grimm's Fairy Tales.*

5. THE FROG is a Russian folktale. It is retold from *The Lazies: Tales of the Peoples of Russia,* translated and edited by Mirra Ginsburg (Macmillan, 1973), and *Baba Yaga's Geese, and Other Russian Stories,* translated and adapted by Bonnie Carey (Indiana University Press, 1973). Carey worked from L. Panteleev, "Dve lyagushki," *Lukomor'e.*

6. Folktales in which someone may live as long as a candle burns exist throughout Europe. Antti Aarne refers to Flemish variants in *The Types of the Folktale* (Burt Franklin, 1971, reprint of 1928 edition). Katharine M. Briggs cites several variants in *A Dictionary of British Folk-Tales in the English Language* (Indiana University Press, 1971). W. B. Yeats included a literary variant in *Irish Fairy Tales* (1892). THE LAWYER AND THE DEVIL is retold from *Irish Folktales,* edited by Henry Glassie (Pantheon, 1985). Glassie worked from Michael J. Murphy's *Now You're Talking* (Belfast: Blackstaff Press, 1975).

7. CROWING KETTLES is a United States folktale retold from *American Folk Tales and Songs,* edited by Richard Chase (New American Library, 1965), who heard it from Smith Harmon in North Carolina. A New Jersey variant has been collected by Henry Charlton Beck in *New York Folklore Quarterly* 4 (1948): 48–49.

8. NEVER SEEN, NEVER HEARD is a folktale about Aesop retold from *Aesop Without Morals*, edited by Lloyd W. Daly (Thomas Yoseloff, 1961). A Russian variant can be found in *Eurasian Folk and Fairy Tales*, edited by I. F. Bulatkin (Criterion, 1965).

9. THE BRAHMAN AND THE BANKER is a Bengali folktale retold from *Popular Tales of Bengal*, by Kasindranath Banerji (Calcutta: H. D. Chattenjee, 1905).

10. A LAST REQUEST is a Chilean folktale retold from *South American Wonder Tales*, translated and edited by Frances Carpenter (Follett, 1969). Carpenter worked from *Folklore Chilien*, Georgette et Jacques Soustelle, Paris Institut International de Coopération Intellectuelle, 1938. A German variant can be found in *The Complete Grimm's Fairy Tales*.

11. OUTWITTING THE KING is an Ethiopian folktale retold from *The Rich Man and the Singer*, told by Mesfin Habte-Mariam and edited by Christine Price (Dutton, 1971). A Haitian variant can be found in *The Magic Orange Tree*, collected by Diane Wolkstein (Knopf, 1978). The Irish and the Celts also have a tale of hiding in the masses, as told in *Celtic Fairy Tales*, edited by Joseph Jacobs (Nutt, 1982).

12. SUNRISE is a Mexican folktale retold from *Tongues of the Monte*, by J. Frank Dobie (Little, Brown, 1947). Variants can be found in *The Golden Bird: Folk Tales from Slovenia*, by Vladimir Kavčič (World, 1969), and Antti Aarne cites several Scandinavian variants in *The Types of the Folktale* (Burt Franklin, 1971, reprint of 1928 edition).

13. THE TALLEST TALE is a Burmese folktale retold from *Burmese Folk-Tales*, edited by Maung Htin Aung (Oxford University Press, 1948). An Ashanti variant can be found in *The Hat-Shaking Dance*, edited by Harold Courlander (Harcourt, 1957), and a Chinese variant can be found in *Floating Clouds, Floating Dreams*, edited by I. K Dunne (Doubleday, 1974).

14. I first heard the basic tale type of THE BET as a contemporary earthy joke about residents of northern Wisconsin in 1985. My telling is an adaptation and blending of this variant and the equally earthy "Tom and the Master," collected by Roger Abrahams in *The Journal of American Folklore* 83 (1970): 235.

15. THE SHIP is a folk mystery that has intrigued philosophers for centuries. It exists in print as far back as the first century A.D. in Plutarch's *Lives*.